STATISTICAL TECHNIQUES FOR ANALYTICAL REVIEW IN AUDITING

STATISTICAL TECHNIQUES FOR ANALYTICAL REVIEW IN AUDITING

KENNETH W. STRINGER

Professor of Accounting
Graduate School of Business Administration
New York University

Retired Partner
Deloitte Haskins & Sells

TREVOR R. STEWART

Partner
Deloitte Haskins & Sells

A Ronald Press Publication

JOHN WILEY & SONS

New York   Chichester   Brisbane   Toronto   Singapore

Library of Congress Cataloging-in-Publication Data:

Stringer, Kenneth W.
    Statistical techniques for analytical review in auditing.

    "A Ronald Press publication."
    Includes indexes.
    1. STAR (Computer program) 2. Auditing—
Statistical methods—Data processing. 3. Auditing,
Internal—Statistical methods—Data processing.
I. Stewart, Trevor R. II. Deloitte Haskins & Sells.
III. Title.

HF5667.S85   1985   657'.45'0285536   85-17874
ISBN 0-471-86076-X

PREFACE

In 1971 Deloitte Haskins & Sells (DH&S) introduced a computer program, known as the STAR Program, into its audit practice. STAR (an acronym for *statistical techniques for analytical review*) integrates audit decisions about materiality, reliability, and other audit objectives with regression analysis and certain other statistical techniques. The effectiveness and efficiency of the STAR Program has been demonstrated in thousands of applications on audit engagements throughout the world in the intervening years.

The primary purpose of this book (which, as far as we know, is the first to be published on the subject) is to explain the concepts and techniques that are implemented through the STAR Program and to encourage their use by other auditors. Because our experience has been principally in financial audits by external auditors, we have written this book from that viewpoint. The STAR Program is readily adaptable, however, for use by internal auditors in business, government, and nonprofit organizations. It may also be adapted for use by management in making budget projections, reviewing variations between budgets and actual results, and making certain types of accounting estimates.

A secondary purpose of this book is to explain the mathematics incorporated in the STAR Program, so that most technical questions that might arise can be answered definitively. We emphasize, however, our view that an auditor does not need to understand all the mathematics to be able to use the STAR Program effectively; we think a good grasp of how the statistical techniques relate to the audit objectives is quite sufficient.

Wherever possible, we have tried to explain the mathematical concepts in a way that we hope will seem intuitively logical to auditors who are not mathematically oriented. In the interest of brevity and clarity, however, we have used customary mathematical formulas and symbols but have supplemented them with numerical examples when we think this will make the mathematics easier to understand.

This book consists of nine chapters and is divided into four parts. In Part I we lay the foundation for the remainder of the book. We describe the audit environment within which the STAR Program is used and the audit philosophy that gave rise to its development. We discuss analytical review techniques in general and provide an overview of the STAR Program and an illustration of its use.

In Part II we present the basic statistical concepts and formulas underlying regression analysis and the other statistical techniques that are incorporated in the STAR Program. We start by explaining simple two-variable models, move on to explain multivariate models, and close with an explanation of the audit interface. Our purpose here is to provide a basis for the auditor's understanding of the statistical concepts so that their relevance to the audit objectives of analytical review procedures will be more apparent. Some of the material that we treat superficially in Part II to achieve this limited purpose is treated more comprehensively in Part IV.

In Part III we deal with auditing applications. Here we discuss audit and statistical objectives, explain the criteria that we suggest for designing and improving audit models for analytical review applications, and provide guidance to help the auditor in understanding and using the results that are obtained from the STAR Program. This part is almost completely nonmathematical and focuses directly on the decisions to be made by the auditor. Although we have written Part III from the perspective of the external auditor, much of the material also applies to use of the STAR Program by internal auditors.

In Part IV we deal with more advanced mathematical and computational aspects of some of the subjects that are introduced in Part II. We explain the details of the statistical tests and transformations that are performed by the STAR Program. We also explain the computational procedure employed by the Program to deal with multivariate models. Part IV is the most mathematically demanding part of the book and is included only for the convenience of readers whose interest might otherwise require them to seek further references. For most readers it will be the least important part because the parallel treatment of the topics in Part II will be sufficient.

Readers who are interested in working through the illustrative calculations in this book should be aware that they may not be able to duplicate exactly the results that are shown. We have tended to show rounded numbers in calculations (to make them more digestible), whereas the STAR Program uses numbers that are accurate to seven significant digits. In addition, to avoid the confusion that can be caused by insignificant differences, we have usually rounded results to make them agree exactly with the comparable results printed by the STAR Program. Readers, therefore, should interpret "=" as "approximately equal" when it is used in a numerical equation and should not assume that the usual rules for rounding numbers have been applied.

Where we have made specific reference to the professional literature, statistical textbooks, or other publications, we have included a number in brackets next to the reference (e.g., "SAS No. 47 [5]") and cited the source at the end of the chapter.

The STAR Program may be licensed from DH&S, and operating instructions for running the Program are included in a *User Guide* that is distributed with it. The Program runs on the IBM Personal Computer™ and many compatible machines. All illustrative applications in this book were prepared using the Program on an IBM Personal Computer™. In some cases we have modified the computer printouts by deleting parts that are not relevant in the context of the example. Several of the tables were prepared with popular spreadsheet programs, which can be used to interface with the STAR Program.

The STAR Program complements the DH&S Audit Sampling Plan, which was developed and adopted for use by the firm in the early 1960s. They are currently the principal quantitative techniques used in the integrated audit philosophy discussed in Part I. One of us (KWS) was primarily responsible for the development of these techniques and the conceptual model for using them in auditing, and had a leading role in introducing the techniques and model into the professional literature. Maurice S. Newman, a retired DH&S partner and now Professor of Accounting at the University of Alabama, made invaluable contributions concerning the statistical techniques and audit interface in the STAR Program, developed the original Program, and participated in initial training and implementation. James L. Kirtland and James L. Kusko of DH&S also made significant contributions to the techniques, model, and initial training.

James L. Kirtland has had a continuing vital role in his capacity as the firm's functional specialist responsible for questions arising in current applications of the Program. In more recent years, Donald F. Behan, director and senior actuary in the firm, provided valuable advice concerning statistical enhancements being considered.

The other of us (TRS) is presently the partner in charge of microcomputer development and support in the firm's Executive Office in New York. He took the initiative leading to preparation of this book, prepared the initial manuscript, and participated heavily in the revisions of it. He also initiated and implemented enhancements to the original computer program and developed the new program for microcomputers. Before being transferred from Johannesburg, South Africa, to New York, he had taken a leading role in introducing the STAR Program in the firm's offices in several countries.

We are grateful to DH&S—and particularly to John W. Queenan, Michael N. Chetkovich, Oscar S. Gellein, and Charles G. Steele—for the encouragement and support provided initially during the development and introduction of the STAR Program into the firm's practice and later during the preparation of this book. We emphasize, however, that the views we express are ours alone and do not necessarily conform with the policies of the firm at the present time or as they may be modified in the future.

We note also that we have used the word *should* liberally to express our views about certain audit decisions that must be made in using the STAR Program. We have done this to avoid the repetitive use of longer but more precise expressions such as *in our opinion, in our judgment,* and so on. We have tried, however, to limit such normative usage to decisions that involve our judgment as to the relevance of certain statistical results to audit objectives, and to avoid extending it to other areas of audit judgment.

We acknowledge with appreciation the assistance of James L. Kirtland and Guy R. Nickerson of DH&S, who read and made many helpful suggestions on the last few drafts of the manuscript; and the cooperation and patience of the following individuals in providing secretarial or other assistance in preparing the manuscript: Genevieve Rodd, Marjorie Lue, Anna Masson, and Arlene McManus. Finally, we are especially grateful to our wives, Catherine Stringer and Margaret Stewart, for their encouragement and understanding throughout the many hours diverted from family activities for preparation of this book.

KENNETH W. STRINGER
TREVOR R. STEWART

New York, New York
October 1985

CONTENTS

STATISTICAL TECHNIQUES
FOR ANALYTICAL REVIEW
IN AUDITING

OVERVIEW

1

THE AUDIT ENVIRONMENT

1.1 Introduction

In this chapter we discuss the conceptual and practical environment in which auditing is conducted. Our purpose is not to explain or expand on that environment, because this book is written for auditors who are already familiar with it. Our purpose is simply to focus attention briefly on those features we think will be helpful in viewing the remaining chapters in perspective against the background of the overall audit environment.

1.2 Nature and Scope of Auditing

A definition of auditing that we like, because of its conceptual clarity and completeness, is that of the American Accounting Association [1]:

> Auditing is a systematic process of objectively obtaining and evaluating evidence regarding assertions about economic actions and events to ascertain the degree of correspondence between those assertions and established criteria and communicating the results to interested users.

The explanatory comments accompanying this definition emphasize the broad range of purposes and subject matter of auditing as follows [1]:

This definition is intentionally quite broad. While it conveys the basic idea that an audit is an investigative process, it is sufficiently comprehensive to encompass the many different purposes for which an audit might be conducted and the variety of subject matter that might be focused on in a specific audit engagement.

Frequently, the term audit (or auditing) is modified by a descriptive word or phrase to indicate either the particular purpose of the audit or the subject matter of the audit or both. For example, we frequently encounter such terms as financial audit, systems audit, management audit, operational audit, performance audit, and compliance audit. While all these terms convey the implication of different types of audit engagements, the above definition is broad enough to include all of them. . . .

Because our experience has been principally in audits of financial statements by independent auditors, we have written this book primarily from that viewpoint. The concepts and techniques presented, however, are readily adaptable for use by internal auditors of business, nonprofit, or governmental organizations. Furthermore, they may also be useful in other management functions, such as the preparation of budgets or other operating plans, the comparison of actual results with those plans, and the preparation of certain kinds of accounting estimates.

1.3   Auditing Standards

Section 150.01 of the *Codification of Statements on Auditing Standards* (CSAS) issued by the American Institute of Certified Public Accountants (AICPA) [2] states that:

Auditing standards differ from auditing procedures in that "procedures" relate to acts to be performed, whereas "standards" deal with measures of the quality of the performance of those acts and the objectives to be attained by the use of the procedures undertaken.

Auditing standards for independent auditors have been established by legislative, regulatory, or professional bodies in the major industrial countries throughout the world. Similar standards have also been established for internal auditors in some countries. At the present time, there is considerable commonality among the standards of different countries, but there are also some important differences. The International Federation of Accountants (IFAC) is trying to achieve greater uniformity by periodically issuing *International Auditing Guidelines*. These guidelines, however, are not binding on auditors in an individual country unless they are formally adopted by the professional or other body that has jurisdiction in that country.

Both the authoritative standards of the respective countries and the *International Auditing Guidelines* are stated in broad general terms, which leave latitude for differences in the underlying audit philosophy and methods of different auditors. For example, generally accepted auditing standards in the United States, which were formally adopted by the profession in 1948 and subsequently codified in *Statement on Auditing Standards* (SAS) 1 [3], include a standard of field work which states that:

> Sufficient competent evidential matter is to be obtained through inspection, observation, inquiries, and confirmations to afford a reasonable basis for an opinion regarding the financial statements under investigation.

Similarly, *International Auditing Guideline* 3 [4], which was issued in 1980, states that:

> The auditor should obtain sufficient appropriate audit evidence through the performance of compliance and substantive procedures to enable him to draw reasonable conclusions therefrom on which to base his opinion on the financial information.

A common element among auditing standards is their recognition that absolute accuracy and reliability of financial statements are not attainable at reasonable cost through the accounting and auditing processes. Accordingly, the standards acknowledge that a reasonable relationship should exist between the costs and benefits of these processes, as is necessary in other economic processes. For the auditor, this cost–benefit constraint manifests itself in two pervasive and interrelated concepts: materiality and audit risk.

Section 150.03 of the CSAS [2] includes the following statement, which is essentially the same as was included in the explanatory comments that accompanied the statement of generally accepted auditing standards adopted in 1948:

> The elements of "materiality" and "relative risk" underlie the application of all of the standards, particularly the standards of field work and reporting.

These concepts have been referred to in numerous pronouncements on auditing standards since that date, and were expressed more formally in SAS 47 [5], issued in 1983.

Because materiality is also an accounting concept, SAS 47 did not define it but rather referred to Financial Accounting Standards Board *Statement of Financial Accounting Concepts* No. 2 [6], which defines materiality as:

> . . . the magnitude of an omission or misstatement of accounting information that, in the light of surrounding circumstances, makes it probable that the judgment of a reasonable person relying on the information would have been changed or influenced by the omission or misstatement.

SAS 47 defines *audit risk* as "the risk that the auditor may unknowingly fail to appropriately modify his opinion on financial statements that are materially misstated."

For the purpose of this chapter, the critical concept in SAS 47 is the recognition that "Audit risk and materiality, among other matters, need to be considered together in determining the nature, timing, and extent of auditing procedures and in evaluating the results of those procedures."

1.4   Auditing Procedures

Auditing standards in the United States recognize four basic types of auditing procedures. The first two, which relate to the study and evaluation of the client's system of internal accounting control, consist of a review and preliminary evaluation of the system and tests of compliance with it. The second two, which are types of substantive tests, include analytical review procedures and tests of details.

The nature, timing, and extent of substantive tests are influenced by the auditor's evaluation of the effectiveness of the system of internal accounting control and the implications of any special audit risks. Because of the inherent limitations on the effectiveness of internal accounting control systems, however, auditors are not permitted to rely completely on any such system but are required, in all cases, to make some substantive tests.

The audit objective of substantive tests is to obtain evidence concerning the validity and accuracy of transactions, balances, and other assertions in the financial statements; or conversely, to obtain evidence of any material misstatements in (including omissions from) the financial statements.

Analytical review procedures are substantive tests of financial information made by a study and comparison of relationships among data. Analytical review is a form of deductive reasoning under which the reliability of individual recorded transactions and balances is inferred from evidence of the reasonableness of the aggregate results.

Tests of details consist of examining samples of transactions or account balances. Tests of details are a form of inductive reasoning under which the reasonableness of the aggregate results is inferred from the evidence of reliability of the details that have been tested.

Analytical review and tests of details are sometimes described as the "top down" and "bottom up" approaches, respectively. Auditing standards permit the auditor's reliance on substantive tests to be derived from analytical review procedures, from tests of details, or from any combination of these procedures that the auditor considers appropriate in the circumstances.

Auditing pronouncements concerning specific areas of an audit generally focus more on the nature of the procedures to be performed than on the extent of their application, and typically indicate only that extent of application is a matter of auditing judgment in the circumstances. This degree of generalization extends quite commonly to the level of implementation in specific audits. Instructions concerning auditing procedures to be applied to particular account balances or classes of transactions usually are provided in the form of audit programs, and such programs frequently include expressions such as "test sufficient items to satisfy yourself that . . . ," "examine a representative number of items," "review the account balances to determine their reasonableness," and other similar expressions. In such instructions, the criteria for satisfying oneself, for being representative, or for being reasonable are hardly more explicit than the general standards themselves. Although such instructions imply the existence of some criteria concerning the assurance desired by the auditor, they generally include no operational means for expressing or measuring it.

1.5 Role of Quantitative Techniques

We believe that auditors can and should use quantitative techniques to express their judgment about audit objectives and to measure the accomplishment of such objectives. Used in this way, the techniques become the focal point for implementing audit judgment. In DH&S statistical sampling was introduced as a technique for tests of details in 1962, and regression analysis was introduced as a technique for analytical review in 1971. Both techniques have been used extensively since their introduction and are important elements in the firm's integrated audit approach. The elements of this approach are described collectively by the term *AuditSCOPE,* which refers to an *Audit System of Coordinated Objectives, Procedures, and Evaluations.*

1.5.1 Audit philosophy and approach

We think a brief explanation of this audit approach and its underlying philosophy will help readers understand the viewpoint from which this book is written. We hasten to emphasize, however, that the techniques described in this book can be used separately from the other elements of Audit-SCOPE.

The following quote from the current DH&S *Audit Practical Manual,* describes the essence of our audit philosophy:

> The ultimate objectives of our audit approach are derived from the profession's generally accepted auditing standards for field work. Our audit approach utilizes a logical framework as a basis for exercising informed professional judgment. We use mathematical methods in our framework to evaluate data that are susceptible to quantification. We use analytical tools to enhance our understanding of the client's business and to adapt our audit techniques to the client's situation.
>
> DH&S has been a leader in the accounting profession for many years in developing and using advanced auditing concepts and techniques. These innovations are an integral part of our audit approach and are designed to help us deal with the increasing complexities of financial systems, to control the costs of audits, to maintain the Firm's quality control standards, and to provide exemplary client service.
>
> Our audit approach is designed to be quantitative, structured, and comprehensive and to allow maximum adaptability to specific client circumstances. Professional judgment is central to adapting our approach to specific circumstances. The following discussion describes each of these characteristics and explains why we believe each is important to the unique DH&S audit approach.
>
> Our audit approach is quantitative in the sense that in an engagement we attempt to measure and evaluate in a practical manner the sufficiency of evidential matter that we either have gathered or plan to gather. We believe quantification is helpful in aggregating and integrating data and individual

judgments related to the various parts of the audit. Specifically, the quantification process provides a useful method of integrating evaluations from internal accounting control, analytical review, and substantive tests of details into a composite judgment of audit reliability.

Not all aspects of information are susceptible to quantification, however, and quantification of certain information is necessarily somewhat subjective. The auditor's professional judgment is the most critical factor in an audit, and quantification is a useful tool in exercising that judgment. Also, we recognize the rational relationship that should be maintained between the cost of quantifying evidential matter and the usefulness of the additional assurance provided by such quantification.

Our approach is structured and comprehensive in the sense that the individual steps in gathering and evaluating audit evidence are integrated and coordinated so that all aspects of the audit are considered from the viewpoint of the audit as a whole. Our auditing objectives, procedures and evaluation methods are integrated into a comprehensive structural framework that is encompassed in policy manuals, audit programs and questionnaires, computer programs, and staff training material developed by the Firm.

The identification of common objectives, procedures, and evaluation methods that can be applied in a variety of circumstances and the incorporation of these common elements into a logically structured system promote both effectiveness and efficiency in auditing. Effectiveness is promoted through the concentrated study that precedes the adoption of particular features of the system, and through the assurance that the inclusion of these features will prevent them from being overlooked in particular audits. Efficiency is promoted through the saving of time that otherwise would be required for repetitive analysis of situations that, although arising in different audits, involve essentially similar problems. Audit judgment and flexibility, of course, are required both in interpreting and in applying common objectives, procedures, and evaluation methods in all cases, and in modifying or supplementing them in unusual cases.

1.5.2   Measures of statistical assurance

The unique feature of statistical techniques that distinguishes them from nonstatistical or subjective techniques in auditing is that they provide measures of the statistical assurance attributable to conclusions drawn from audit tests of details or analytical review procedures. The terms used to describe these measures are not standardized in statistical literature and practice. In this book we use *reliability* and *precision* as the measures of statistical assurance. In this context, reliability is the complement of detection risk, as the latter term is defined in SAS 47 [5].

Reliability and precision are dual measures that can be defined jointly for our purpose at this stage as follows:

> Reliability is a measure of the mathematical probability reasonably attributable to a conclusion that an upper precision limit, properly calculated from the results of a statistical sample or statistical analytical review, will exceed the total errors in the population sampled or the data reviewed, assuming that any errors in the sample items examined or in the fluctuations investigated in the review are recognized by the auditor.

Statistical concepts and computations pertaining to these measures of assurance are discussed in later chapters.

From the definition given, it is clear that the statistical measures of reliability and precision can be related to the auditing concepts of reasonable assurance (or audit risk) and materiality, respectively. Consequently, an auditor's judgment about a reasonable level of audit assurance or risk and about materiality in financial statements can be expressed objectively by specifying the reliability level and precision limit desired from substantive audit tests. These specifications can be used first in planning the extent of audit tests, and second in evaluating the results of the tests.

1.5.3   Audit judgment and statistical techniques

We think it is important for readers to understand the relationship between audit judgment and statistical techniques in the design and evaluation of audit tests. Misunderstanding in this respect is often the cause of misguided opposition to the use of such techniques.

The relationship can be explained best by emphasizing that the auditor's judgment is really a combination of two separable decisions. The first decision relates to the audit objectives; the second relates to the extent of tests and the evaluation of the results that are necessary to accomplish the objectives.

An auditor's training and experience provide the best basis for judgment about the objectives of audit tests. They are not, however, the best basis for determining the extent and evaluating the results necessary to achieve those objectives. Decisions on these matters involve, implicitly or explicitly, consideration of the probabilities of forming correct or incorrect conclusions from the evidence obtained from audit tests. A generally accepted body of statistical concepts and techniques is available and is used widely and successfully in many other fields for dealing with similar probabilities and inferences.

We think that the use of statistical techniques, wherever practicable, as a means of expressing and implementing audit judgment about objectives is the best way to combine the professional expertise available in the auditing and statistical disciplines. Conversely, we think that the failure to use such techniques telescopes two separable decisions into one subjective process, in which the audit objectives are not expressed explicitly and the extent of tests and evaluation of results are determined without reference to the probabilities that inevitably are involved.

Early research and experience in DH&S and a growing body of academic research concerning decision-making processes in auditing and other fields tend to support the foregoing views. This research indicates that individuals are proficient in identifying relevant factors to be considered, but generally are not proficient in integrating the effect of several interrelated factors that are relevant to their decisions. For example, Libby [7], on page 104, commented on this subject as follows:

> The limited ability of people to integrate information from different sources appears to be the most consistent finding of the literature reviewed in this book. . . . While some experimental results may overstate the magnitude of this problem, . . . [the] conclusion that "experts are much better at selecting and coding information than they are at integrating it" appears applicable to accountants and users of their information.

1.5.4   Systems and models

We think it is useful to view the underlying philosophy just expressed in the broader perspective of *systems* and *models,* as these terms are used in current literature in other fields of study.

A *system* can be thought of somewhat abstractly as a set of elements that interact or are interrelated in a way that is worthy of study for some purpose. For our purpose, systems have three general characteristics. First, they pertain to reality—real processes, events, results, conditions, and so on. For example, we may refer to the solar system, the social system, or the economic system. Second, individual systems usually are a part of larger systems and may interact with those or other systems. As a part of the economic system, for example, we might consider systems relating to banking, transportation, financial markets, or other sectors of economic activity. Third, the perception of a system depends on the purpose for which it is being studied. For example, an engineer might perceive the parts of an airplane as a flying system and be concerned with the laws of aerodynamics to optimize physical performance, while an economist might view the airplane as part of a transportation system and be concerned with payloads and flight schedules to optimize economic performance.

The principal systems with which accountants and auditors are concerned include the general economic system, the system of business operations that generates the transactions of a particular entity, and the accounting and internal accounting control systems of the entity.

Models are simplified representations of the systems to which they relate. Models are needed when factors such as time, cost, physical conditions, or other constraints make it impracticable to study systems completely.

The principal models with which accountants are concerned are the accounting model (e.g., the historical-cost or current-cost model), as defined by the applicable set of accounting principles, and financial statements of a particular entity. Such statements constitute a model of the system of business operations of the entity.

In addition to accounting models, auditors are concerned with audit models such as:

- Models of the client's accounting and internal accounting control systems, which usually are in the form of questionnaires, flowcharts, or narrative descriptions, and the results of compliance tests
- Models of the system of business operations of the client, in the form of information obtained through substantive tests of details and analytical review procedures
- An implicit or explicit materiality and audit risk model, used for combining the audit reliance on internal accounting control and on substantive tests to form an opinion on the financial statements being audited

Mathematical models highlight and clarify decisions about fundamental relationships and assumptions, the quantification of parameters, and uses of the model. This clarity invites, and often results in, criticism of the decisions by others. Such criticism sometimes may be constructive and result in improvement of the models. The imperfections present in an explicit mathematical model, however, are likely to be present to an equal or greater degree, but not be recognized, in a vague subjective model.

To underscore this practical perspective that is so often ignored, we close this section with the following quotation from Forrester [8], which coincides with our point of view regarding mathematical models:

> The validity and usefulness of dynamic (mathematical) models should be judged, not against an imaginary perfection, but in comparison with the mental and descriptive models which we would otherwise use. We should judge the formal models by their clarity of structure and compare this clarity to the confusion and incompleteness so often found in a verbal description. We should judge the models by whether or not the underlying assumptions are more clearly exposed than in the veiled background of our thought processes. We should judge the models by the certainty with which they show the correct time-varying consequences of the statements made in the models compared to the unreliable conclusions we often reach in extending our mental image of system structure to its behavioral implications. We should judge the models by the ease of communicating their structure compared to the difficulty in conveying a verbal description. By constructing a formal model, our mental image of the system is clearly exposed. General statements of size, magnitude, and influence are given numerical values. As soon as the model is so precisely stated, one is usually asked how he knows that the model is "right." A controversy often develops over whether or not reality is exactly as presented in the model. But such questions miss the first purpose of a model, which is to be clear and to provide concrete statements that can be easily communicated.
>
> There is nothing in either the physical or social sciences about which we have perfect information. We can never prove that any model is an exact representation of "reality." Conversely, among those things of which we are aware, there is nothing of which we know absolutely nothing. So we always deal with information which is of intermediate quality—it is better than nothing and short of perfection. Models are then to be judged, not on an absolute scale that condemns them for failure to be perfect, but on a relative scale that approves them if they succeed in clarifying our knowledge and our insights into systems.

To summarize the views expressed in this section, we believe that statistical concepts and techniques are the best available means for implementing auditors' judgments about the objectives and results of audit tests and, accordingly, should be used wherever practicable. The remainder of this book is written from this perspective and is intended to encourage and facilitate the application of this philosophy in the performance of analytical review procedures.

References

1. American Accounting Association, "A Statement of Basic Auditing Concepts." *Studies in Accounting Research* No. 6, 1973.
2. American Institute of Certified Public Accountants, *Codification of Statements on Auditing Standards,* 1984.
3. American Institute of Certified Public Accountants, "Codification of Auditing Standards and Procedures." *Statement on Auditing Standards* 1, 1972.
4. International Federation of Accountants, "Basic Principles Governing an Audit." *International Auditing Guideline* No. 3, 1980.
5. American Institute of Certified Public Accountants, "Audit Risk and Materiality in Conducting an Audit." *Statement on Auditing Standards* 47, 1983.
6. Financial Accounting Standards Board, "Qualitative Characteristics of Accounting Information." *Statement of Financial Accounting Concepts* No. 2, 1980.
7. Robert Libby, *Accounting and Human Information Processing: Theory and Applications.* Englewood Cliffs, N.J.: Prentice-Hall, 1981.
8. Jay W. Forrester, *Principles of Systems.* Cambridge, Mass.: Wright Allen, 1968.

2

ANALYTICAL REVIEW

2.1 Introduction

In this chapter we first discuss the background and basic concepts underlying the analytical review process. Next we discuss the techniques commonly used in subjective or nonstatistical analytical reviews, and present an overview of the statistical techniques for analytical review that are the major topic of this book. We close the chapter with a comparison of statistical and nonstatistical techniques.

2.2 Analytical Review Process

Under one name or another, analytical review procedures have been performed as long as audits have been conducted. For example, we have located a bulletin on the subject that was issued for inclusion in the procedures manual of DH&S in the 1930s, and this bulletin undoubtedly was a formalization of already existing practices.

To the best of our knowledge, the first use of the descriptive term *analytical review* in the authoritative professional pronouncements was in *Statement on Auditing Procedures* No. 54 [1], which was issued by the American Institute of Certified Public Accountants in 1972 and was subsequently included as CSAS Section 320 [2]. A further pronouncement dealing with the subject in more detail was issued as SAS 23 in 1978 [3] and was subsequently codified as CSAS Section 318. That statement includes the following definition: "Analytical review procedures are substantive tests of financial information made by a study and comparison of relationships among data."

International Auditing Guideline No. 8, "Audit Evidence," issued by IFAC in 1982 [4], defines analytical review as follows: "Analytical review consists of studying significant ratios and trends and investigating unusual fluctuations and items."

SAS 23 [3] describes the following general analytical review procedures:

- Comparison of the financial information with information for comparable prior period(s)
- Comparison of the financial information with anticipated results (for example, budgets and forecasts)
- Study of the relationship of elements of financial information that would be expected to conform to a predictable pattern based on the entity's experience
- Comparison of the financial information with similar information regarding the industry in which the entity operates
- Study of the relationship of the financial information with relevant non-financial information

SAS 23 goes on to explain the relationship of analytical review to tests of details as follows: "The auditor's reliance on substantive tests may be derived from tests of details of transactions and balances, from analytical review procedures, or from any combination of both."

Auditing standards, therefore, permit auditors to rely on analytical review procedures, on tests of details, or on any combination of these substantive tests that they consider appropriate in the circumstances. Our experience indicates that most auditors tend to rely relatively more on analytical review of operating accounts and on tests of details of balance-sheet accounts. When tests of details of balances are performed as of an interim date, auditors often place substantial reliance on analytical review procedures in updating their tests through the balance-sheet date.

Analytical review is a form of deductive reasoning in which the propriety of the individual details in inferred from evidence of the reasonableness of the aggregate results. It involves a comparison of the recorded financial results with results that may reasonably be expected in the circumstances. This comparison should either provide audit evidence of the reasonableness of the recorded amount or identify significant fluctuations from expected results that merit further investigation.

Two questions that are inherent in analytical review must be answered, either implicitly or explicitly, however the review is performed: (1) What results may reasonably be expected? (2) How much fluctuation from those results should be considered significant?

The concepts of reasonably expected results and of significant fluctuations from those results imply the existence of some system that can be studied and understood in sufficient depth to allow the development of a satisfactory model. Whether this task is feasible depends on factors such as the complexity of the system, its relative stability or volatility, the availability of information needed to study it, and the time and cost constraints on obtaining such information. In certain cases, analytical review may not be an effective and efficient substantive test. An auditor's principal alternative in these situations is to obtain more reliance from tests of details than otherwise would be necessary.

2.3 Subjective Techniques

We refer to techniques that do not provide statistical measurements of the reliability and precision attributable to the results of analytical review procedures as subjective techniques. We discuss these techniques briefly here to provide a frame of reference for comparison with the statistical techniques presented later.

Subjective techniques involve an intuitive modeling process that is so instinctive and automatic that it is seldom recognized as such. An intuitive modeling process is inherent even in making simple comparisons. For example, auditors often compare results for the current year with the budget for the current year or results for the prior year. The model inherent in this process is that these amounts provide a reasonable expectation of current results. If this were not the case, the comparison would be pointless.

In making comparisons with prior years, auditors may revise the data for such years to eliminate unusual transactions or events in those years, or to adjust them for the estimated effects of general inflation or specific changes in sales prices or costs. Such revisions are conscious efforts to improve the model. Similarly, the use of an average, a trend, or a growth rate based on more than one year implies that a longer period is expected to improve the model. Comparing information for corresponding months of one or more years implies that seasonality may be expected. Models used in subjective reviews may also be expanded to include relationships between the accounts of interest to the auditor and other information, such as gross profit rates, turnover rates, unit costs, number of days outstanding, and similar statistics.

We believe that the preceding paragraphs describe the models that generally are used in subjective analytical reviews. However, subjective techniques for determining how much fluctuation from expected results is sufficient to require investigation by the auditor are more difficult to describe. The only comments in CSAS Section 318 that pertain to this problem are as follows:

> When analytical review procedures identify fluctuations that are not expected, or the absence of fluctuations when they are expected, or other items that appear unusual, the auditor should investigate them if he believes that they are indicative of matters that have a significant effect on his examination.

To the best of our knowledge, when subjective techniques are used for analytical review, the fluctuations to be investigated are determined either completely subjectively or by the use of subjectively established cutoff points that are expressed as absolute amounts or as percentages of the related recorded amounts. In either event, the amounts selected for investigation typically show no direct link to audit decisions about materiality and audit risk.

2.4   Overview of Statistical Techniques

In this section we present a brief overview of the principal statistical techniques discussed in this book, of a computer program that is used to implement these techniques, and of the actions required by an auditor in a simple application of the techniques and the program. This overview is intended only as an introduction to the further discussion of these matters in later chapters. Accordingly, this section will leave many questions unanswered. Those that pertain to statistical concepts and calculations are discussed in Part II of this book, and those that relate to auditing decisions are discussed in Part III.

The program we will refer to is called STAR (an acronym for *Statistical Techniques for Analytical Review*). It has been used extensively since the early 1970s when DH&S introduced it into the firm's audit practice. The STAR Program melds audit decisions about materiality, reliability, and other audit objectives with regression analysis and certain other statistical techniques into a tool that is able to produce results directly relevant to, and usable by, the auditor. The Program was developed for use on a commercial timesharing network. It was used extensively on that network for several years before being transferred to the DH&S timesharing network. More recently, it has been revised and rewritten for the IBM Personal Computer and certain compatible computers.

The STAR Program incorporates an audit model for regression analysis, which combines the general regression model with an audit interface. The general regression model underlies the application of regression analysis for any purpose, while the audit interface is an extension that adapts the general model to serve the auditing purposes of analytical review.

The steps involved in a STAR application are:

Designing the audit model

Running the STAR Program

Reviewing the Program printouts

Investigating unusual fluctuations

Evaluating audit results

These steps are discussed in the following subsections. They are illustrated in a specific example, which will reappear several times in this book.

The example relates to the analytical review of revenue for a fictitious computer software company, "Gamma Company," or Gamma for short. Gamma Company employs around 270 computer professionals who provide service to Gamma's clients for programming projects. Three categories of personnel are employed by Gamma—programmers, senior programmers, and analysts. Their latest hourly billing rates are $45, $70, and $100, respectively. The exact numbers fluctuate, but there are usually about 200 programmers, 50 senior programmers, and 20 analysts on the payroll at any one time. Gamma Company bills customers on the basis of time and expenses, although the company typically does not bill 100% of the time charged to each job. Historically, the company's realization has been around 90%. Everyone at Gamma fills out a monthly time report, which is used as the basis for the billing of customers.

The audit of revenue is clearly of central importance. The auditor has decided to review the relationship of recorded revenue to time at standard billing rates.

2.4.1 Designing the audit model

In the system-design phase, the auditor specifies his or her objectives and perception of the system, including the plausible relationships among elements of the system. In this phase, the auditor needs to draw on personal knowledge of the client's business and accounting practices. The information needed to develop the model is identified at this stage.

The auditor's first design decision has been indicated in the example. The audit purpose of the application is to test recorded revenue, and this becomes the *dependent variable,* in regression terminology.

Next the auditor needs to decide what data to use in the application. For the Gamma example, we assume that the recorded revenue for a series of months is to be used. These monthly amounts are described as *observations* or *observed values* of the dependent variable, and the set for all of the months used is a part of the *data profile.* Because the observations cover a series of consecutive time periods, they are described as *time-series* observations, and that term is also used to describe the related data profile. The auditor might have decided to use the amount of revenue from each customer, in which case such amounts would have been known as *cross-sectional* observations and the data profile would have been described by the same term.

The auditor must also decide how many observations are to be included in the data profile. For the Gamma Company example, we assume that the profile is to include the 36 months preceding the year being audited and the 12 months of that year. In this book we refer to the observations for the 36 months as the *base profile,* and those for the 12 months as the *projection profile.* The remaining elements of the audit objective are established by the auditor's decisions about the direction of the test (i.e., for overstatement or understatement) and the reliability level and precision limit desired.

Once the audit objectives are specified, the remaining step for the auditor in designing the audit model is to specify the *independent variables* to be used. These consist of the balances, transactions, or other data that might have a relationship to the dependent variable and that would be useful in determining reasonably expected values for the latter.

For the Gamma Company example, we assume that the auditor decides to use hourly billing rates, hours worked, and recorded revenue for each month, all of which are readily available from Gamma's records. We also assume that the auditor creates another variable that represents standard revenue, based on hours worked and standard billing rates, which is called TIME AT STANDARD.

Table 2.1 shows a printout of the data profile, including the derived variable. This table also shows EXPENSES charged to clients, and COST OF SERVICES. These two variables are not used in this example, but are included here for reference in later examples.

2.4.2   Running the STAR Program

The STAR Program comes with a User Guide that provides specific instructions for running it in the applicable computer environment. Therefore this phase of an application is not discussed further in this book.

2.4.3   Reviewing the program printouts

As will be explained in Chapter 7, the program printouts should be reviewed to determine whether they suggest any possibilities for improvements in the audit model. For our purpose at this stage, we describe briefly the general content of the printouts. A complete STAR Program printout is included as Printout B.1.

A printout describing the data profile for the Gamma Company is shown in Figure 2.1. Each variable is given a *label* by the STAR Program. The original variables are labeled C01, C02, and so on (C stands for *column*); the mathematically derived variable is labeled M07. Each variable can be

Table 2.1 Gamma Company data profile

		Rate			Hours Worked					
Obs.	Analysts	Senior Prgmrs	Prgmrs	Analysts	Senior Prgmrs	Prgmrs	Time at Standard	Expense	Revenue	Cost of Services
No.	C01	C02	C03	C04	C05	C06	M07	C08	C09	C10
1	75	50	30	3946	7218	30560	1574	802	2107	1527
2	75	50	30	3499	7760	28427	1503	785	1915	1531
3	75	50	30	3813	7345	33064	1645	711	1873	1507
4	75	50	30	2816	6465	28180	1380	844	1978	1681
5	75	50	30	3085	8476	30831	1580	761	2010	1443
6	75	50	30	4486	7426	28951	1576	716	1969	1507
7	90	55	30	4221	7782	31475	1752	724	2228	1545
8	90	55	30	3057	5443	32467	1549	753	2152	1376
9	90	55	30	2983	8313	30888	1652	1020	2439	1870
10	90	55	30	3463	7700	30506	1650	878	2318	1744
11	90	55	30	2726	6990	28881	1496	841	2244	1547
12	90	55	30	3741	7287	31124	1671	900	2357	1864
13	90	55	30	2778	8582	31896	1679	794	2103	1622
14	90	55	30	3522	8353	33510	1782	873	2457	1699
15	90	55	30	3730	7403	30291	1652	929	2606	1683
16	90	55	30	3176	9325	31909	1756	875	2493	1712
17	90	55	30	2210	6850	32639	1555	794	2264	1603
18	90	55	30	3225	8467	28834	1621	813	2058	1550
19	90	55	40	3420	7725	31241	1982	886	2516	1830
20	90	55	40	3930	8186	31153	2050	913	2533	2052
21	90	55	40	3109	6954	32419	1959	990	2958	1855
22	90	55	40	2838	6868	30074	1836	963	2564	1759
23	90	55	40	3318	7425	32467	2006	855	2318	1830
24	90	55	40	4158	6325	36060	2164	1058	2928	2333
25	90	55	40	2589	7508	28354	1780	1059	2754	2005
26	90	55	40	2857	7740	34268	2054	966	2678	2000
27	90	55	40	4061	9582	34320	2265	983	3189	2024
28	90	55	40	3796	7814	33633	2117	956	3067	2182
29	90	55	40	2878	8256	31058	1955	1077	2735	1981
30	90	55	40	3708	8428	31541	2059	1108	3029	2073
31	100	60	40	2711	8026	32661	2059	813	2531	1921
32	100	60	40	3405	7704	32333	2096	1101	2765	2110
33	100	60	40	3444	8208	34092	2201	1186	3074	2120
34	100	60	40	3074	6843	32455	2016	1092	2651	2058
35	100	60	40	3648	7560	34471	2197	915	3056	2039
36	100	60	40	2603	9140	31848	2083	1062	3155	2157
37	100	60	40	2018	8085	34712	2075	909	2757	1979
38	100	60	40	2379	8458	30965	1984	999	2869	2046
39	100	60	40	3804	9241	35275	2346	1035	3168	2072
40	100	60	40	3815	8055	34734	2254	956	3210	1933
41	100	60	40	3733	7572	33451	2166	1348	2958	2433
42	100	60	40	3297	8499	29327	2013	1157	2698	2250
43	100	70	45	3642	8548	33947	2490	969	3412	2224
44	100	70	45	3460	6103	31237	2179	1176	2872	2288
45	100	70	45	2765	6572	33515	2245	1331	3263	2421
46	100	70	45	2892	8929	35569	2515	1140	3506	2447
47	100	70	45	3224	8267	33055	2389	1347	3452	2338
48	100	70	45	2712	9023	33030	2389	1159	2993	2312

22

```
CLIENT    = GAMMA COMPANY
YEAR END  = DECEMBER 31 1984
```

NAME OF VARIABLE		SOURCE/DESCRIPTION OF VARIABLE	UNITS	BYPASS
C01	RATE-ANALYSTS	RATE - ANALYSTS	1	NONE
C02	RATE-SNR PRGRMRS	RATE - SENIOR PROGRAMMERS	1	NONE
C03	RATE-PRGMRS	RATE - PROGRAMMERS	1	NONE
C04	HRS-ANALYSTS	HOURS WORKED - ANALYSTS	1	NONE
C05	HRS-SNR PRGMRS	HOURS WORKED - SENIOR PROGRAMMERS	1	NONE
C06	HRS-PRGMRS	HOURS WORKED - PROGRAMMERS	1	NONE
M07	TIME AT STANDARD	(C01*C04+C02*C05+C03*C06)/1000	1000	NONE
C08	EXPENSES		1000	NONE
C09	REVENUE		1000	NONE
C10	COST OF SERVICES		1000	NONE

```
NUMBER OF OBSERVATIONS :
   IN BASE PERIOD                    36
   IN PROJECTION PERIOD              12
                                   ────
   TOTAL                             48
                                   ════
```

THE DATA PROFILE IS TIME SERIES

THERE ARE 12 PERIODS PER YEAR

Figure 2.1   Gamma Company, STAR Program printout describing the data profile. The observations themselves are shown in Table 2.1. Note that the variables are "labeled" C01, C02, etc. The "C" stands for column. The variable in the seventh column is labeled M07 to signify that is has been derived mathematically from the other columns. The formula that was used to derive it is also shown.

given a name and an extended description as illustrated here. A *units* field is used to show the unit in which each variable is expressed, and a *bypass* field can be used to cause the Program to ignore a certain number of beginning or ending values of the variable.

To keep things simple at this stage, we assume that TIME AT STANDARD was the only independent variable specified by the auditor. Because EXPENSES are also billed to clients, and thus will explain part of the recorded REVENUE, we should also include EXPENSES as an independent variable. However, we will not do so until Chapter 4.

STAR uses regression analysis to compute the *regression function* that expresses the closest linear relationship that has been found between the dependent variable and the independent variable in the base profile. A regression function with only one independent variable is particularly easy to visualize. It is a straight line passing through a scatter of points that

SCATTER DIAGRAM OF REVENUE VS TIME AT STANDARD

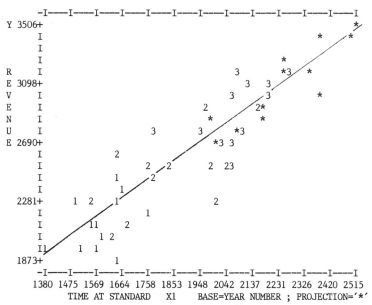

Figure 2.2 Gamma Company. Scatter diagram and line of best fit. The base observations are represented by the number of the year to which they belong. The line of best fit has been fitted to those base observations. The observations from the projection profile are represented by asterisks.

represent the base observations. This is illustrated in Figure 2.2. Such a function can be represented by an equation of the form

$$\hat{Y}_t = a + bX_t$$

where $\hat{Y}$ (pronounced "Y-hat") represents the estimate of the dependent variable provided by the line, and X represents the value of the independent variable. The subscript t indicates that the values are those for observation t.

The symbols a and b represent the two parameters of the regression function: a is called the *regression constant* and b is the *regression coefficient* or simply the *coefficient* of X. The regression function for the Gamma Company example is shown in Figure 2.3 in slightly different symbols than those we are using here. In our symbols, it is

$$\hat{Y}_t = 13.7629 + 1.3582\,X_t$$

| | INPUT DATA | | REGRESSION FUNCTION ETC. | |
DESCRIPTION	MEAN	STANDARD ERROR	CONSTANT OR COEFFICIENT	STANDARD ERROR
CONSTANT			13.7629	
INDEPENDENT VARIABLES X1 TIME AT STANDARD	1832.0000	246.1553	1.3582	0.1359
DEPENDENT VARIABLE Y REVENUE Y' REGRESSION ESTIMATE	2502.0000	387.0976	2502.0000	197.9585
COEFFICIENT OF : CORRELATION REGRESSION IMPROVEMENT RESIDUAL VARIATION			0.8637 0.4886 0.0791	

REGRESSION ESTIMATE [Y'(t)] OF REVENUE FOR OBSERVATION t :
$Y'(t) = 13.7629 + 1.3582*X1(t)$

MONETARY PRECISION = 600 (SAME UNITS AS DEPENDENT VARIABLE)
RELIABILITY FACTOR = 3
DIRECTION OF TEST IS UNDERSTATEMENT

---------------------- REGRESSION PROJECTIONS ----------------------

| | | | | | OPTIONAL SAMPLE DATA | | |
OBS NO	RECORDED AMOUNT	REGRESSION ESTIMATE	RESIDUAL	EXCESS TO BE INVESTIGATED	SELECTION INTERVAL	RANDOM START	MAXIMUM ITEMS
37	2757	2832	−75				
38	2869	2708	161				
39	3168	3200	−32				
40	3210	3075	135				
41	2958	2956	2				
42	2698	2748	−50				
43	3412	3396	16				
44	2872	2973	−101				
45	3263	3063	200				
46	3506	3430	76				
47	3452	3259	193				
48	2993	3259	−266	138	384	331	8
	37158	36899	259	138			8

Figure 2.3 Gamma Company. STAR Printout showing the regression function that relates REVENUE as the dependent variable to TIME AT STANDARD as the independent variable. The bottom part of the printout shows the audit interface.

25

The calculation of the regression function and the other regression statistics shown on the printout and the meaning of the statistics are explained in Chapter 3. In the equation shown on the printout, the independent variable has been designated X_1. If there were several independent variables, we would use X_1, X_2, X_3, and so on to represent the independent variables, and b_1, b_2, and b_3 to represent their respective coefficients. We have used a further subscript, t, to indicate that the variables represent amounts for period t.

The regression function is used to calculate a *regression estimate* for each observation of the dependent variable by simply substituting the corresponding value of the independent variable into the equation. The differences between the actual values of the dependent variable and the regression estimates are known as the *residuals*.

The regression function is developed from the base profile by use of the regression module of the STAR Program. The audit interface module uses the regression function and the observations of the independent variable in the projection profile to calculate the results shown in the "Regression Projections" section of the printout shown in Figure 2.3.

The regression estimate and residuals are calculated as just explained. The *excess to be investigated* is calculated from the reliability, precision, and direction of test specified by the auditor and from statistical calculations of the standard error of the estimates and of the most adverse possible distribution of errors among the observations of the dependent variable. The latter is a critical feature of the audit interface, because a material amount of error could occur in any one of the observations of the dependent variable or could be distributed equally or disproportionately among any number of them. The *optional sample data* are provided to assist the auditor in designing a sample for use in a test of details, if the auditor decides that such a test is needed. The audit interface calculations are explained in Chapter 5.

2.4.4   Investigating unusual fluctuations and evaluating audit results

Having identified excess residuals that warrant investigation in the light of the auditor's specified objectives and the statistical characteristics of the data profile, the STAR Program has accomplished its purpose. Methods of investigating excesses that the Program has identified and of evaluating audit results are independent of the Program and are in the realm of audit judgment.

The fluctuations identified for investigation could result from any of the following causes:

- An error in the recorded amount of the dependent variable
- An unusual transaction or event, or a change in conditions
- An error in an independent variable, some imperfection in the audit model, or an extreme random fluctuation

Although the primary reason for investigating an excess is to determine whether it is caused by errors in the dependent variable, the result of the investigation may have other effects. For example, it may raise questions that need to be considered in relation to disclosures or to other phases of the audit. It may also reveal information that helps the auditor make constructive suggestions about the client's business operations. Precautions to be taken to avoid errors in independent variables or significant imperfections in the audit model are discussed in Chapters 6 and 7.

The investigation of an identified excess may be performed by either (1) obtaining a satisfactory analytical explanation of the excess or (2) performing additional tests of details of the pertinent balances or transactions. If the amount of the excess is substantial in relation to the recorded amount, the analytical approach generally is preferable. If the excess is relatively small, a satisfactory analytical explanation is less likely to be obtainable, and therefore additional tests of details may be the preferable alternative. As indicated earlier, the optional sample data shown on the printout are provided to assist the auditor in designing and selecting an integrated statistical sample if the latter alternative is to be followed. The investigation of excesses and the evaluation of audit results are discussed further in Chapter 7.

2.5 Comparison of Subjective and Statistical Techniques

Although the basic concepts underlying analytical review are the same regardless of the techniques used in performing the review, we believe that statistical techniques offer some important advantages over subjective techniques. We summarize our views on this issue in this section.

The statistical techniques described in this book can be used for making all of the types of comparisons and studies of relationships that are set forth in SAS 23 and quoted in Section 2.2 of this chapter, with one general exception. That exception applies to situations in which the comparisons or studies are confined to aggregate annual data for the current audit period and for only one period or for very few other periods. In such situations, the number of observations is likely to be either insufficient to permit regression computations or inadequate to provide useful results.

In these cases the statistical techniques tend to highlight the basic problem, which arises from the sparsity of the data being used rather than from the technique itself. The same problem, of course, is present but not highlighted when subjective techniques are used. We think that this problem can be avoided in the majority of audits by the use of data from more years or, preferably, from shorter periods (e.g., quarters or months).

The two principal advantages that we perceive for using statistical techniques for analytical review relate to audit effectiveness. The first is the ability of statistical techniques to provide more realistic estimates of the expected amounts of the dependent variable. We think that the regression estimates are more realistic, because they are determined more objectively and comprehend more complex relationships than is the case with subjective estimates. The dispassionate mathematical analysis performed by the STAR Program is an effective safeguard against any subjective bias toward presuming that recorded amounts are correct. Further, the Program obviously is capable of assimilating and analyzing far more complex relationships than can be handled subjectively. The limited ability of people to handle these functions is one of the most consistent findings in research on human information processing, as noted in the quotation presented in Section 1.5.3.

The second advantage of statistical techniques lies in their ability to measure the reliability and precision that can be attributed to the audit results of a STAR application. Our views on the usefulness of these measurements and their relationship to audit objectives and judgment have already been expressed in Chapter 1.

The efficiency of statistical techniques should be assessed by weighing the costs against the benefits. The costs relate principally to development of the data profile. Our experience indicates, however, that those costs are not prohibitive initially and that subsequent costs tend to be insignificant.

The benefits of statistical techniques, from the most practical point of view, lie in their effect on the relative reliance to be assigned by the auditor to analytical review and tests of details. We think that the extra effectiveness of statistical techniques ordinarily provides a reasonable basis to support an increase in the relative reliance that is appropriate for analytical review and a resulting decrease in the extent of tests of details that is necessary.

References

1. American Institute of Certified Public Accountants, "The Auditor's Study and Evaluation of Internal Control." *Statement on Auditing Procedures* No. 54, 1972.
2. American Institute of Certified Public Accountants. *Codification of Statements on Auditing Standards* No. 1 to No. 47, 1984.
3. American Institute of Certified Public Accountants, "Analytical Review Procedures." *Statement on Auditing Standards* 23, 1978.
4. International Federation of Accountants, "Audit Evidence." *International Auditing Guideline* No. 8, 1982.

BASIC CONCEPTS OF REGRESSION ANALYSIS

3

THE SIMPLE REGRESSION MODEL

3.1 Introduction

The simplest type of regression model is one that relates a dependent variable to only one independent variable as a linear function. Not only is this two-variable function relatively easy to calculate, it is also easy to visualize because it can be depicted as a straight-line graph. By contrast, a multiple or multivariate regression function that relates a dependent variable to two or more independent variables is difficult to graph and is considerably more complex to calculate.

In this chapter we will show how to calculate a simple regression function and other regression statistics, and we will explain the nature and purpose of the latter. Spending the time needed to understand the properties of simple regression functions is worthwhile, because many of these properties apply with little change to the multivariate functions that are discussed in subsequent chapters.

Before dealing with regression functions, we will introduce some basic statistical concepts and notations to which we will be referring in the remainder of this book.

3.2 Basic Statistical Concepts and Notation

In mathematics it is traditional to use the symbol Σ, the Greek capital letter sigma, to indicate the process of summing a sequence of numbers. For example, if Y_t represents sales in period t, the sum of sales in periods 1 through 4 (namely, $Y_1 + Y_2 + Y_3 + Y_4$) can be written as

$$\sum_{t=1}^{4} Y_t$$

In a more general context

$$\sum_{t=m}^{n} Y_t$$

is the sum of the quantities Y_m through Y_n. The variable t is the *index* of the summation, and m through n is its *range*. When the range of the index is obvious from the context, the sum may be written more cleanly and simply as ΣY_t, or as ΣY.

The most used and simplest type of statistical estimate is the *mean estimate*. It may also be the best estimate in situations in which there is no significant independent variable. We will explain this type of estimate as a prelude to regression estimates, because many of the concepts carry over to the latter, more complex case.

A mean estimate is made by calculating the mean of a set of sample observations and using that mean to estimate future results. For example, Table 3.1 shows the six most recent monthly payroll totals for Company A. In the absence of any further information, it might be reasonable to use the mean of those results to estimate payroll costs for period 7. Doing this,

Table 3.1   Company A payroll

Period	$'000
1	97
2	103
3	98
4	105
5	96
6	101
Total	600
Mean	100

of course, implies a model of some underlying process that, in the short term at least, tends to cause payroll costs to fluctuate around the same mean.

The mean of n observations $Y_1, Y_2, \ldots, Y_n$ of a variable Y is

$$\bar{Y} = \frac{\sum\limits_{t=1}^{n} Y_t}{n}$$

The symbol $\bar{Y}$ is pronounced "Y bar." In the previous example

$$\bar{Y} = \frac{\sum\limits_{t=1}^{6} Y_t}{6} = \frac{600}{6} = 100$$

In audit applications, a mean estimate can be useful, provided that the assumption is fair that the same process that generated the base results will also generate the audit period results; more particularly, that the audit period results will tend to fluctuate around the same mean. A mean estimate is said to be *unbiased* if, on average, it will yield the true value of the underlying process, even though individual estimates might deviate.

How accurate a mean estimate is likely to be depends, in part, on how much deviation from the mean is expected. In the case of Company A, the payrolls for periods 1 through 6 cluster quite closely around their mean. If these observations are typical, then an estimate of 100 for period 7 is likely to be reasonably accurate.

By contrast with the amounts for Company A, the amounts for Company B, shown in Table 3.2, are much more widely dispersed about their mean, although the mean is the same as that for Company A. All other things being equal, and assuming that the observed degrees of dispersion are representative of the actual variability of the underlying processes, a mean estimate for Company A is likely to be more accurate than a mean estimate for Company B.

These examples illustrate the well-known point that averages can be misleading unless it is known how well they represent the data. A facetious example is that of someone with feet in the freezer and head in the oven who is "comfortable on average." Clearly there is a need to measure the variability in data.

Table 3.2   Company B payroll

Period	$'000
1	73
2	109
3	101
4	110
5	80
6	127
Total	600
Mean	100

Several statistics are used to measure the variability of data. Their common starting point is the sum of the squares of the deviations from the mean. These squared differences for Company A and Company B are shown in Table 3.3, together with several other statistics that we shall now explain.

A useful convention, which is observed in this book, is that original variables are represented by uppercase letters while deviations from means are represented by the corresponding lowercase letters. Thus if Y_t is used to designate payroll cost for period t and $\bar{Y}$ is the mean, then the deviations $Y_t - \bar{Y}$ are designated by y_t. The sum of the squares of the deviations is

$$\Sigma y_t^2 = \Sigma (Y_t - \bar{Y})^2$$

Table 3.3   Measures of variation for sample data

Period	Company A Y	Company A y	Company A y^2	Company B Y	Company B y	Company B y^2
1	97	−3	9	73	−27	729
2	103	3	9	109	9	81
3	98	−2	4	101	1	1
4	105	5	25	110	10	100
5	96	−4	16	80	−20	400
6	101	1	1	127	27	729
Totals	600	0	64	600	0	2,040
Variance			12.8			408.0
Standard Deviation			3.6			20.2
Coefficient of Variation			0.036			0.202

If there are n items, their *variance* is defined as

$$s_y^2 = \frac{\Sigma y_t^2}{n - 1}$$

This statistic measures the "average" squared variability in n items and is also known as the *mean square error*. (It is not quite an average because the divisor is $n-1$ rather than n.) For Company A, the variance is

$$s_y^2 = \frac{64}{5} = 12.8$$

Table 3.3 shows the payroll amounts (Y) for Companies A and B, the deviations of those amounts from their respective means (y), and the squares of those deviations (y^2). The derived statistics are explained in the text for Company A.

Just as the calculated mean is an estimate of the mean of the underlying process, the calculated variance is an estimate of the variance of that process. It might seem odd to divide by $n-1$ rather than by n in the formula just given. The reason (which we state without proof) is to ensure that the calculated variance is an *unbiased* estimate of the variance of the underlying process. (This means that, on average, the variance based on the sample observations can be expected to equal the variance of the underlying process.) The divisor, $n-1$, has a special name. It is called the number of *degrees of freedom*. As we will explain in Section 3.4.2, the general formula for the number of degrees of freedom in regression analysis is $n-k-1$, where k is the number of independent variables used. In the case of a mean estimate, there are no independent variables.

The variance is difficult to interpret, because it is expressed in squared units rather than in the original units of the variable. A statistic that relates better to the original variable is the *standard deviation,* or *standard error*. It is the square root of the variance

$$s_y = \sqrt{s_y^2}$$

The *coefficient of variation* measures the standard error relative to the mean of Y. For Company A, this is

$$v = \frac{s_y}{\bar{Y}} = \frac{3.6}{100} = 0.036$$

In other words, payroll costs have fluctuated by about 3.6% from their mean over the six periods.

The variance, standard error, and coefficient of variation are statistics that are estimates of the equivalent parameters of the assumed underlying process. The symbol σ_y^2 (σ is the Greek lowercase letter sigma) is used to denote the variance of the underlying process to distinguish it from s_y^2, the statistic that is an estimate of it. Similarly, σ_y is the standard error of the underlying process that is estimated by s_y.

In this book, the terms *variance* and *standard error* are used strictly as defined here. *Variance* should not be confused with its accounting usage in relation to standard cost or budget systems, or with the general concepts of variability or variation in the broader statistical sense. The term *error* should not be confused with error in the accounting or auditing context. The use of that term originated from the application of statistics to the analysis of errors that are inherent in methods of scientific measurement.

3.3   Regression Function

If the relationship between a dependent variable and one independent variable is exactly linear, it can be depicted as a straight line on a graph and expressed by an equation of the form

$$Y = \alpha + \beta X$$

where α is the *constant* and β is the *coefficient* of X. For example, if the rates for a rental car are $15/day plus 20¢/mile, the rental for one day is expressed by the function

$$Y = 15.00 + 0.20X$$

where X is miles driven and Y is the daily rental cost. The relationship can be depicted by the line shown in Figure 3.1. This line intercepts the Y axis at $15 (the rental if X is zero) and has a slope of 0.2. The slope indicates that the line rises by 20¢ with each additional mile. Accordingly, the con-

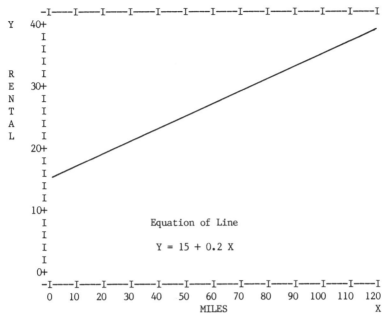

Figure 3.1   Linear function depicting the relationship between miles driven and daily car rental cost assuming a rate of $15 per day plus 20 cents per mile. Notice that the line intercepts the Y axis at 15 and that the slope of the line is 0.2.

stant and the regression coefficient are often referred to as the *intercept* and the *slope,* respectively.

In this example, the linear function can be used to compute an exact value for Y given any value of X. Auditors are seldom able to work with relationships that are such exact predictors. They nearly always have to deal with an element of variability that, for all intents and purposes, is random. This variability can be dealt with by assuming that the relationship between X and Y can be represented by some *underlying linear relationship* (ULR) (like that for the car rental example) plus a factor to account for the random variability from the ULR. Such a model can be expressed as

$$Y_t = \alpha + \beta X_t + u_t$$

where $\alpha + \beta X_t$ is the part that represents the ULR and u_t is the part that represents the random variability. The variable u_t is also known as the *dis-*

turbance term because it represents the disturbance from an otherwise exact relationship in period *t*. In statistics, a variable such as u_t that represents unpredictable and essentially random events is called a *random variable*. It is because the u_t's can be regarded as random variables that the powerful analytical tools of modern statistics can be used.

One of the most important parameters of the ULR is the *standard error of the disturbance*. It measures the expected size of the disturbances which, in auditing terms, is the expected variability from the ULR. The standard error of the disturbance is denoted by σ_u.

Another important difference between the car rental example and most audit applications is that, in the car rental example, the coefficient and the constant are fixed by a rental agreement; in most audit applications, the coefficient and the constant must be estimated from empirical observations. Regression analysis provides a means of estimating the parameters α and β of the ULR from a sample of base observations. These estimates are usually denoted by *a* and *b*, respectively. The resulting regression function is written as

$$Y_t = a + bX_t + e_t$$

where $a + bX_t$ is an estimate of the ULR and e_t is the *residual* that approximates the disturbance u_t. The residuals can be used to calculate the *standard error of the regression function*. This is denoted by s_u and is an estimate of σ_u, the standard error of the disturbance. We will explain how to calculate it in Section 3.4.

It is important to remember that the constant, the coefficient, and the standard error of the regression function are estimates of the parameters of the ULR and, as such, are subject to a certain amount of error. Had the underlying processes of the business yielded a different sample of base observations, the resulting regression function would have been slightly different. This is one of the factors that is taken into account in the audit interface.

The *method of least squares* is used to calculate a "line of best fit" for the observed data, such as the one shown in Figure 2.2 in Chapter 2. This method, first suggested in the early nineteenth century by the French mathematician, Adrien Legendre, results in a line that is "best" in the sense that it minimizes the sum of the squared deviations from the line.

Following the method of least squares, the coefficient and constant for the regression function are calculated as follows:

1. Calculate the means of the X's and the Y's.

$$\bar{X} = \frac{\Sigma X_t}{n}$$

$$\bar{Y} = \frac{\Sigma Y_t}{n}$$

2. Calculate the deviation of each observation from the related mean.

$$x_t = (X_t - \bar{X})$$
$$y_t = (Y_t - \bar{Y})$$

3. Calculate the *sum of the squares* of the deviations x_t.

$$\Sigma x_t^2$$

4. Calculate the *sum of the cross products* of the deviations.

$$\Sigma x_t y_t$$

5. Calculate the regression coefficient.

$$b = \frac{\Sigma x_t y_t}{\Sigma x_t^2}$$

6. Calculate the regression constant.

$$a = \bar{Y} - b\bar{X}$$

The deviations from the mean, the squared deviations, and the cross products of the deviations for the Gamma Company data of Table 2.1 are shown in Table 3.4. Although not needed for computing the regression function, the squared deviations of the Y values are shown because they will be used later.

Table 3.4 Gamma Company basic calculations required for regression

Obs. No.	Original Variables X	Original Variables Y	Deviations from Means x	Deviations from Means y	Squares and Cross Products x^2	Squares and Cross Products xy	Squares and Cross Products y^2
1	1,574	2,107	(258)	(395)	66,564	101,910	156,025
2	1,503	1,915	(329)	(587)	108,241	193,123	344,569
3	1,645	1,873	(187)	(629)	34,969	117,623	395,641
4	1,380	1,978	(452)	(524)	204,304	236,848	274,576
5	1,580	2,010	(252)	(492)	63,504	123,984	242,064
6	1,576	1,969	(256)	(533)	65,536	136,448	284,089
7	1,752	2,228	(80)	(274)	6,400	21,920	75,076
8	1,549	2,152	(283)	(350)	80,089	99,050	122,500
9	1,652	2,439	(180)	(63)	32,400	11,340	3,969
10	1,650	2,318	(182)	(184)	33,124	33,488	33,856
11	1,496	2,244	(336)	(258)	112,896	86,688	66,564
12	1,671	2,357	(161)	(145)	25,921	23,345	21,025
13	1,679	2,103	(153)	(399)	23,409	61,047	159,201
14	1,782	2,457	(50)	(45)	2,500	2,250	2,025
15	1,652	2,606	(180)	104	32,400	(18,720)	10,816
16	1,756	2,493	(76)	(9)	5,776	684	81
17	1,555	2,264	(277)	(238)	76,729	65,926	56,644
18	1,621	2,058	(211)	(444)	44,521	93,684	197,136
19	1,982	2,516	150	14	22,500	2,100	196
20	2,050	2,533	218	31	47,524	6,758	961
21	1,959	2,958	127	456	16,129	57,912	207,936
22	1,836	2,564	4	62	16	248	3,844
23	2,006	2,318	174	(184)	30,276	(32,016)	33,856
24	2,164	2,928	332	426	110,224	141,432	181,476
25	1,780	2,754	(52)	252	2,704	(13,104)	63,504
26	2,054	2,678	222	176	49,284	39,072	30,976
27	2,265	3,189	433	687	187,489	297,471	471,969
28	2,117	3,067	285	565	81,225	161,025	319,225
29	1,955	2,735	123	233	15,129	28,659	54,289
30	2,059	3,029	227	527	51,529	119,629	277,729
31	2,059	2,531	227	29	51,529	6,583	841
32	2,096	2,765	264	263	69,696	69,432	69,169
33	2,201	3,074	369	572	136,161	211,068	327,184
34	2,016	2,651	184	149	33,856	27,416	22,201
35	2,197	3,056	365	554	133,225	202,210	306,916
36	2,083	3,155	251	653	63,001	163,903	426,409
	65,952	90,072	0	0	2,120,780	2,880,436	5,244,538
Mean	1,832	2,502					

The calculations for the Gamma Company are

$$b = \frac{\Sigma x_t y_t}{\Sigma x_t^2} = \frac{2,880,436}{2,120,780} = 1.3582$$

$$a = \bar{Y} - b\bar{X} = 2502 - 1.3582 \times 1832 = 13.7629$$

Therefore the Gamma Company regression function is

$$\hat{Y}_t = 13.7629 + 1.3582X_t$$

The regression line for this function is illustrated in Figure 2.3 in Chapter 2.

To distinguish it from certain more exotic functions (which will be referred to in later chapters), a regression function that is calculated according to the method just given is often referred to as an *ordinary least squares* (OLS) function. A feature of an OLS function is that it always passes through the center of the points in the scatter diagram—the point that represents the mean of the variables, (1832, 2502) in the example. This guarantees that the residuals related to the observations used to develop the OLS regression function will net to zero.

Once computed, the regression function can be used to calculate the estimated Y value and the residual for each observation. These amounts and the squares of the residuals for the Gamma Company are shown in Table 3.5.

3.3.1 Mathematical note on the method of least squares

The least squares method determines the values of a and b that minimize the sum of the squared residuals in the equation

$$Y_t = a + bX_t + e_t$$

To show how this is done, we first rewrite the basic equation as

$$e_t = Y_t - a - bX_t$$

Table 3.5 Gamma Company calculation of residuals and squared residuals. The regression estimate is 13.7629 + 1.3582X. The residual is Y minus the regression estimate

Obs. No.	Original Variables		Regression Estimate	Residual	Squared Residual
	X	Y	$\hat{Y}$	e	e^2
1	1,574	2,107	2,152	(45)	1,988
2	1,503	1,915	2,055	(140)	19,643
3	1,645	1,873	2,248	(375)	140,638
4	1,380	1,978	1,888	90	8,083
5	1,580	2,010	2,160	(150)	22,420
6	1,576	1,969	2,154	(185)	34,337
7	1,752	2,228	2,393	(165)	27,339
8	1,549	2,152	2,118	34	1,181
9	1,652	2,439	2,258	181	32,933
10	1,650	2,318	2,255	63	3,993
11	1,496	2,244	2,046	198	39,344
12	1,671	2,357	2,283	74	5,427
13	1,679	2,103	2,294	(191)	36,556
14	1,782	2,457	2,434	23	525
15	1,652	2,606	2,258	348	121,435
16	1,756	2,493	2,399	94	8,878
17	1,555	2,264	2,126	138	19,105
18	1,621	2,058	2,215	(157)	24,781
19	1,982	2,516	2,706	(190)	35,997
20	2,050	2,533	2,798	(265)	70,271
21	1,959	2,958	2,674	284	80,377
22	1,836	2,564	2,507	57	3,200
23	2,006	2,318	2,738	(420)	176,674
24	2,164	2,928	2,953	(25)	621
25	1,780	2,754	2,431	323	104,088
26	2,054	2,678	2,804	(126)	15,755
27	2,265	3,189	3,090	99	9,781
28	2,117	3,067	2,889	178	31,653
29	1,955	2,735	2,669	66	4,348
30	2,059	3,029	2,810	219	47,825
31	2,059	2,531	2,810	(279)	78,014
32	2,096	2,765	2,861	(96)	9,132
33	2,201	3,074	3,003	71	5,016
34	2,016	2,651	2,752	(101)	10,182
35	2,197	3,056	2,998	58	3,394
36	2,083	3,155	2,843	312	97,402
	65,952	90,072	90,072	0	1,332,340

For the n base profile observations, we have

$$e_1 = Y_1 - a - bX_1$$
$$e_2 = Y_2 - a - bX_2$$
$$\cdot$$
$$\cdot$$
$$\cdot$$
$$e_n = Y_n - a - bX_n$$

Squaring each side of each equation and summing the results we get

$$\Sigma e_t^2 = \Sigma(Y_t - a - bX_t)^2$$

Because Σe_t^2 is a function of a and b, we can write

$$f(a,b) = \Sigma(Y_t - a - bX_t)^2$$

where f is the function whose value is to be minimized.

Differential calculus provides a technique for just this kind of minimization problem. The technique is to differentiate f with respect to a and to b, to set both derivatives equal to zero, and to solve simultaneously for a and b. The function $f(a,b,)$ will be a minimum for these values of a and b. Differentiating, we get

$$\frac{df}{da} = -2\Sigma(Y_t - a - bX_t)$$

$$\frac{df}{db} = -2\Sigma X_t(Y_t - a - bX_t)$$

Setting these two equations equal to zero, we get

$$\Sigma(Y_t - a - bX_t) = 0$$
$$\Sigma X_t(Y_t - a - bX_t) = 0$$

which may be written in what is known as the "normal form"

$$an + b\Sigma X_t = \Sigma Y_t$$

$$a\Sigma X_t + b\Sigma X_t^2 = \Sigma X_t Y_t$$

Solving these simultaneous equations for b, we get

$$b = \frac{\Sigma X_t Y_t - (\Sigma X_t)(\Sigma Y_t)/n}{\Sigma X_t^2 - (\Sigma X_t)^2/n}$$

This formula for b can be written in terms of deviations from the means $\bar{X}$ and $\bar{Y}$ as

$$b = \frac{\Sigma(X_t - \bar{X})(Y_t - \bar{Y})}{\Sigma(X_t - \bar{X})^2} = \frac{\Sigma x_t y_t}{\Sigma x_t^2}$$

The constant a can be obtained by solving the first of the two normal equations

$$a = \frac{\Sigma Y_t}{n} - b\frac{\Sigma X_t}{n}$$

$$= \bar{Y} - b\bar{X}$$

The method of least squares results in estimates of α and β that are known as *best linear unbiased* (or BLU) estimates. Although other methods of estimation are possible, it is the BLU property of the least squares estimators that has ensured their enduring popularity. The fact that a and b are BLU can be proved mathematically. (See, for example, Johnston [1], pp. 18–24.)

The fact that a and b are "linear" estimators means that they can be expressed as linear functions of the observed Y values. That they are "unbiased" means that, if the regression procedure were to be repeated again and again with different sets of observations on X and Y, the estimates a and b would, on average, equal the parameters α and β. A biased estimate is one that, on average, does not equal the true value. That a and b are "best" linear unbiased estimators means that, of all possible linear unbiased estimators of α and β, a and b have the smallest variance. That is, they will have values that, on average, are closer to those of α and β than any other linear unbiased estimators.

3.4 Other Regression Statistics

In addition to the regression function, several interesting statistics are computed by the STAR Program. We will discuss their purpose and computation in the remainder of this section.

3.4.1 Measures of variation in regression analysis

If the observations of a dependent variable are viewed by themselves, simply as an isolated set of data without reference to the values of any independent variables, then, as we explained in Section 3.2, the fluctuations that are measured are those of the variable about its mean. Regression analysis seeks to improve on the mean estimate by "explaining" the fluctuation of the dependent variable from its mean. Several statistics are used to measure the extent to which this objective has been achieved. The starting point in the calculation of these statistics is the analysis of total variation.

$$Y_t - \bar{Y} = (\hat{Y}_t - \bar{Y}) + (Y_t - \hat{Y}_t)$$

or, in terms of the lower case convention

$$y_t = \hat{y}_t + e_t$$

The first component, y_t, measures the difference between the regression estimate and the mean estimate—the amount of variation that has been "explained by" the regression. The second component, e_t, is the "unexplained" or residual variation arising from the deviation of the recorded value from the regression estimate. The sum of the two components is the total variation.

Because of the way in which the regression line is calculated, it turns out that the analysis of total variation as applied to each observation also holds true for the total squared variation for all observations. Therefore

$$\Sigma y_t^2 = \Sigma \hat{y}_t^2 + \Sigma e_t^2$$

In other words

$$\text{Total sum of squares} = \text{Explained sum of squares} + \text{Residual sum of squares}$$

Rearranging the terms, we get

$$\Sigma \hat{y}_t^2 = \Sigma y_t^2 - \Sigma e_t^2$$

which highlights the fact that the variation explained by the regression analysis is simply the total variation less the variation that remains unexplained after the regression analysis.

For the Gamma Company example, the total squared variation, 5,244,538, is shown in the "y^2" column in Table 3.4. The squared unexplained variation, 1,332,340, is shown in the "e^2" column in Table 3.5. The explained variation is the difference, 3,912,198.

3.4.2 Measures of "goodness of fit"

From this point forward, we will sometimes refer to a regression function's relative success in minimizing the unexplained variation, and thus maximizing the explained variation, as its *goodness of fit*. While this is not an elegant term, it is nevertheless commonly used and is concisely descriptive of the concepts that need to be communicated.

The goodness of fit of a regression function is measured using various statistics that analyze, from somewhat different perspectives, the improvement in the estimate that is brought about by regression analysis. Some of these statistics focus on the explained portion of the variation, while others focus on the unexplained portion. Most of them are not used directly in the STAR Program, but all may be of interest to the user for general descriptive purposes or for comparisons among different applications.

The basic measure of unexplained variation in regression analysis is the *standard error of the regression function,* denoted by s_u. (Some authors describe this measure as the *standard error of the estimate*. We have not because we have used it to describe another measure in Section 3.5.) The standard error of the regression function is essential to the analysis that is performed by STAR, because it is used in the process of identifying fluctuations that are statistically significant. The formula for the standard error of the regression function is

$$s_u = \sqrt{\frac{\Sigma e_t^2}{n - 2}}$$

The divisor, $n - 2$, is the degrees of freedom; it "averages" the residual sum of squares to produce a *mean square error*. Thus in a sense the standard error measures the "average" of the variability represented by the residuals. In general, if there are k independent variables in the regression, then the number of degrees of freedom is $n - k - 1$. When a mean estimate rather than a regression estimate is used and there are therefore no independent variables, $k = 0$ and the number of degrees of freedom is $n - 1$ (See Section 3.2). When one independent variable has been used, $k = 1$. Taking the square root of the mean square error reduces the latter to original units.

The standard error of the regression function is an estimate of the standard error of the disturbances from the underlying linear model. Dividing by the degrees of freedom, $n - k - 1$, rather than by the number of observations, n, yields an unbiased estimate of σ_u, the standard error of the ULR.

In the Gamma Company example, the standard error of the regression function is

$$s_u = \sqrt{\frac{1,332,340}{36 - 2}} = 197.9585$$

as shown on the STAR printout in Figure 2.3. Thus 197.9585 is the best estimate that can be made of σ_u, the standard error of the disturbances from the ULR. (The calculation as shown actually works out to 197.9557. The difference is due to rounding and to the fact that, as explained in Chapter 9, STAR uses a somewhat different computational procedure.)

Because the standard error of the regression function is a measure of the variation between the regression estimates and observed values of the dependent variable, its relative size generally can be expressed meaningfully in relation to the mean of the dependent variable. This statistic is known as the *coefficient of residual variation*. It is

$$v = \frac{s_u}{\bar{Y}}$$

In the Gamma Company application

$$v = \frac{197.9585}{2502} = 0.0791$$

which indicates that the standard error is slightly less than 8% of the average value of the dependent variable.

A measure of goodness of fit that is based on explained rather than unexplained variation is the *coefficient of determination*. This coefficient, denoted by R^2, is the ratio of the explained sum of squares to the total sum of squares. Thus

$$R^2 = \frac{\Sigma \hat{y}_t^2}{\Sigma y_t^2}$$

Since the coefficient of determination is derived from squared deviations, many people prefer to use its square root, which is called the *coefficient of correlation*

$$R = \sqrt{R^2}$$

For the Gamma Company application

$$R^2 = \frac{3,912,198}{5,244,538} = 0.74596$$

$$R = \sqrt{0.74596} = 0.8637$$

An alternative formula for the coefficient of correlation that is often used in practice is

$$R = \frac{\Sigma x_t y_t}{\sqrt{\Sigma x_t^2}\sqrt{y_t^2}}$$

The formula expressed in this way is quite illuminating, because it shows how correlation depends on the interaction of the dependent and independent variables. As an illustration, the scatter diagram for Y and X is divided into quadrants in Figure 3.2. Since the center of the quadrants is exactly in the middle of the scatter (at the mean of Y and X), the deviations from the means (y and x) determine into which quadrants the points fall.

If most of the points fall into quadrants one and three (as they do in Figure 3.2), then positive y's tend to be accompanied by positive x's and negative y's tend to be accompanied by negative x's. In both cases, the *cross product* $x_t y_t$ is positive. This indicates a positive correlation between them. Positive y's accompanied by negative x's and negative y's accompanied by positive x's (negative cross products) are indications of negative correlation. The sum of the cross products, $\Sigma x_t y_t$, measures the total interaction between x and y. It is divided by $\sqrt{\Sigma x_t^2}$ and $\sqrt{\Sigma y_t^2}$ to reduce it to standard units that measure the relative strength of the correlation.

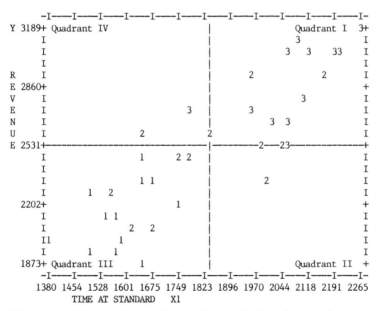

SCATTER DIAGRAM OF REVENUE VS TIME AT STANDARD

```
      -I----I----I----I----I----I----I----I----I----I----I----I----I-
 Y 3189+ Quadrant IV                |            Quadrant I   3+
     I                              |                3         I
     I                              |            3   3    33   I
     I                              |                         I
 R   I                              |    2            2       I
 E 2860+                            |                         +
 V   I                              |            3            I
 E   I                       3      |   3                     I
 N   I                              |        3  3             I
 U   I               2            2 |                         I
 E 2531+---------------------------|--------2---23------------+
     I               1        2 2   |                         I
     I                              |                         I
     I                   1 1        |        2                I
     I          1   2              |                         I
  2202+                     1       |                         +
     I           1 1                |                         I
     I                2   2         |                         I
    I1                1             |                         I
     I          1   1              |                         I
 1873+ Quadrant III     1          |            Quadrant II   +
      -I----I----I----I----I----I----I----I----I----I----I----I----I-
      1380 1454 1528 1601 1675 1749 1823 1896 1970 2044 2118 2191 2265
          TIME AT STANDARD    X1
```

Figure 3.2 Gamma Company. Scatter diagram showing division of observations into quadrants. The predominance of points in Quadrants I and III is indicative of positive correlation. In these quadrants, xy is positive. In Quadrants II and IV, xy is negative.

In the Gamma Company example, the coefficient of correlation can be recalculated as

$$R = \frac{2,880,436}{\sqrt{2,120,780}\sqrt{5,244,538}} = 0.8637$$

which is the same as the square root of the coefficient of determination.

A third measure of goodness of fit is the *coefficient of regression improvement*. This coefficient measures the proportionate reduction in the standard error that has been achieved by use of estimates based on the regression function instead of estimates based on the mean of the dependent variable. This coefficient is computed as

$$I = 1 - \frac{s_u}{s_y}$$

For the Gamma Company example

$$I = 1 - \frac{197.9585}{387.0976} = 0.4886$$

Figure 3.3 illustrates how the coefficients of correlation and regression improvement vary with the coefficient of determination. All three of these statistics are closely related (as shown in Figure 3.3). Because the coefficient of correlation is the most widely used, however, it is the one that will be referred to most often in the rest of this book.

3.4.3   Standard error of the regression coefficient

In many applications of regression analysis, the main purpose of the application is calculation of the slope of the regression line. For instance, in an economic model that relates consumption to income, the coefficient (i.e., the slope) of the line represents the estimated marginal propensity to consume. In such applications the regression coefficient is an estimate of the coefficient of the ULR, and it is often important to know how accurate the estimate is. Because the regression function is computed from a sample of data, the regression coefficient is affected by the random variability in the sample data. If the regression function were to be computed over and over

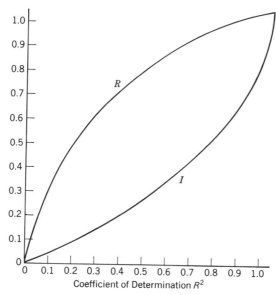

Figure 3.3 Relationship between the coefficient of correlation (R), the coefficient of regression improvement (I), and the coefficient of determination.

again, each time from a different set of sample data, a degree of variability would be observed in the regression coefficient. The *standard error of the regression coefficient* measures the average of that variability.

One factor that affects the standard error of the regression coefficient is the standard error of the regression function. If the observations were all very close to the regression function, the standard error of regression would be small and it would be reasonable to suppose that, if the regression line were to be recalculated based on another set of observations, the new line would be very similar to the original one.

A second factor that affects the standard error of the regression coefficient is the total spread of values of the independent variable as measured by the sum of the squared deviations from its mean. This, in turn, depends on the number of observations (the more, the better) and the sizes of the individual deviations (the larger, the better). A function based on a large number of widely spread observations on the independent variable will have a coefficient with a lower standard error than one based on fewer observations or a narrower spread.

The formula for the standard error of the coefficient reflects all three of these factors

$$s_b = \frac{s_u}{\sqrt{\Sigma x^2}}$$

In the Gamma Company example, the calculation is

$$s_b = \frac{197.9585}{\sqrt{2,120,780}} = 0.1359$$

3.5   Standard Error of Individual Residuals

In Section 3.3 we explained that the disturbance u_t represents the amount by which the dependent variable fluctuates from the ULR in period t. We further explained that the expected size of the fluctuation is represented by σ_u, the standard error of the disturbance, and that the standard error of the regression function, s_u, is an estimate of σ_u. In practice, of course, the exact formula for the ULR is not known; neither are the exact sizes of the disturbances. Instead, interest is focused on the regression function and on the residuals from that function. For reasons that are explained in Chapter 5, it is important to know the standard error of each residual in the audit period. In this section, we will show how to estimate it.

There are two elements of variability that explain why the recorded value of a dependent variable differs from its regression estimate. First, the dependent variable might differ from the ULR. (It differs by the amount of the disturbance.) Second, the regression function, being an estimate of the ULR, might differ from the ULR. These elements of variability can be seen more clearly if the residual is expressed as

$$e_t = Y_t - \hat{Y}_t = (Y_t - \text{ULR}_t) + (\text{ULR}_t - \hat{Y}_t)$$

This difference is illustrated in Figure 3.4. Because the residual can be expressed in this manner, its standard error can be expressed as a combination of the standard errors of the two terms on the right-hand side of the equation. The easy part is the standard error of $Y_t - \text{ULR}_t$. In terms of the linear model, the standard error is σ_u. It is approximated by s_u.

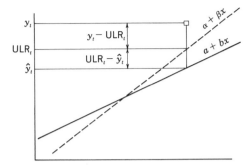

Figure 3.4   Elements of variability. This diagram shows that the variation of the recorded amount from the regression estimate can be analyzed into two parts: the part that represents the variation from the ULR, and the part that represents the difference between the ULR and the regression estimate.

The term $\text{ULR}_t - \hat{Y}_t$ represents the difference between the regression estimate for observation t and the projection that would be obtained if the formula for the ULR were known. Naturally, this difference will vary depending on the particular observations that were used to generate the regression function. Its standard error is called the *standard error of the regression estimate.*

The standard error of the regression estimate depends on a number of factors.

1.   On σ_u, the inherent variability of the disturbances from the ULR. The greater this variability, the greater the variability in the various regression functions that could be generated.

2.   On n, the number of base observations. The more observations that are used, the less variation is likely between the various functions that could be generated.

3.   On the total spread of the X values on which the function has been based. If this spread is wide, the function is more likely to be a good estimate of the ULR over a broader range of X values than if the function were more narrowly based. This total spread is measured by Σx^2, the sum of the squared differences of the base X values from their mean.

4.   On the position of the X value being used for the estimate. For X values near the center of those used to generate the function, we

would expect estimates closer to the ULR than for X values toward and beyond the fringe of the base values. This is simply because, at the center of the scatter, all the points will tend to confirm and corroborate the position of the regression function. At the fringe of the scatter, the position of the regression function is based on more tenuous information.

All these factors are brought together in the formula for the standard error of the regression estimate

$$\sigma(\text{ULR}_t - \hat{Y}_t) = \sqrt{\frac{\sigma_u^2}{n} + \frac{(X_t - \bar{X})^2}{\Sigma x^2} \sigma_u^2}$$

It is readily apparent that the value of the first term on the right-hand side of the equation varies directly with σ_u, the standard error of the ULR, and inversely with n, the number of base-period observations. The second term also varies directly with σ_u and with the distance between the particular X value and the mean of the X's. This illustrates that the standard error is smallest when X_t equals the mean of the X's, and becomes larger the further X_t is from the center. Also the second term varies inversely with the sum of the squared deviations of the X's from their mean. This illustrates that the greater the total spread of X values, the smaller will be the standard error.

Under certain conditions, the standard error of the sum of two random variables is the square root of the sum of the squared standard errors of the variables. The conditions are met in this case and therefore the *standard error of the individual residual* is

$$\sigma(e_t) = \sqrt{\sigma_u^2 + \frac{\sigma_u^2}{n} + \frac{(X_t - \bar{X})^2}{\Sigma x^2} \sigma_u^2}$$

which simplifies to

$$\sigma(e_t) = \sigma_u \sqrt{1 + \frac{1}{n} + \frac{(X_t - \bar{X})^2}{\Sigma x^2}}$$

One remaining problem is that this formula depends on σ_u, the true standard error of the disturbances, which is unknown. Thus σ_u must be replaced by its estimator s_u, which, like the residuals on which it is based, is subject to a certain amount of random variability. The formula therefore becomes

$$s(e_t) = s_u \sqrt{1 + \frac{1}{n} + \frac{(X_t - \bar{X})^2}{\Sigma x^2}}$$

As we shall show in the next section, this adjustment has a subtle effect on the distribution of the residual.

3.6 Distribution of Residuals

When the disturbance u_t is viewed as a *random variable,* it becomes meaningful to talk about the *probability* that it will be greater than some amount, less than some amount, or between two amounts. The probabilistic behavior of random variables is the subject of a highly developed branch of mathematics known as *probability theory.* The foundations of probability theory were laid largely in the eighteenth century by French mathematicians who were hired for the highly practical job of calculating gambling odds.

As an example of how random variables occur, let us consider what might happen in 100 fair tosses of a balanced coin. Let H denote the number of heads observed in a set of 100 tosses. No formal knowledge about probability theory is needed to understand certain things about the behavior of the random variable H. For example:

- Although it is impossible to determine in advance how many heads will be observed, the most likely number is $H = 50$.
- The probability of observing exactly 50 heads in any given set of 100 tosses is fairly low because of the variability that is inherent in the underlying process.
- The probability that H will be greater than 50 is the same as the probability that it will be less than 50.
- The probability that H will be between, say, 35 and 45 is the same as the probability that it will be between 55 and 65. In other words, the probability distribution of H is symmetrical.
- The probability that H will be between 35 and 45 is greater than the probability that H will be between 25 and 35. In other words, extreme values of H are less probable than values closer to 50.

The probabilistic behavior of H can be described precisely by the so-called *binomial probability distribution*. This distribution is based on a mathematical function that can be used to determine the probability that H will lie within any range of values. Although the binomial distribution is the exact distribution of H, the behavior of H can be very well approximated by the so-called *normal probability distribution*. The graph of the normal approximation to the probability distribution of H is shown in Figure 3.5. The probability that H will lie between any two values is represented by the relative area under the curve between those two values. For example, the probability that H will be between 50 and 55, inclusive, is 34%. The probability that H will be greater than 60 is only 2%.

It can be shown that the standard error of H is 5. That is, if the experiment (tossing the coin 100 times) were to be repeated again and again *ad infinitum*, the "average" variation that would be observed is 5. A property of the normal distribution, shown in Figure 3.5, is that about 68% of the observed values of H will fall within 1 standard error of the mean (i.e., 45 to 55 heads), and about 95% will fall within 2 standard errors (i.e., 40 to 60 heads). In fact, the probability of H being greater or less than any specified amount or between any two specified amounts can be approximated from the normal distribution.

In the example, it so happens that H can only take on integer values between 0 and 100. The kind of random variables that are ordinarily dealt with in analytical review can take on any values, not just whole numbers. The normal distribution is specifically applicable to such variables. If H is

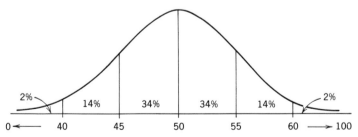

Figure 3.5   Approximate probability distribution of H, the number of heads in 100 fair tosses of a balanced coin. Although the binomial distribution is the exact distribution of H, the normal distribution shown above is a good approximation. The probability that H will be within any range of values is represented by the area under the curve within that range. The total area is 1. Example: the area under the curve between 50 and 55 is 0.34, and therefore, the probability of 50 to 55 heads is 34 percent.

simply redefined as a random variable that is normally distributed with a mean of 50 and a standard error of 5, and the condition that it can only take on integer values is dropped, then the distribution of H as illustrated in Figure 3.5 is exact.

The normal probability distribution was derived in 1738 by De Moivre, an English mathematician of French origin, after he had done considerable work on the theory of games of chance. This distribution is of central importance in modern statistics not so much because of its applicability to games of chance, but because the behavior of a surprising number of things can be measured and described by statistics with probability distributions that are normal, approximately normal, or closely related to the normal. Besides the empirical evidence that supports the use of the normal distribution, there is a strong case for its use that is proved by the so-called *central limit theorem* of statistics.

The gist of the central limit theorem is that, under remarkably general conditions, the distribution of a random variable that is the net effect of a number of independent random events will tend to normality. An assumption in regression analysis, ordinarily very reasonable in practice, is that each disturbance from the ULR is the net effect of many minor unpredictable factors, or random events. Under such conditions, the central limit theorem provides strong theoretical grounds for belief that the disturbance will behave normally. In other words, if it were possible to keep the independent variable constant and to make many observations of the related Y value, the disturbance term would be seen to follow an approximately normal distribution.

The significance of this is that an observed Y value that is significantly improbable according to the normal probability distribution provides prima facie evidence that some unusual factor (possibly an error or irregularity) has induced the disturbance. An analogous situation would occur in the coin-tossing experiment if, say, a total of 90 heads was observed in 100 tosses. Although this event can occur, the probability of its occurring if the coin is balanced and the tosses are fair is so remote that its actual occurrence would be prima facie evidence that the coin is not balanced or had not been tossed fairly.

The "shape" of a particular normal distribution depends on the standard error of the random variable. A random variable with a large standard error will have a flatter distribution than one with a small standard error. To avoid dealing with different-shaped distributions, statisticians frequently divide the random variable by the amount of its standard error. This yields a random variable with a standard error of 1. Therefore, if the disturbance term u_t is normally distributed with mean 0 and standard error σ_u, then u_t/σ_u has a normal distribution with a mean of 0 and a standard error of 1. Similarly, the *standardized residual*

$$\frac{e_t}{\sigma(e_t)}$$

has a normal distribution with a mean of 0 and a standard error of 1. Because the normal distribution with a mean of 0 and a standard error of 1 is used so frequently, it is given a special name, *the standard normal distribution.*

As we indicated at the end of the previous section, one problem with the formula just given for the standardized residual is that the denominator $\sigma(e_t)$ uses the true standard error of the disturbances σ_u, which is unknown. Therefore σ_u must be replaced by its estimator, s_u. The standardized residual thus becomes

$$\frac{e_t}{s(e_t)}$$

The difference between $s(e_t)$ and $\sigma(e_t)$ is that $\sigma(e_t)$ is the true (though unknown) standard error of e_t and therefore is a constant value; $s(e_t)$ is an estimate of $\sigma(e_t)$ and as such is susceptible to a certain amount of random variability. In other words, $s(e_t)$ is a random variable with its own probability distribution. Thus the ratio $e_t/s(e_t)$ is the ratio of two random variables, each with its own probability distribution. The distribution of the ratio is the so-called *Student's t distribution,* or just *t distribution.*

When the regression function is based on a large number of degrees of freedom, the variability in $s(e_t)$ is very small, and the use of $s(e_t)$ instead of $\sigma(e_t)$ makes practically no difference. The distribution of the standardized residual will, for all intents and purposes, be well approximated by the standard normal distribution. However, when the degrees of freedom are few, as they often are, the use of $s(e_t)$ makes the standard normal distribution inappropriate. In fact, the derivation of the t distribution in 1908 by W. S. Gosset was motivated by a need to deal correctly with small samples. Gosset worked for Messrs. Guiness, the Irish brewing company, and needed the t

distribution to deal statistically with the variety of small sample experiments required to operate the brewery properly. He published his works under the pen name "A Student": hence Student's t distribution. From a computational point of view, there is little difference between working with a normal distribution or a t distribution. Therefore, STAR always uses the t distribution.

Whereas there is only one standard normal distribution, there is a different t distribution for every number of degrees of freedom. Therefore, a random variable is often described as being "distributed as t with v degrees of freedom" to identify the appropriate t distribution. The degrees of freedom, v, is the same as the degrees of freedom associated with the standard error used to standardize the random variable. Because the estimated standard error of the residual has $n - k - 1$ degrees of freedom (k is the number of independent variables used), the standardized residual $e_t/s(e_t)$ is distributed as t with $n - k - 1$ degrees of freedom.

In the Gamma Company example, the t distribution has 34 degrees of freedom because there are 36 base observations and 1 independent variable ($36 - 1 - 1 = 34$). A graph of the t distribution with 34 degrees of freedom is shown in Figure 3.6.

3.6.1 Illustrative calculation of standardized residual

We will show how the calculations are made for period 48 for the Gamma Company example. Because period 48 is the one period in which an excess to be investigated was identified (see Figure 2.4), we will use these results again when we discuss the audit interface in Chapter 5.

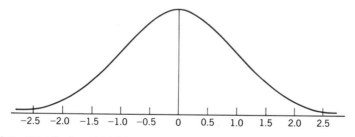

Figure 3.6 t Distribution with 34 degrees of freedom. The probability that t will fall between any two values on the horizontal axis is equal to the relative area under the curve.

The estimated standard error of e_{48} (the residual in period 48) can be calculated from the formula

$$s(e_{48}) = s_u \sqrt{1 + \frac{1}{n} + \frac{(X_{48} - \bar{X})^2}{\Sigma x^2}}$$

and the standardized residual is

$$\frac{e_{48}}{s(e_{48})}$$

All the factors that are needed for this calculation have been derived in this chapter. Some of them also appear on the STAR printout shown as Figure 2.4. They are

s_u	197.9585	Figure 2.4
n	36	Figure 2.2
X_{48}	2,389	Table 2.1
$\bar{X}$	1,832	Table 3.4
Σx^2	2,120,780	Table 3.4

Therefore

$$s(e_{48}) = 197.9585 \sqrt{1 + \frac{1}{36} + \frac{(2389 - 1832)^2}{2,120,780}} = 214.497$$

The degrees of freedom associated with this standard error are $36 - 1 - 1 = 34$. Therefore

$$\frac{e_{48}}{214.497}$$

is a point on the t distribution with 34 degrees of freedom.

Because the actual observed residual for period 48 shown in the STAR printout of Figure 2.4 is -266, the standardized residual is

$$\frac{-266}{214.497} = -1.24$$

standard errors.

The t distribution can be used to make some statements about how the residual is expected to behave, assuming that it does not contain any error. For example, there is a 95% probability that the residual will be less than 1.69 standard errors (see Table A.2 in Appendix A or Figure 3.4). Since 1 standard error equals 214.497, there is a 95% probability that the residual will be less than 362 (that is, 1.69×214.497). It is also possible to work backward from the observed residual and make statements about the probability that a residual of that size could occur. If the residual is so large as to be significantly improbable, a reasonable conclusion is that it might have been affected by an error or some other factor not comprehended by the model. In Chapter 5 we will show how the standard error, the probability distribution, and the audit parameters relating to reliability and materiality are combined to provide results that are meaningful in an audit context.

3.7   Nonlinear Relationships

The discussion to this point has been confined to linear relationships, for which the regression function has been expressed as

$$Y = a + bX + e$$

A function in this form is described as a *linear function* because all of its parameters are linear. Aside from extensions to include more independent variables as discussed in the next chapter, a regression function in any other form is described as a *nonlinear function*. For example,

$$Y = a + bX^2 + e$$

is a nonlinear function because X^2 is a nonlinear term. In the remainder of this section we are concerned with $\hat{Y}$ (the estimate of Y) and therefore omit the residual e from the formulas given.

Our experience indicates that linear functions ordinarily are satisfactory for auditing purposes. For some auditing and nonauditing applications, however, the regression model may be improved by specifying a nonlinear function. Possibilities for such improvement may be indicated by (1) knowledge of underlying conditions that cause a nonlinear relationship to be expected, or (2) observation of a nonlinear pattern in a graph of the variables. The STAR Program includes an option to print such graphs. The remainder of this section deals with certain mathematical aspects of nonlinear functions. The discussion in Chapter 6 relating to auditing matters to be considered in designing models applies to both linear and nonlinear functions.

3.7.1   Classification and general approach

Nonlinear regression functions can be classified broadly as (1) those that are *intrinsically nonlinear* or (2) those that are *intrinsically linear* but have nonlinear parameters. The basic distinction is that a function of the second type can be transformed into a linear form by transformation of its parameters so that the method of least squares can be applied, while a function of the first type cannot. Intrinsically nonlinear functions require the use of more complicated mathematics; they are not dealt with in this book nor can they be handled by the present version of the STAR Program.

Intrinsically linear functions can be classified further as those in which the transformation involves (1) only the independent variables or (2) the dependent variable, either alone or in addition to the independent variables. In the remainder of this section we assume that the model includes only one independent variable, but the general approach that we discuss can be extended to models that include more independent variables.

The number of possible curves that can be described by nonlinear functions is unlimited, but only a few types of curves are commonly used for statistical analysis. A judicious selection from the commonly used functions is generally considered adequate for most applications of regression analysis, and should, we think, be adequate for auditing applications. A few of the commonly used functions and their general characteristics are discussed in the next two subsections, and numerical illustrations are included in Section 3.7.4. The purpose of this discussion and the illustrations is to assist readers in identifying nonlinear functions that may improve regression models and in making the necessary transformations.

3.7.2 Transformations of the independent variable only

If the transformation involves the independent variable only, the transformed variable can simply be substituted for the original variable and the results from the STAR Program can be used in the usual way for typical analytical review applications. The only change that affects the use of the results in this case is that the coefficient b of the independent variable relates to the transformed variable. This is important only if the coefficient is a feature of interest, which ordinarily is not the case in STAR applications.

The following three transformations are examples of transformations that involve only the independent variable:

Type	Nonlinear Function	Transformation	Linear Function
Log	$\hat{Y} = a + b \ln X$	$X' = \ln X$	$\hat{Y} = a + bX'$
Reciprocal	$\hat{Y} = a + b\,(1/X)$	$X' = 1/X$	$\hat{Y} = a + bX'$
Power	$\hat{Y} = a + bx^p$	$X' = X^p$	$\hat{Y} = a + bX'$

In these examples $\hat{Y}$ is the estimate of the dependent variable, X is the original independent variable, X' is the transformed independent variable, ln is the natural logarithm, and p is a power of X.

For each of these transformations we discuss briefly the general characteristics of the related functions and present graphs illustrating segments of the curves generated by them. The graphs on the left sides of the figures are for positive correlation between $\hat{Y}$ and X' and those on the right are for negative correlation, as indicated by the respective signs of the coefficient b. The sign of the coefficient, of course, depends on the data and thus is not a matter of choice. However, the type of transformation, if any, to be used is a matter to be specified in designing the model. The material presented below shows that a discerning choice among these transformations can accommodate a variety of nonlinear relationships.

Independent log transformation. For positive coefficients in the function generated by this transformation, the value of $\hat{Y}$ increases, but at a decreasing rate, as X increases; for negative coefficients, $\hat{Y}$ decreases at an increasing rate. In both cases the curve is convex when viewed from above,

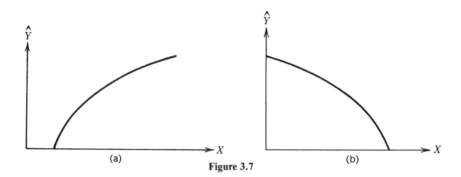

Figure 3.7

and becomes asymptotic (almost parallel) to the X axis when X is very large. This is illustrated in Figure 3.7. This curve can be inverted so that it becomes concave from above by using the following modified transformation, in which X_{max} is the largest value of X in the data being used:

$$X' = \ln X_{max} - \ln X$$

Independent reciprocal transformation.   For positive coefficients in the function resulting from this transformation, the value of $\hat{Y}$ decreases at a decreasing rate as X increases and the curve is concave from above; for negative coefficients, $\hat{Y}$ increases at a decreasing rate and the curve is convex. In both cases the curve becomes asymptotic to the X axis when X is very large. This is illustrated in Figure 3.8. This curve can be inverted so that the characteristics just described are reversed by using the following modified transformation:

$$X' = 1 - 1/X$$

Independent power transformation.   The shape of the power curve that results from this transformation depends on both the sign of the coefficient b and the value of the power p. If b is positive and p is greater than 1, the value of $\hat{Y}$ increases at an increasing rate as X increases. If b is positive and p is between 0 and 1, $\hat{Y}$ increases but at a decreasing rate. These curves are illustrated in Figure 3.9a. If b is negative, the characteristics just described are reversed, as illustrated in Figure 3.9b.

The square root transformation, which is equivalent to a power of 0.5, is a common example of this type of transformation. Since the auditor can

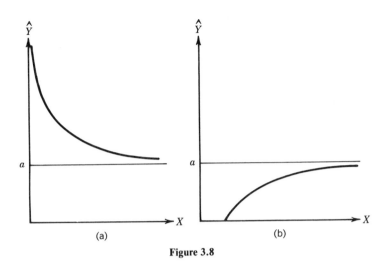

Figure 3.8

specify any value for the power p this transformation is potentially more useful for STAR applications than the two described previously. However, the value to be specified is not likely to be intuitively apparent. If the auditor has any knowledge of underlying conditions or previous experience that is relevant for this purpose, such information obviously should be used for guidance. Otherwise, the power to be specified can be determined by

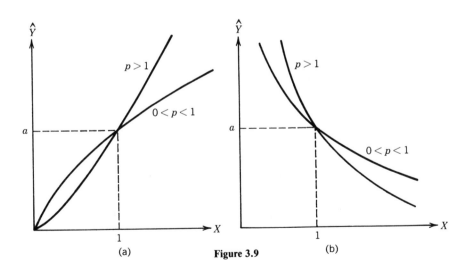

Figure 3.9

an examination of a scatter diagram of the variables and some experimentation.

Figure 3.9a may be helpful in choosing an appropriate power. The concave curve results from the equation

$$Y = a + bX^{1.5}$$

A more concave curve would indicate a power higher than 1.5. Less concavity would indicate a power lower than 1.5. The convex curve in Figure 3.9a results from the equation

$$Y = a + bX^{0.5}$$

A more convex curve would indicate a power lower than 0.5. Less convexity would indicate a power greater than 0.5. Some experimentation with different powers of X in the region of that suggested by an examination of the scatter diagram should produce a regression function with an approximately minimal coefficient of residual variation. A numerical example of such an experimental approach is given in Section 3.7.4.

3.7.3 Transformations of the dependent variable

Several common types of transformation involve the dependent variable, either alone or in addition to the independent variable. For all of these, the regression estimates and the related residuals and standard errors will be expressed in terms of the transformed dependent variable. If, for example, that variable is the logarithm of Y all of the results will be expressed as logarithms and the residuals cannot be used in the audit interface in the usual way. Consequently the statistical properties of the regression function, including the best least squares fit, apply to the transformed variables but not necessarily to the original variables.

If regression results are needed in terms of the original dependent variable, it becomes necessary to retransform the estimates and to recalculate the related residuals and standard errors. This makes the calculation of excesses to be investigated (see Chapter 5) more complicated. For this reason, we discourage the direct use of transformations that affect the dependent variable in typical STAR applications.

3.7.4 Numerical illustrations

In this section we include a few illustrations to demonstrate the concepts and computations we have just discussed and to give some general indication of the numerical effects of the transformations. The information shown in these illustrations is taken from portions of the STAR printouts that are relevant for our purpose. Where necessary a scaling factor has been used in making the transformations so that the transformed variable will be expressed in whole numbers.

Independent log transformation. Figure 3.10 shows a STAR printout of two variables. The variable labeled C01 is the Y variable and was derived exactly from the variable labeled C02 (the X variable) through the formula

$$Y = -4028 + 1749.8 \ln X$$

VARIABLES ON FILE

OBS#	C01	C02
1	4030	100
2	5243	200
3	5952	300
4	6456	400
5	6846	500
6	7165	600
7	7435	700
8	7669	800
9	7875	900
10	8059	1000
11	8226	1100
12	8378	1200
13	8518	1300
14	8648	1400
15	8769	1500
16	8882	1600
17	8988	1700
18	9088	1800
19	9182	1900
20	9272	2000
	154681	21000

Figure 3.10 Data for independent log function.

The STAR printout in Figure 3.11 shows what happens when Y is regressed against 1000 ln X (denoted by 1000 $*$ log(X) by STAR). Not surprisingly, the fit is exact apart from minor aberrations caused by rounding. Notice that the coefficient is 1.7498 rather than 1749.8. This reflects the fact that the Y is regressed against 1000 ln X rather than against ln X.

STEPWISE MULTIPLE REGRESSION MODEL

DESCRIPTION	INPUT DATA: MEAN	INPUT DATA: STANDARD ERROR	REGRESSION FUNCTION ETC.: CONSTANT OR COEFFICIENT	REGRESSION FUNCTION ETC.: STANDARD ERROR
CONSTANT			-4028.7380	
INDEPENDENT VARIABLES				
X1 LOG(X)*1000	6721.9502	812.7220	1.7499	0.0000
DEPENDENT VARIABLE				
Y YVAR	7734.0498	1422.1630		
Y' REGRESSION ESTIMATE			7734.0498	0.0000
COEFFICIENT OF :				
CORRELATION			0.9999	
REGRESSION IMPROVEMENT			1.0000	
RESIDUAL VARIATION			0.0000	

REGRESSION ESTIMATE [Y'(t)] OF VARIABLE 2 FOR OBSERVATION t :

Y'(t) = -4028.738 + 1.7499*X1(t)

Figure 3.11 Model for independent log function.

For comparative purposes Figure 3.12 shows the STAR printout that results when Y is regressed against the original X. The residual plot in Figure 3.13 reveals a curve that is characteristic of an underlying logarithmic relationship. This clear pattern, however, results from the fact that the observations of the independent variable are in ascending order in these illustrations, which ordinarily would not be the case in either time-series or cross-sectional applications.

STEPWISE MULTIPLE REGRESSION MODEL

| DESCRIPTION | INPUT DATA | | REGRESSION FUNCTION ETC. | |
	MEAN	STANDARD ERROR	CONSTANT OR COEFFICIENT	STANDARD ERROR
CONSTANT			5383.3052	
INDEPENDENT VARIABLES X1 XVAR	1050.0000	591.6080	2.2388	0.2064
DEPENDENT VARIABLE Y YVAR Y' REGRESSION ESTIMATE	7734.0498	1422.1630	7734.0498	532.1338
COEFFICIENT OF : CORRELATION REGRESSION IMPROVEMENT RESIDUAL VARIATION			0.9313 0.6258 0.0688	

REGRESSION ESTIMATE [Y'(t)] OF YVAR FOR OBSERVATION t :
Y'(t) = 5383.305 + 2.2388*X1(t)

Figure 3.12 Linear model for comparison with model in Figure 3.11.

RESULTS BASED ON THE REGRESSION FUNCTION

OBS#	RECORDED AMOUNT	REGRESSION ESTIMATE	RESIDUAL	RESIDUALS GRAPHED IN UNITS OF 1 STD. ERROR (532.133)	OBS#
				−4 −3 −2 −1 0 1 2 3 4 −I—I—I—I—I—I—I—I—I-	
1	4030	5607	−1577	-I * I I I I-	1
2	5243	5831	−588	-I I * I I I-	2
3	5952	6055	−103	-I I *I I I-	3
4	6456	6279	177	-I I I* I I-	4
5	6846	6503	343	-I I I * I I-	5
6	7165	6727	438	-I I I * I I-	6
7	7435	6950	485	-I I I * I I-	7
8	7669	7174	495	-I I I * I I-	8
9	7875	7398	477	-I I I * I I-	9
10	8059	7622	437	-I I I * I I-	10
11	8226	7846	380	-I I I * I I-	11
12	8378	8070	308	-I I I * I I-	12
13	8518	8294	224	-I I I* I I-	13
14	8648	8518	130	-I I I* I I-	14
15	8769	8742	27	-I I * I I-	15
16	8882	8965	−83	-I I * I I-	16
17	8988	9189	−201	-I I *I I I-	17
18	9088	9413	−325	-I I * I I I-	18
19	9182	9637	−455	-I I * I I I-	19
20	9272	9861	−589	-I I * I I I-	20
				-I—I—I—I—I—I—I—I—I-	

Figure 3.13 Regression results for the linear model in Figure 3.12.

Independent power transformation.   Figure 3.14 shows a STAR printout of two variables. The variable labelled C01 is the Y variable and was derived exactly from the variable labelled C02 (the X variable) through the formula

$$Y = X^{1.5}$$

The STAR printout in Figure 3.15 shows what happens when Y is regressed against $X^{1.5}$ (denoted by $X^{\wedge}1.5$ by STAR). Not surprisingly, the fit is exact apart from minor aberrations caused by rounding.

For comparative purposes Figure 3.16 shows the STAR printout that results when Y is regressed against the original X. The residual plot in Figure 3.17 reveals a curve that is characteristic of an underlying power ($p > 1$) relationship. This clear pattern, however, results from the fact that the observations of the independent variable are in ascending order in these illustrations, which ordinarily would not be the case in either time-series or cross-sectional applications.

VARIABLES ON FILE

OBS#	C01	C02
1	1000	100
2	2828	200
3	5196	300
4	8000	400
5	11180	500
6	14697	600
7	18520	700
8	22627	800
9	27000	900
10	31623	1000
11	36483	1100
12	41569	1200
13	46872	1300
14	52383	1400
15	58095	1500
16	64000	1600
17	70093	1700
18	76368	1800
19	82819	1900
20	89443	2000
	760796	21000

Figure 3.14   Data for independent power function.

STEPWISE MULTIPLE REGRESSION MODEL

DESCRIPTION	INPUT DATA MEAN	INPUT DATA STANDARD ERROR	REGRESSION FUNCTION ETC. CONSTANT OR COEFFICIENT	REGRESSION FUNCTION ETC. STANDARD ERROR
CONSTANT			-0.2188	
INDEPENDENT VARIABLES				
X1 X^1.5	38039.8280	28246.4902	1.0000	0.0000
DEPENDENT VARIABLE				
Y YVAR	38039.8010	28246.6309		
Y' REGRESSION ESTIMATE			38039.8010	0.0000
COEFFICIENT OF :				
CORRELATION			0.9999	
REGRESSION IMPROVEMENT			1.0000	
RESIDUAL VARIATION			0.0000	

REGRESSION ESTIMATE [Y'(t)] OF YVAR FOR OBSERVATION t :
Y'(t) = -.2187 + 1*X1(t)

Figure 3.15 Model for independent power function.

STEPWISE MULTIPLE REGRESSION MODEL

DESCRIPTION	INPUT DATA MEAN	INPUT DATA STANDARD ERROR	REGRESSION FUNCTION ETC. CONSTANT OR COEFFICIENT	REGRESSION FUNCTION ETC. STANDARD ERROR
CONSTANT			-11645.5996	
INDEPENDENT VARIABLES				
X1 XVAR	1050.0000	591.6080	47.3194	1.5001
DEPENDENT VARIABLE				
Y YVAR	38039.8010	28246.6309		
Y' REGRESSION ESTIMATE			38039.8010	3868.4629
COEFFICIENT OF :				
CORRELATION			0.9911	
REGRESSION IMPROVEMENT			0.8630	
RESIDUAL VARIATION			0.1017	

REGRESSION ESTIMATE [Y'(t)] OF YVAR FOR OBSERVATION t :
Y'(t) = -11645.6 + 47.3194*X1(t)

Figure 3.16 Linear model for comparison with model in Figure 3.15.

RESULTS BASED ON THE REGRESSION FUNCTION

OBS#	RECORDED AMOUNT	REGRESSION ESTIMATE	RESIDUAL	RESIDUALS GRAPHED IN UNITS OF 1 STD. ERROR (3868.46)		OBS#
				-4 -3 -2 -1 0 1 2 3 4		
				-I—I—I—I—I—I—I—I—I-		
1	1000	-6914	7914	-I I I * I-		1
2	2828	-2182	5010	-I I I * I I-		2
3	5196	2550	2646	-I I I * I I-		3
4	8000	7282	718	-I I I* I I-		4
5	11180	12014	-834	-I I *I I I-		5
6	14697	16746	-2049	-I I * I I I-		6
7	18520	21478	-2958	-I I * I I I-		7
8	22627	26210	-3583	-I I * I I I-		8
9	27000	30942	-3942	-I I * I I I-		9
10	31623	35674	-4051	-I I * I I I-		10
11	36483	40406	-3923	-I I * I I I-		11
12	41569	45138	-3569	-I I * I I I-		12
13	46872	49870	-2998	-I I * I I I-		13
14	52383	54602	-2219	-I I * I I I-		14
15	58095	59334	-1239	-I I *I I I-		15
16	64000	64065	-65	-I I * I I-		16
17	70093	68797	1296	-I I I* I I-		17
18	76368	73529	2839	-I I I * I I-		18
19	82819	78261	4558	-I I I * I I-		19
20	89443	82993	6450	-I I I *I I-		20
				-I—I—I—I—I—I—I—I—I-		

Figure 3.17   Regression results for the linear model in Figure 3.16.

Experimental determination of a power.   Figure 3.18 shows two variables. A scatter diagram depicting their relationship is shown in Figure 3.19.

The first step in the experimental procedure is to compare the scatter diagram with Figure 3.9a. This comparison reveals that a concave function would be appropriate. A first approximation using a value of 1.5 for p seems reasonable. This value of p is used to transform the X values into values of $X' = X^{1.5}$. Then Y is regressed against X'. The STAR printout for this model is shown in Figure 3.20, and the result is summarized as iteration 1 in Table 3.6.

A better value than 1.50 might lie on either side of 1.50. We start by choosing a value a little greater, say 1.51. This value is used to transform X into X' and Y is regressed against X'. The result for this model is shown as iteration 2 in Table 3.6. Clearly we are moving in the right direction from 1.50, since otherwise the coefficients of residual variation would have increased rather than decreased.

VARIABLES ON FILE

OBS#	C01	C02
1	382	100
2	2686	200
3	4599	300
4	8593	400
5	12482	500
6	13787	600
7	18249	700
8	21180	800
9	26607	900
10	32246	1000
11	35276	1100
12	40949	1200
13	46949	1300
14	51745	1400
15	57222	1500
16	65723	1600
17	70106	1700
18	76023	1800
19	81759	1900
20	90647	2000
TOT	757210	21000
HASH	757210	21000

Figure 3.18 Variables related by power function.

SCATTER DIAGRAM OF YVAR VS XVAR

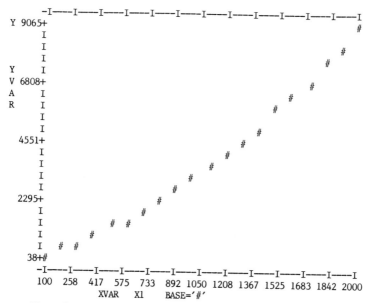

Figure 3.19 Scatter diagram relating variables shown in Figure 3.18.

STEPWISE MULTIPLE REGRESSION MODEL

	INPUT DATA		REGRESSION FUNCTION ETC.	
DESCRIPTION	MEAN	STANDARD ERROR	CONSTANT OR COEFFICIENT	STANDARD ERROR
CONSTANT			−339.9648	
INDEPENDENT VARIABLES X1 XVAR^1.5	38039.8280	28246.4902	1.0042	0.0072
DEPENDENT VARIABLE Y YVAR Y′ REGRESSION ESTIMATE	37860.5000	28378.8691	37860.5000	885.5335
COEFFICIENT OF : CORRELATION REGRESSION IMPROVEMENT RESIDUAL VARIATION			0.9995 0.9688 0.0234	

REGRESSION ESTIMATE [Y′(t)] OF YVAR FOR OBSERVATION t :
Y′(t) = −339.9648 + 1.0042*X1(t)

Figure 3.20   Regression function obtained after relating Y to $X^{1.5}$.

We continue in the same direction and try $p = 1.52$ and then $p = 1.53$. For the latter value the residual variation increases as shown in Table 3.6. Therefore $p = 1.52$ is the best value of p that we have.

Table 3.6   Summarized results for experimental determination of a power

Iteration	Trial Value	Regression Model		Correlation	Residual Variation
		Constant	Coefficient		
1	1.50	−339.7773	1.0042	.9995	0.0234
2	1.51	−175.1328	.9302	.9995	0.0231
3	1.52	−12.1992	.8616	.9996	0.0230
4	1.53	149.0625	.7981	.9996	0.0231

At this point we could try to determine whether the actual "best" p is between 1.51 and 1.52 or between 1.52 and 1.53. For practical purposes, however, $p = 1.52$ will be quite accurate enough. A STAR printout for the value $p = 1.52$ is shown in Figure 3.21. The residuals from the regression function are also shown in Figure 3.21.

The time required in using the STAR Program for the interactions illustrated in Table 3.6 is nominal, and the results shown can be read from the screen without requiring printouts.

STEPWISE MULTIPLE REGRESSION MODEL

| | INPUT DATA | | REGRESSION FUNCTION ETC. | |
DESCRIPTION	MEAN	STANDARD ERROR	CONSTANT OR COEFFICIENT	STANDARD ERROR
CONSTANT			−12.2344	
INDEPENDENT VARIABLES X1 XVAR^1.52	43955.2890	32921.9100	0.8616	0.0061
DEPENDENT VARIABLE Y YVAR Y' REGRESSION ESTIMATE	37860.5000	28378.8691	37860.5000	872.4189
COEFFICIENT OF : CORRELATION REGRESSION IMPROVEMENT RESIDUAL VARIATION			0.9996 0.9693 0.0230	

REGRESSION ESTIMATE [Y'(t)] OF YVAR FOR OBSERVATION t :
Y'(t) = −12.2344 + .8616*X1(t)

RESULTS BASED ON THE REGRESSION FUNCTION

OBS#	RECORDED AMOUNT	REGRESSION ESTIMATE	RESIDUAL	RESIDUALS GRAPHED IN UNITS OF 1 STD. ERROR (872.419)	OBS#
				−4 −3 −2 −1 0 1 2 3 4 −I—I—I—I—I—I—I—I—I—	
1	382	933	−551	−I I * I I I−	1
2	2686	2697	−11	−I I * I I−	2
3	4599	5006	−407	−I I *I I I−	3
4	8593	7758	835	−I I I * I I−	4
5	12482	10896	1586	−I I I *I I−	5
6	13787	14379	−592	−I I * I I I−	6
7	18249	18179	70	−I I * I I−	7
8	21180	22273	−1093	−I I * I I I−	8
9	26607	26642	−35	−I I * I I−	9
10	32246	31271	975	−I I I * I I−	10
11	35276	36148	−872	−I I * I I I−	11
12	40949	41261	−312	−I I *I I I−	12
13	46949	46601	348	−I I I* I I−	13
14	51745	52159	−414	−I I *I I I−	14
15	57222	57927	−705	−I I * I I I−	15
16	65723	63899	1824	−I I I * I−	16
17	70106	70068	38	−I I * I I−	17
18	76023	76429	−406	−I I *I I I−	18
19	81759	82977	−1218	−I I * I I I−	19
20	90647	89706	941	−I I I * I I−	20
				−I—I—I—I—I—I—I—I—I−	

Figure 3.21 Regression function obtained after relating Y to $X^{1.52}$.

References

1. J. Johnston, *Econometric Methods,* 2nd ed. New York: McGraw-Hill, 1972.

General References

S. Chaterjee, *Regression Analysis by Example.* New York: Wiley, 1977.

N. R. Draper and H. Smith, *Applied Regression Analysis.* New York: Wiley, 1981.

M. Ezekiel and K. A. Fox, *Methods of Correlation and Regression Analysis,* 3rd ed. New York: Wiley, 1959.

A. Koutsoyiannis, *Theory of Econometrics,* 2nd ed. London: Macmillan, 1977.

M. S. Lewis-Beck, *Applied Regression: An Introduction.* Beverly Hills, CA: Sage Publications, 1980.

J. Neper, *Applied Linear Regression Models.* Homewood, IL: R. D. Irwin, 1983.

K. W. Smillie, *An Introduction to Regression and Correlation.* New York: Academic Press, 1966.

4

THE GENERAL REGRESSION MODEL

4.1 Introduction

The simple regression model (with one independent variable) described in Chapter 3 is important as the starting point for understanding regression analysis, and it is adequate for many applications. There is no need, however, to limit applications to only one independent variable, and in some cases the regression function can be improved significantly by the inclusion of several independent variables.

In some fields, such as econometrics, it is sometimes necessary to study the simultaneous effect of dozens of independent variables. Auditors, however, seldom need to focus on the fundamental social and economic factors that ultimately determine dependent variables. Instead they are normally more concerned with the relationships between a few key variables. In practice, the ability of the STAR Program to handle up to 25 variables simultaneously is more than adequate for audit applications.

In this chapter we illustrate the extension of the simple two-variable model (one dependent and one independent variable) to the three-variable model (one dependent and two independent variables). We continue the Gamma Company example from Chapter 3 to illustrate the concepts and computations.

When several independent variables are specified by the auditor, it often happens that some do not contribute significantly to the explanatory power of the model. The STAR Program and many other regression programs incorporate a procedure that is designed to ensure that only the significant variables are included. In this chapter we give a brief overview of this procedure. Some of the statistical aspects are explained in Chapter 8, and a detailed analysis of the computational methods used in the STAR Program is provided in Chapter 9.

The final section of this chapter contains an introductory discussion of the statistical assumptions that underlie the use of regression analysis, their audit implications, and what the STAR Program does about them. A more detailed analysis is provided in Chapter 8.

4.2   Regression with Two Independent Variables

Just as two variables can be represented in a two-dimensional scatter diagram, three variables can be displayed in three dimensions. The three-dimensional equivalent of graph paper can be visualized as a box divided into small cubes. The independent variables are graded along two horizontal edges of the box, and the dependent variable is graded along a vertical edge. First, every combination of the two independent variables is marked as a dot on the floor of the box. Second, each dot is raised vertically by the amount of the dependent variable. The result is a swarm of dots in the box.

The relationship between the three variables can be represented by a flat plane that passes through the swarm of dots. The *plane of best fit* is the one that best fits the scatter in the sense of minimizing the sum of the squared deviations from the plane. It is the three-dimensional equivalent of a line of best fit (see Figure 2.2). A three-dimensional scatter diagram and plane of best fit are shown in Figure 4.1. A residual in this case is the vertical difference between the height of a dot and the height of the plane of best fit at the point of the plane lying directly above or below the dot. The method of least squares is used to calculate the plane that minimizes the sum of the squared residuals.

4.2.1   Regression function

The formulas for calculating the regression function for the model with two independent variables are similar to those for the model with one indepen-

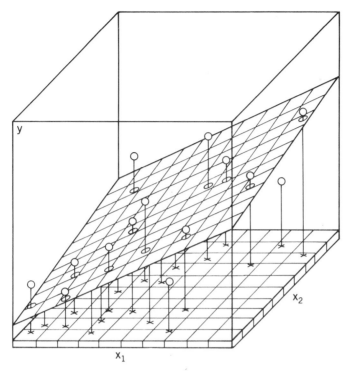

Figure 4.1   Three-dimensional scatter diagram. The points are depicted in a box. The floor of the box contains the X_1, X_2 coordinates. Each point lies directly above its X_1, X_2 coordinate. The Y coordinate is measured along a vertical edge as shown. A plane of best fit is also shown. The coefficient of X_1 is the slope of the plane in the X_1 direction; the coefficient of X_2 is the slope of the plane in the X_2 direction; and the constant is the point on the Y axis that is intercepted by the plane.

dent variable in that they involve the squares and cross products of deviations from the means of the variables; but they are more complex in that they require more combinations of these results. The data required for the Gamma Company calculations are shown in Table 4.1. (Of course, to a computer program the extra calculations just involve manipulation of more columns of data, and there is very little difference between calculating a regression with one independent variable and calculating a function with several variables. A printout from the STAR Program that shows the effect of including EXPENSES as a variable in the Gamma Company case is shown in Figure 4.3 in Section 4.3.)

Table 4.1 Gamma Company calculations for

Obs.	Observations			Deviations		
No.	X_1	X_2	Y	x_1	x_2	y
1	1,574	802	2,107	(258)	(109)	(395)
2	1,503	785	1,915	(329)	(126)	(587)
3	1,645	711	1,873	(187)	(200)	(629)
4	1,380	844	1,978	(452)	(67)	(524)
5	1,580	761	2,010	(252)	(150)	(492)
6	1,576	716	1,969	(256)	(195)	(533)
7	1,752	724	2,228	(80)	(187)	(274)
8	1,549	753	2,152	(283)	(158)	(350)
9	1,652	1,020	2,439	(180)	109	(63)
10	1,650	878	2,318	(182)	(33)	(184)
11	1,496	841	2,244	(336)	(70)	(258)
12	1,671	900	2,357	(161)	(11)	(145)
13	1,679	794	2,103	(153)	(117)	(399)
14	1,782	873	2,457	(50)	(38)	(45)
15	1,652	929	2,606	(180)	18	104
16	1,756	875	2,493	(76)	(36)	(9)
17	1,555	794	2,264	(277)	(117)	(238)
18	1,621	813	2,058	(211)	(98)	(444)
19	1,982	886	2,516	150	(25)	14
20	2,050	913	2,533	218	2	31
21	1,959	990	2,958	127	79	456
22	1,836	963	2,564	4	52	62
23	2,006	855	2,318	174	(56)	(184)
24	2,164	1,058	2,928	332	147	426
25	1,780	1,059	2,754	(52)	148	252
26	2,054	966	2,678	222	55	176
27	2,265	983	3,189	433	72	687
28	2,117	956	3,067	285	45	565
29	1,955	1,077	2,735	123	166	233
30	2,059	1,108	3,029	227	197	527
31	2,059	813	2,531	227	(98)	29
32	2,096	1,101	2,765	264	190	263
33	2,201	1,186	3,074	369	275	572
34	2,016	1,092	2,651	184	181	149
35	2,197	915	3,056	365	4	554
36	2,083	1,062	3,155	251	151	653
Total	65,952	32,796	90,072	0	0	0
Mean	1,832	911	2,502			

regression with two independent variables

Obs. No.	Squared Deviations x_1^2	x_2^2	y^2	Cross Products x_1x_2	x_1y	x_2y
1	66,564	11,881	156,025	28,122	101,910	43,055
2	108,241	15,876	344,569	41,454	193,123	73,962
3	34,969	40,000	395,641	37,400	117,623	125,800
4	204,304	4,489	274,576	30,284	236,848	35,108
5	63,504	22,500	242,064	37,800	123,984	73,800
6	65,536	38,025	284,089	49,920	136,448	103,935
7	6,400	34,969	75,076	14,960	21,920	51,238
8	80,089	24,964	122,500	44,714	99,050	55,300
9	32,400	11,881	3,969	(19,620)	11,340	(6,867)
10	33,124	1,089	33,856	6,006	33,488	6,072
11	112,896	4,900	66,564	23,520	86,688	18,060
12	25,921	121	21,025	1,771	23,345	1,595
13	23,409	13,689	159,201	17,901	61,047	46,683
14	2,500	1,444	2,025	1,900	2,250	1,710
15	32,400	324	10,816	(3,240)	(18,720)	1,872
16	5,776	1,296	81	2,736	684	324
17	76,729	13,689	56,644	32,409	65,926	27,846
18	44,521	9,604	197,136	20,678	93,684	43,512
19	22,500	625	196	(3,750)	2,100	(350)
20	47,524	4	961	436	6,758	62
21	16,129	6,241	207,936	10,033	57,912	36,024
22	16	2,704	3,844	208	248	3,224
23	30,276	3,136	33,856	(9,744)	(32,016)	10,304
24	110,224	21,609	181,476	48,804	141,432	62,622
25	2,704	21,904	63,504	(7,696)	(13,104)	37,296
26	49,284	3,025	30,976	12,210	39,072	9,680
27	187,489	5,184	471,969	31,176	297,471	49,464
28	81,225	2,025	319,225	12,825	161,025	25,425
29	15,129	27,556	54,289	20,418	28,659	38,678
30	51,529	38,809	277,729	44,719	119,629	103,819
31	51,529	9,604	341	(22,246)	6,583	(2,842)
32	69,696	36,100	69,169	50,160	69,432	49,970
33	136,161	75,625	327,184	101,475	211,068	157,300
34	33,856	32,761	22,201	33,304	27,416	26,969
35	133,225	16	306,916	1,460	202,210	2,216
36	63,001	22,801	426,409	37,901	163,903	98,603
	2,120,780	560,470	5,244,538	730,408	2,880,436	1,411,469

The formulas for the regression function and the illustrative calculations for the Gamma Company are

$$b_1 = \frac{(\Sigma x_1 y)(\Sigma x_2^2) - (\Sigma x_2 y)(\Sigma x_1 x_2)}{(\Sigma x_1^2)(\Sigma x_2^2) - (\Sigma x_1 x_2)^2}$$

$$= \frac{2{,}880{,}436 \times 560{,}470 - 1{,}411{,}469 \times 730{,}408}{2{,}120{,}780 \times 560{,}470 - 730{,}408^2}$$

$$= 0.8906$$

$$b_2 = \frac{(\Sigma x_2 y)(\Sigma x_1^2) - (\Sigma x_1 y)(\Sigma x_1 x_2)}{(\Sigma x_1^2)(\Sigma x_2^2) - (\Sigma x_1 x_2)^2}$$

$$= \frac{1{,}411{,}469 \times 2{,}120{,}780 - 2{,}880{,}436 \times 730{,}408}{2{,}120{,}780 \times 560{,}470 - 730{,}408^2}$$

$$= 1.3578$$

$$a = \bar{Y} - b_1 \bar{X}_1 - b_2 \bar{X}_2$$

$$= 2502 - 0.8906 \times 1832 - 1.3578 \times 911$$

$$= -366.4614$$

Thus the regression function for Gamma Company is

$$Y_t = -366.4614 + 0.8906 \, X_{1t} + 1.3578 \, X_{2t} + e_t$$

This is the best estimate of the ULR

$$Y_t = \alpha + \beta_1 X_{1t} + \beta_2 X_{2t} + u_t$$

The formula for a is the same as in the case of one independent variable, except for the addition of the term $b_2 \bar{X}_2$. Also the left-most terms in the numerator and denominator in the formula for b_1 are those used to compute b in the model with one independent variable, and the additional terms are those needed to compute the effect of X_2. Finally, the numerators in the formulas for b_1 and b_2 are symmetrical, and their denominators are identical.

The regression coefficients can be determined by an alternative procedure that we think is more intuitively appealing. An explanation of that procedure follows.

In the simple model derived in Chapter 3, in which X_1 is the only independent variable, the extent to which X_1 has failed to explain the behavior of Y is represented by the residuals from that function. Thus if X_2 has the potential to improve the estimates of Y, it must contribute information about the previously unexplained behavior of Y. In other words, X_2 must be correlated with the residuals.

The information that can be contributed by X_2 may overlap somewhat with information that has already been contributed by X_1. To determine the *marginal* contribution of X_2 it is first necessary to remove the influence of X_1 from X_2. This is done by regressing X_2 as a dependent variable against X_1. The residuals from that regression represent the marginal information content of X_2. The ideal situation is to have a very low degree of correlation between X_1 and X_2 because then the overlap will be minimal.

The correlation between the two sets of residuals (from Y versus X_1 and from X_2 versus X_1) represents the marginal influence of X_2. In fact, the coefficient b_2 can be calculated by regressing the residuals from Y versus X_1 as the dependent variable against those from X_2 versus X_1 as the independent variable.

In the Gamma Company example (explained in Chapter 3) Y is regressed against X_1, and the regression function is

$$\hat{Y}_t = 13.7629 + 1.3582 \, X_{1t}$$

The residuals from this function are

$$e_t = Y_t - (13.7629 + 1.3582 \, X_{1t})$$

If X_2 is regressed against X_1, the function is

$$\hat{X}_{2t} = 280.0363 + 0.3444 \, X_{1t}$$

The residuals from this function (designated by f to distinguish them from those previously designated by e) are

$$f_t = X_{2t} - (280.0363 + 0.3444 \, X_{1t})$$

Finally, if e is regressed as the dependent variable against f as the independent variable, the resulting regression function is

$$\hat{e}_t = 1.3578\, f_t$$

The point of interest in the last function is that the coefficient of f is the same as the coefficient of X_2 in the regression function with two independent variables. (Readers may also note that this coefficient is very close to 1.3582, the coefficient of X_1 in the original regression function with one independent variable. This closeness is purely coincidental, and readers should not attribute any significance to it.)

There is no regression constant in the function relating e and f. This is because a regression function always passes through the mean of the variables and, since the variables in this case are actually residuals from previous regressions, their means are zero. As a result, the regression line for this regression passes through the point (0,0).

The coefficient of correlation between e and f is .6533. This is called the *partial correlation coefficient between Y and X_2 after removing the influence of X_1*. It is a measure of the degree to which X_2 explains the variability that remains after the initial regression of Y against X_1.

We have shown how to calculate the coefficient of X_2 given that X_1 has already been included in the function. If the respective subscripts and narrative references in the previous discussion are reversed, the same procedure can be used to calculate the coefficient of X_1 given that X_2 has been included.

We summarize in Figure 4.2 the alternative procedure illustrated in this subsection, and extend the illustration to include the reverse calculations.

4.2.2   Other regression statistics

The other regression statistics for the model with two independent variables closely parallel those for the model with one independent variable. We therefore present the results with minimum comment.

Total variation can be analyzed as follows:

Explained sum of squares	$\Sigma\, \hat{y}_t^2$	4,481,633
Residual sum of squares	$\Sigma\, e_t^2$	762,905
Total sum of squares	$\Sigma\, y_t^2$	$\overline{5{,}244{,}538}$

First Set of Regressions

Regression Number	1	2	3	4
Variables:				
Dependent	Y	X_2	Y	X_1
Independent	X_1	X_1	X_2	X_2
Regression Function:				
Constant	13.7629	280.0363	207.7515	644.7664
Coefficient	1.3582	.3444	2.5184	1.3032
Correlation	.8637	.6700	.8203	.6700

Second Set of Regressions

Regression Number	5	6
Variables - residuals from the regressions above:		
Dependent	1	3
Independent	2	4
Regression Function:		
Constant	- - -	- - -
Coefficient - Applicable in three-variable model to:		
X_1	- - -	.8906
X_2	1.3578	- - -
Partial correlation	.6533	.7407

Figure 4.2 Interaction between the variables in the Gamma Company example.

The standard error of the regression function is

$$s_u = \sqrt{\frac{\Sigma e_t^2}{n - k - 1}} = \sqrt{\frac{762,905}{33}} = 152.0471$$

The number of degrees of freedom is 33, which is 1 less than for the function with one independent variable. The coefficient of residual variation is

$$v = \frac{s_u}{\bar{Y}} = \frac{152.0471}{2502} = 0.0608$$

The coefficient of determination is

$$R^2 = \frac{\Sigma \hat{y}_t^2}{\Sigma y_t^2} = \frac{4,481,633}{5,244,538} = 0.8545$$

The coefficient of correlation is

$$R = \sqrt{R^2} = 0.9244$$

The coefficient of regression improvement is

$$I = 1 - \frac{s_u}{s_y} = 1 - \frac{152.0471}{387.0976} = 0.6072$$

4.2.3   Comparison of examples

Table 4.2 shows a comparison of the regression statistics for the models with one and two independent variables, respectively.

4.3   Many Independent Variables

The basic concepts explained for the model with two independent variables hold also for extensions to three or more independent variables. However, the complexity of the formulas expands exponentially as more variables are added. For such models, the concise notation of matrix algebra and more efficient computational methods are needed. In Chapter 9, for readers who

Table 4.2   Gamma Company comparison of regression statistics for one and two independent variables, respectively

Statistics	One Variable	Two Variables
Regression Constant	13.7629	−366.4614
Regression Coefficients		
X_1	1.3582	0.8906
X_2	−	1.3578
Standard Error of Regression Function	197.9585	152.0471
Coefficients of		
Residual Variation	0.0791	0.0608
Determination	0.7460	0.8545
Correlation	0.8637	0.9244
Regression Improvement	0.4886	0.6072

are interested, we present a matrix formulation of regression analysis and a detailed account of the computational procedure that is used in the STAR Program. In this section we provide an intuitive treatment of the same subject matter.

When a large set of independent variables is available to the auditor, a decision has to be made about which particular subset results in the "best" regression function. One extreme is to use all the variables; another is to use none or perhaps only one. Between these two extremes there is a wide range of choices. For example, if 15 independent variables are available, over 32,000 different regression functions could be developed.

Some method must be used for selection of the "best" regression function from among the many possibilities. On the one hand, there is an inclination to include as many of the independent variables as possible, because it is desirable that the regression function should explain as much as possible about the behavior of the dependent variable. On the other hand, there is a cost associated with each additional independent variable, so the conflicting inclination is to use a smaller set of independent variables. Clearly a compromise is needed.

The ideal is a small but powerful set of independent variables. Variables that are superfluous because they do not contribute much to the explanatory power of the regression function should be left out, but variables that make a significant contribution should be included. The STAR Program incorporates a variable selection procedure that ensures the selection of such a set. The statistical basis for this selection process is discussed in Chapter 8. The audit decisions that should precede and follow the automatic selection process are discussed in Chapter 6.

There are various statistical procedures for selecting the best regression function. One rather cumbersome approach is to have the computer generate all possible regressions and then to select the "best" one judgmentally. Another approach is to compute the regression function that includes all the independent variables and then use a *backward elimination* procedure to eliminate, one by one, the variables that make the least significant contribution. After each elimination, the regression function is recomputed. The procedure ends when the least significant variable in the regression function nevertheless still makes a statistically significant contribution.

Yet another approach is to start with no variables in the regression and use a *forward selection* procedure to enter, one by one, the variables that make the most significant contribution to the regression. After each admission of a variable, the regression function is recomputed. The procedure ends when the most significant remaining variable would make only a statistically insignificant contribution to the regression were it to be included in the function.

The STAR Program uses a procedure that includes a forward selection procedure for admitting new variables one at a time, as well as a backward elimination procedure for removing variables that become redundant as a result of subsequent admissions. Known as *stepwise regression,* this procedure is widely regarded as one of the best procedures currently available. Its goal is to ensure that all the independent variables that are included in the final regression function contribute significantly to it in a statistical sense.

In Figure 4.3, a STAR Program printout is shown for a Gamma Company model in which TIME AT STANDARD (X_1), EXPENSES (X_2), and COST OF SERVICES (X_3) were specified as the independent variables. In the stepwise regression procedure, X_3 was the first independent variable to be admitted to the function, because it is the one that correlates most highly with Y. Thereafter X_1 and X_2 were admitted, in that order. Finally, in a backward elimination process, X_3 was eliminated from the function, because it had been rendered redundant by the combined effect of X_1 and X_2. The net result is the regression function with two independent variables that was discussed in Section 4.2. We will explain this example in greater detail in Chapter 9.

4.4   Statistical Assumptions, Tests, and Transformations

The soundness of an inference based on a model is usually affected by the validity of certain assumptions about that model. In regression analysis, certain statistical assumptions are implicit in the use of the model. Although the expectation that these assumptions will be appropriate for most applications is reasonable, the assumptions ordinarily cannot be proven to be true or false for any particular analysis. Nevertheless, statistical tests can be made to determine whether they appear to be reasonable. These tests help to ensure that the auditor is alerted to problems that may affect the usefulness of the application.

In this section we present an introduction to the statistical assumptions,

SPECIFICATIONS FOR MODEL

NAME OF VARIABLE	SOURCE/DESCRIPTION OF VARIABLE	UNITS	BYPASS
Y REVENUE	C09	1000	NONE
X1 TIME AT STANDARD	M07 = (C01*C04+C02*C05+C03*C06)/1000	1000	NONE
X2 EXPENSES	C08	1000	NONE
X3 COST OF SERVICES	C10	1000	NONE

STEPWISE MULTIPLE REGRESSION MODEL

	INPUT DATA		REGRESSION FUNCTION ETC.	
DESCRIPTION	MEAN	STANDARD ERROR	CONSTANT OR COEFFICIENT	STANDARD ERROR
CONSTANT			−366.4614	
INDEPENDENT VARIABLES				
X1 TIME AT STANDARD	1832.0000	246.1553	0.8906	0.1406
X2 EXPENSES	911.0000	126.5435	1.3578	0.2736
DEPENDENT VARIABLE				
Y REVENUE	2502.0000	387.0976		
Y' REGRESSION ESTIMATE			2502.0000	152.0471
COEFFICIENT OF :				
CORRELATION			0.9244	
REGRESSION IMPROVEMENT			0.6072	
RESIDUAL VARIATION			0.0608	

REGRESSION ESTIMATE [Y'(t)] OF REVENUE FOR OBSERVATION t :
Y'(t) = −366.4614 + .8906*X1(t) + 1.3578*X2(t)

Figure 4.3 Gamma Company. In this application, three independent variables were specified. In the stepwise multiple regression procedure, X_3, COST OF SERVICES, was the first variable to be admitted to the function because it is the variable that is most highly correlated with Y. In the following steps, X_1, TIME AT STANDARD, and then X_2, EXPENSES, were admitted. In the final step, X_3 was eliminated because that variable was rendered redundant by the joint effect of X_1 and X_2.

tests, and transformations of regression. A more detailed and mathematical treatment is set forth in Chapter 8.

4.4.1 Discontinuity of the regression function

One assumption that is implied in the linear model is that of *continuity;* that is, that the same underlying linear relationship applies throughout the range of the observations. Its opposite, *discontinuity,* can occur within the base period or between the base period and the audit period. The STAR Program applies tests for both types of discontinuity to time-series applications.

The data shown in Table 4.3 display discontinuity. These data relate to the production of a chemical for 1972, 1973, and 1974. The two variables are PRODUCTION COSTS and QUANTITY PRODUCED. A significant discontinuity occurred after the price of oil began to skyrocket in late 1973. The discontinuity is apparent from Figure 4.4, where it can be seen that the regression function that best represents the first 24 months is very different from the function that represents the last 12 months; and neither coincides with the function that best represents the full 36 months of the base period.

A partial STAR printout for the regression is shown in Figure 4.5. A complete printout is included as Printout B.2. The discontinuity clearly shows up in the graph of the residuals.

Table 4.3 Universal Chemicals data for 1972 to 1974

| | ----------1972---------- | | | ----------1973---------- | | | ----------1974---------- | |
| | Prod. Costs | Quantity | | Prod. Costs | Quantity | | Prod. Costs | Quantity |
Obs#	Y	X_1	Obs#	Y	X_1	Obs#	Y	X_1
1	312	388	13	568	739	25	414	581
2	320	392	14	448	604	26	528	614
3	320	422	15	613	787	27	1010	1152
4	363	494	16	452	644	28	699	733
5	512	721	17	540	734	29	831	916
6	334	470	18	531	653	30	638	673
7	390	567	19	621	815	31	675	707
8	185	263	20	363	467	32	710	750
9	528	683	21	515	698	33	711	692
10	395	483	22	605	825	34	723	742
11	380	499	23	546	717	35	660	679
12	375	496	24	629	805	36	633	626

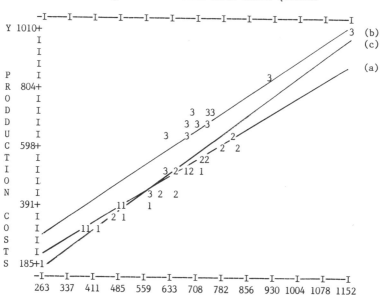

Scatter Diagram of PRODUCTION COSTS versus QUANTITY

Figure 4.4 Universal Chemicals. The scatter diagram relates PRODUCTION COSTS to QUANTITY PRODUCED. The points on the diagram are represented by the number of the year in which the observation occurred. Three regression functions are shown:

a. $\hat{Y} = 3.7545 + 0.7489X$. This is the line of best fit for the first 24 periods (years 1 and 2).

b. $\hat{Y} = 42.0620 + 0.8717X$. This is the line of best fit for the last 12 periods (year 3).

c. $\hat{Y} = -67.9933 + 0.9266X$. This is the line of best fit for the entire 36 periods (years 1, 2, and 3).

The discontinuity between the data for the first 24 months and the last 12 months is apparent.

A statistical indication of discontinuity within the base period can sometimes occur in situations in which the practical significance of the discontinuity is negligible. These situations can arise when, in spite of the discontinuity, the regression function still manages to fit the observations for the entire base period very well. As a result, the STAR Program does not test for discontinuity when the coefficient of correlation is 95% or greater.

Discontinuity is typically caused by changes in conditions. If these are anticipated when the model is first specified, the problem of discontinuity

RESULTS BASED ON THE REGRESSION FUNCTION

OBS#	RECORDED AMOUNT	REGRESSION ESTIMATE	RESIDUAL	RESIDUALS GRAPHED IN UNITS OF 1 STD. ERROR (65.6605)	OBS#
				-4 -3 -2 -1 0 1 2 3 4	
				-I—I—I—I—I—I—I—I—I-	
1	312	292	20	-I I I* I I-	1
2	320	295	25	-I I I* I I-	2
3	320	323	-3	-I I * I I-	3
4	363	390	-27	-I I *I I I-	4
5	512	600	-88	-I I * I I I-	5
6	334	367	-33	-I I * I I I-	6
7	390	457	-67	-I I * I I I-	7
8	185	176	9	-I I * I I-	8
9	528	565	-37	-I I * I I I-	9
10	395	380	15	-I I I* I I-	10
11	380	394	-14	-I I *I I I-	11
12	375	392	-17	-I I *I I I-	12
				-I—I—I—I—I—I—I—I—I-	
13	568	617	-49	-I I * I I I-	13
14	448	492	-44	-I I * I I I-	14
15	613	661	-48	-I I * I I I-	15
16	452	529	-77	-I I * I I I-	16
17	540	612	-72	-I I * I I I-	17
18	531	537	-6	-I I * I I-	18
19	621	687	-66	-I I * I I I-	19
20	363	365	-2	-I I * I I-	20
21	515	579	-64	-I I * I I I-	21
22	605	696	-91	-I I * I I I-	22
23	546	596	-50	-I I * I I I-	23
24	629	678	-49	-I I * I I I-	24
				-I—I—I—I—I—I—I—I—I-	
25	414	470	-56	-I I * I I I-	25
26	528	501	27	-I I I* I I-	26
27	1010	999	11	-I I * I I-	27
28	699	611	88	-I I I * I I-	28
29	831	781	50	-I I I * I I-	29
30	638	556	82	-I I I * I I-	30
31	675	587	88	-I I I * I I-	31
32	710	627	83	-I I I * I I-	32
33	711	573	138	-I I I * I-	33
34	723	620	103	-I I I *I I-	34
35	660	561	99	-I I I *I I-	35
36	633	512	121	-I I I * I-	36
				-I—I—I—I—I—I—I—I—I-	

Figure 4.5 Universal Chemicals. This is a plot of the residuals from a regression function that relates PRODUCTION COSTS to QUANTITY PRODUCED. The regression function has been based on the full 36-month base. Notice the discontinuity that occurs at around period 26. This was due to the increase in the price of oil at about that time.

can sometimes be avoided. If discontinuity occurs, the cause can sometimes be found by reviewing the residuals. This review could suggest a new independent variable, the inclusion of which might eliminate the discontinuity. It might suggest, on the other hand, that the discontinuity is best eliminated by discarding the observations for the first year in the base profile. Because the consequences of discontinuity within the base period can be quite significant, the STAR Program does not allow a model that is discontinuous in the base period to be used for audit purposes.

The test for discontinuity between the base period and the audit period is similar in concept to the test for discontinuity within the base period, although the mechanics are somewhat different.

When discontinuity is detected between the base period and the audit period, the STAR Program prints a message to alert the auditor. The presence of such discontinuity should not be interpreted to mean that the regression function is inappropriate for performing analytical review. In many cases the reason for the apparent discontinuity is the very effectiveness of the regression function in identifying that errors or unusual transactions occurred in the audit period. All the facts of the particular circumstance should be considered in deciding whether the application is appropriate for the auditor's analytical review objective.

4.4.2 Autocorrelation

An assumption that is implicit in the ULR is that the disturbances from the ULR are statistically independent of one another over time. In other words, that a regression estimate in period t could not be improved by knowledge of what the residual was in period $t - 1$ or any other prior period.

In the business world, events frequently move in a time-related pattern. When those events are the minor factors that underlie the behavior of the residuals, a pattern in the residuals may result. In this case the assumption of statistical independence is not valid, because regression estimates can be improved by factoring in the pattern in the residuals.

A systematic pattern of interdependence over time is known as *autocorrelation* or *serial correlation* of the disturbances. It ordinarily results in a visible pattern in the residuals from the regression function. If significant autocorrelation is ignored and the ordinary regression function is used, two things could happen. First, the regression projections might not be as good as they could be because the pattern would be ignored rather than factored in. Second, the calculations of the standard error might be distorted. It is desirable therefore to test for autocorrelation and, if possible, to circumvent the problem that autocorrelation can cause.

Because significant autocorrelation is a potentially serious problem, the STAR Program automatically tests for it and then, if necessary, adjusts for it by calculating a so-called *generalized regression function*. This test is performed only in time-series applications (not in cross-sectional applications), because autocorrelation relates to patterns over time.

Although it is possible to consider patterns that are highly complex, a satisfactory assumption for most purposes is that autocorrelated disturbances follow a so-called *first-order autoregressive scheme*. This means that the disturbance in period t consists of a part that depends on the residual in period $t - 1$, the previous period, and a part that is random and independent.

Figure 4.6 contains three graphs showing zero autocorrelation and two different degrees of first-order autocorrelation. The coefficients of autocorrelation that are illustrated are positive numbers between 0 and 1. Accordingly, the related patterns are such that runs of positive residuals and runs of negative residuals are observed. A scatter diagram in which the residuals were plotted against themselves lagged by one period would show noticeable positive correlation.

Negative autocorrelation is also possible. In that case, the coefficient of autocorrelation is a negative number between 0 and -1, and successive residuals tend to flip-flop between positive and negative to a greater extent than they would when there is no autocorrelation. A scatter diagram of the residuals plotted against themselves lagged one period would show a negative correlation. Negative autocorrelation is seldom a factor in business data and therefore is not dealt with in the STAR Program or in this book.

To illustrate what STAR does about autocorrelation, we will use the data for a company called Autocorp Inc. that are shown in Table 4.4. Figure 4.7 shows how the STAR Program handled the application, in which WAGES was regressed against HOURS WORKED. The residuals from the generalized function show very little pattern, whereas the residuals from the original function show a strong pattern. A complete STAR Program printout is included as Printout B.3.

The generalized function for the Autocorp application is shown in Figure 4.7. How it was calculated is explained in detail in Chapter 8. The function

<pre>
      Coefficient of   Coefficient of   Coefficient of
  Autocorrelation = 0.0   Autocorrelation = 0.6   Autocorrelation = 0.9
  ---------------------   ---------------------   ---------------------

 4 -3 -2 -1 0 1 2 3 4 -4 -3 -2 -1 0 1 2 3 4 -4 -3 -2 -1 0 1 2 3 4
-I—I—I—I—I—I—I—I—I—I—I—I—I—I—I—I—I—I—I—I—I—I—I—I—I—I—I-
-I   I * I   I   I—I   I * I   I   I—I   I   *   I   I-
-I   I   I * I   I—I   I   I * I   I—I   I   I * I   I-
-I   I * I   I   I—I   I   *   I   I—I   I   I*   I   I-
-I   I   I * I   I—I   I   I * I   I—I   I   I * I   I-
-I   I   I   *   I—I   I   I * I   I—I   I   I * I   I-
-I   I   I * I   I—I   I   I   *   I—I   I   I   *   I-
-I   I   I* I   I—I   I   I   *   I—I   I   I   I*   I-
-I   I * I   I   I—I   I   I*   I   I—I   I   I * I   I-
-I   I   I * I   I—I   I   I * I   I—I   I   I   I*   I-
-I   I* I   I   I—I   I   *I   I   I—I   I   I * I   ·I-
-I   I * I   I   I—I   I * I   I   I—I   I   I*   I   I-
-I   I * I   I   I—I   I *   I   I   I—I   I   *   I   I-
-I   I   I * I   I—I   I   *   I   I—I   I   I*   I   I-
-I   I*   I   I   I—I   I*   I   I   I—I   I * I   I   I-
-I   I   I * I   I—I   I * I   I   I—I   I   *I   I   I-
-I   I*   I   I   I—I   *   I   I   I—I   I*   I   I   I-
-I   I   *   I   I—I   I *   I   I   I—I   I*   I   I   I-
-I   I *I   I   I—I   I * I   I   I—I   I*   I   I   I-
-I   I *I   I   I—I   I * I   I   I—I   I*   I   I   I-
-I   I   I * I   I—I   I   I*   I   I—I   I * I   I   I-
-I   I   I* I   I—I   I   I* I   I—I   I * I   I   I-
-I   I   I * I   I—I   I   I * I   I—I   I   *   I   I-
-I   I   I   * I   I—I   I   I   *I   I—I   I   I * I   I-
-I   I *I   I   I—I   I   I * I   I—I   I   I*   I   I-
-I   I   I * I   I—I   I   I * I   I—I   I   I * I   I-
-I   I *I   I   I—I   I   I * I   I—I   I   I * I   I-
-I   I   I * I   I—I   I   I * I   I—I   I   I * I   I-
-I   I *I   I   I—I   I   *   I   I—I   I   I*   I   I-
-I   I   I* I   I—I   I   I* I   I—I   I   I*   I   I-
-I   I*   I   I   I—I   I * I   I   I—I   I * I   I   I-
-I   I * I   I   I—I   I*   I   I   I—I   I * I   I   I-
-I   I   I* I   I—I   I * I   I   I—I   I * I   I   I-
-I   I *I   I   I—I   I * I   I   I—I   I * I   I   I-
-I   I*   I   I   I—I   *   I   I   I—I   *   I   I   I-
-I   I   *   I   I—I   I *   I   I   I—I   *   I   I   I-
-I   I*· I   I   I—I   I * I   I   I—I   I * I   I   I-
-I   I   I* I   I—I   I   *I   I   I—I   I * I   I   I-
-I   I   I* I   I—I   I   *   I   I—I   I   * I   I   I-
-I   I * I   I   I—I   I   *I   I   I—I   I   *I   I   I-
-I   I   I* I   I—I   I   *   I   I—I   I   *   I   I-
-I   I *I   I   I—I   I   *I   I   I—I   I   *I   I   I-
-I   I   I * I   I—I   I   I* I   I—I   I   *   I   I-
-I   I   *   I   I—I   I   *   I   I—I   I   *   I   I-
-I   I   *   I   I—I   I   *   I   I—I   I   *   I   I-
-I   I   I * I   I—I   I   I * I   I—I   I   I * I   I-
-I   I   *   I   I—I   I   I *   I   I—I   I   I * I   I-
-I   I *I   I   I—I   I   I* I   I—I   I   I * I   I-
-I—I—I—I—I—I—I—I—I—I—I—I—I—I—I—I—I—I—I—I—I—I—I—I—I—I—I—I-
</pre>

Figure 4.6 Three graphs, showing residuals that have been generated by different autoregressive schemes. The autoregressive parameters (coefficients of autocorrelation) that have been used are, from left to right, 0.0, 0.6, and 0.9. Notice how the pattern in the residuals gets more pronounced as the coefficient of autocorrelation increases.

97

Table 4.4   Autocorp Inc. wages and hours worked data

Obs#	Wages Y	Hours X_1	Obs#	Wages Y	Hours X_1
1	649	287	25	986	406
2	660	303	26	887	370
3	766	355	27	989	401
4	747	347	28	1042	425
5	804	356	29	943	394
6	686	299	30	905	383
7	709	312	31	963	382
8	745	319	32	945	419
9	904	370	33	820	352
10	968	384	34	862	378
11	824	342	35	786	360
12	806	328	36	805	417
13	928	373			
14	884	346	Total Base	31372	13236
15	881	362			
16	901	396			
17	986	411			
18	863	346			
19	987	393	37	867	442
20	989	377	38	925	482
21	945	389	39	1200	537
22	980	401			
23	885	363	Total Audit	2992	1461
24	942	390			

shows that, for periods 2 through 39, regression estimates are made with the formula

$$\hat{Y}_t = 118.8505 + 2.0386\, X_t + 0.6209\, e_{t-1}$$

where .6209 is the coefficient of autocorrelation and

$$e_t = Y_t - (118.8505 + 2.0386\, X_t)$$

The generalized function works rather like an ordinary regression function except that it includes a term that factors in the previous residual. For example, to calculate the regression estimate for period 38, it is necessary first to calculate e_{37}.

$$e_{37} = 867 - (118.8505 + 2.0386 \times 442) = -153$$

				Plot of Residuals from Ordinary Least Squares Regression Function.			Plot of Residuals from Generalized Regression Function
#	Y	Est	e		Est	f	

```
                    Plot of Residuals from              Plot of Residuals from
                    Ordinary Least Squares              Generalized Regression
 #   Y    Est   e   Regression Function.     Est    f        Function
                    -4 -3 -2 -1 0 1 2 3 4             -4 -3 -2 -1 0 1 2 3 4
                    -I—I—I—I—I—I—I—I—I                -I—I—I—I—I—I—I—I—I-
 1  649  665  -16  -I    I   *I    I      I 661  -12 -I    I     *I    I    I-
 2  660  706  -46  -I    I *  I    I      I 702  -42 -I    I  *  I     I    I-
 3  766  839  -73  -I    I *   I   I      I 795  -29 -I    I   * I     I    I-
 4  747  819  -72  -I    I *   I   I      I 779  -32 -I    I   * I     I    I-
 5  804  842  -38  -I    I  *  I   I      I 795    9 -I    I      I*    I    I-
 6  686  696  -10  -I    I    *I   I      I 703  -17 -I    I    *I     I    I-
 7  709  729  -20  -I    I    *I   I      I 729  -20 -I    I    *I     I    I-
 8  745  747   -2  -I    I     *    I     I 741    4 -I    I     *      I    I-
 9  904  877   27  -I    I     I *  I     I 858   46 -I    I     I  *   I    I-
10  968  913   55  -I    I     I  * I     I 921   47 -I    I     I  *   I    I-
11  824  806   18  -I    I     I*   I     I 857  -33 -I    I   * I      I    I-
12  806  770   36  -I    I     I *  I     I 792   14 -I    I     I*     I    I-
                    -I—I—I—I—I—I—I—I—I                -I—I—I—I—I—I—I—I—I-
13  928  885   43  -I    I     I * I      I 891   37 -I    I     I *    I    I-
14  884  816   68  -I    I     I   * I    I 854   30 -I    I     I *    I    I-
15  881  857   24  -I    I     I*   I     I 894  -13 -I    I    *I      I    I-
16  901  944  -43  -I    I  *  I    I     I 941  -40 -I    I  *  I      I    I-
17  986  982    4  -I    I     *    I     I 941   45 -I    I     I  *   I    I-
18  863  816   47  -I    I     I *  I     I 842   21 -I    I     I*     I    I-
19  987  936   51  -I    I     I  * I     I 944   43 -I    I     I *    I    I-
20  989  895   94  -I    I     I   *I     I 929   60 -I    I     I   *  I    I-
21  945  926   19  -I    I     I*   I     I 975  -30 -I    I   * I      I    I-
22  980  957   23  -I    I     I*   I     I 957   23 -I    I     I*     I   ,I-
23  885  860   25  -I    I     I*   I     I 886   -1 -I    I     *      I    I-
24  942  929   13  -I    I     I*   I     I 930   12 -I    I     I*     I    I-
                    -I—I—I—I—I—I—I—I—I                -I—I—I—I—I—I—I—I—I-
25  986  969   17  -I    I     I*   I     I 964   22 -I    I     I*     I    I-
26  887  877   10  -I    I     I*   I     I 898  -11 -I    I    *I      I    I-
27  989  957   32  -I    I     I *  I     I 945   44 -I    I     I  *   I    I-
28 1042 1018   24  -I    I     I*   I     I1018   24 -I    I     I*     I    I-
29  943  939    4  -I    I     *    I     I 957  -14 -I    I    *I      I    I-
30  905  911   -6  -I    I     *    I     I 913   -8 -I    I     *      I    I-
31  963  908   55  -I    I     I  * I     I 901   62 -I    I     I   *  I    I-
32  945 1003  -58  -I    I  *  I    I     I1014  -69 -I    I *   I      I    I-
33  820  831  -11  -I    I    *I    I     I 819    1 -I    I     *      I    I-
34  862  898  -36  -I    I  *  I    I     I 879  -17 -I    I    *I      I    I-
35  786  852  -66  -I    I *   I    I     I 836  -50 -I    I  *  I      I    I-
36  805  998 -193  -I*    I    I    I     I 928 -123 -I   *I     I      I    I-
                    -I—I—I—I—I—I—I—I—I                -I—I—I—I—I—I—I—I—I-
37  867 1061 -194  -1*    I    I    I     I 918  -51 -I    I  *  I      I    I-
38  925 1164 -239  -*     I    I    I     I1007  -82 -I   I*     I      I    I-
39 1200 1304 -104  -I     *    I    I     I1104   96 -I    I     I      *    I-
                    -I—I—I—I—I—I—I—I—I                -I—I—I—I—I—I—I—I—I-
```

Figure 4.7 Autocorp, Inc. The ordinary least squares regression function is

$$\hat{Y} = -68.0822 + 2.5554X_t$$

The generalized regression function (after the second iteration) is

$$\hat{Y}_1 = 118.8505 + 2.0386X_1 + \sqrt{1 - .6209^2}\, e_1$$

$$\hat{Y}_t = 118.8505 + 2.0386X_t + .6209e_{t-1}, \text{ for } t > 1$$

where $e_t = Y_t - (118.8505 + 2.0386X_t)$

Notice how the pattern that is apparent in the left-hand plot has been eliminated in the right-hand plot.

Then the generalized regression estimate is

$$\hat{Y}_{38} = 118.8505 + 2.0386 \times 482 + 0.6209 \times (-153) = 1007$$

In period 1, because the previous residual is not known, the regression estimate is made with a different formula ($Y_1 = 649$ and $X_1 = 287$):

$$e_1 = 649 - (118.8505 + 2.0386 \times 287) = -55$$
$$\hat{Y}_1 = 118.8505 + 2.0386 \times 287 + \sqrt{1 - 0.6209^2} \times (-55) = 661$$

If the adjustment has worked, the generalized function will not be autocorrelated. If on the other hand the generalized regression function is autocorrelated, the function is treated only as a first approximation and the procedure is repeated, this time the generalized function being treated as though it were the original ordinary function. The result is a new generalized regression function. The STAR Program goes through three iterations like this. If the function is still autocorrelated after the third iteration, the application is treated as fatally flawed. In the Autocorp application, the program took two iterations to develop an approximation to the coefficient of autocorrelation that was sufficiently good to eliminate the autocorrelation. These iterations will be explained in Chapter 8.

Autocorrelation can often be attributed to a major cause. In such cases it is ordinarily better to include in the regression function a variable that accounts for the cause of the autocorrelation than to use the generalized function.

4.4.3 Heteroscedasticity

Another assumption made in ordinary regression analysis is that the standard error is constant from point to point along the ULR. This condition is called *homoscedasticity*. To illustrate this condition assume that it were possible to select any X value along the ULR and, while holding it constant, observe a large number of Y values corresponding to that X. The standard error of the disturbances could be calculated at that point. Homoscedasticity means that standard errors calculated in this way would be the same at all points of the ULR.

In practice, disturbances are not always homoscedastic. For example, in a cross-sectional analysis of sales across the branches of a retail company, the sales of large stores might fluctuate more from the ULR (the disturbances will have a greater standard error) in terms of absolute dollars than the sales of small stores. Disturbances from the ULR that do not have a constant standard error are said to be *heteroscedastic.* Heteroscedasticity can also be observed in a time-series analysis in which the size of the variables increases over time because of either growth or inflation. Disturbances are heteroscedastic if their standard error varies in absolute dollar terms, even though it may not vary in relative terms.

The scatter diagrams in Figure 4.8 illustrate the difference between well-behaved homoscedastic disturbances and heteroscedastic disturbances. When the disturbances are homoscedastic, the standard error of the regression function can be used as an estimate of the standard error of the disturbances from the ULR. When they are heteroscedastic, the standard error of the regression function cannot be used without modification. In the example of heteroscedastic residuals shown in Figure 4.8, the standard error of the regression function will tend to overestimate the standard error of the smaller disturbances and to underestimate that of the larger disturbances.

Heteroscedasticity can take many different forms. For audit applications of regression analysis, however, it is ordinarily reasonable to assume that, where heteroscedasticity exists, the size of the disturbances will vary in proportion to one of the independent variables. This is the assumption made in the STAR Program, and it provides the basis on which the Program tests for and compensates for heteroscedasticity. Where there is significant heteroscedasticity, STAR performs *weighted regression,* in which the observations are weighted to compensate for the effect of the independent variable on the standard error.

An example of heteroscedasticity is provided by the Heteroco application in which RENT COST and FLOOR AREA are regressed against SALES in a cross-sectional application. A printout of the data for this application is shown in Table 4.5. In this example, the OLS function computed from the original variables is

$$Y_t = 29.6635 + 2.945X_{1t} + 0.8393X_{2t} + e_t$$

A strong correlation between the absolute residuals and X_1 in the Heteroco example is apparent from the scatter diagram shown in Figure 4.9.

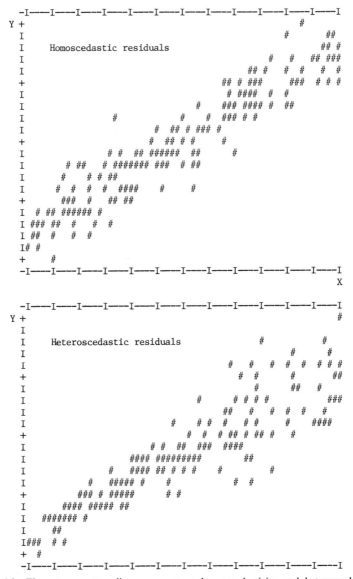

Figure 4.8 These two scatter diagrams contrast homoscedasticity and heteroscedasticity. Homoscedastic residuals show approximately the same standard error from observation to observation. Heteroscedastic residuals typically show a standard error that increases as the independent variable increases.

Table 4.5 Heteroco Inc. cross-sectional data across operating units

Obs#	Sales Y	Rent Cost X_1	Floor Area X_2	Obs#	Sales Y	Rent Cost X_1	Floor Area X2
1	2787	347	2050	17	2440	229	2096
2	3095	437	2052	18	3126	479	1970
3	3184	517	1944	19	4776	1002	1951
4	2084	139	1978	20	2030	100	2035
5	2287	189	2022	21	2070	138	1963
6	3228	551	1901	22	4949	1144	1945
7	4842	1076	2058	23	2862	371	2087
8	2210	194	1912	24	2347	185	2082
9	2565	276	2081	25	2912	388	2030
10	2494	297	1912	26	2259	234	1875
11	2422	241	2030	27	2730	393	1822
12	3090	444	2077	28	2106	153	1944
13	2287	229	1899	29	2274	200	1967
14	2669	297	2151	30	2444	212	2087
15	3204	467	2123				
16	2105	171	1886	31	2200	300	2000

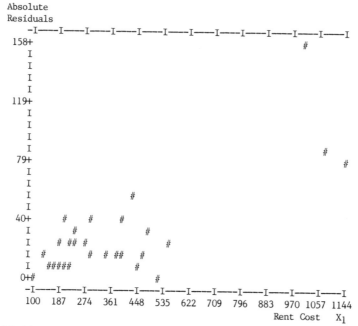

Figure 4.9 Heteroco, Inc. Scatter diagram of absolute residuals against rent cost. There is a strong positive correlation between them, indicating heteroscedasticity.

The weighted regression function is

$$Y_t = -97.5193 + 2.9701 \ X_{1t} + 0.8987 \ X_{2t} + e_t$$

Its standard error is $0.08754 \ X_{1t}$ for observation t. The inclusion of X_{1t} ensures that the standard error will vary from observation to observation. A complete STAR Program printout for this application is included as Printout B.4.

4.4.4   Abnormality

In Section 3.6 we indicated that there are strong theoretical grounds for believing that disturbances from the ULR will tend to be normally distributed. There is not really any way of confirming that a particular disturbance is normally distributed because, ordinarily, only one residual is observed for that period. If it were possible to hold a value of the independent variable constant for period t and observe repeated values of the residual, a frequency distribution of the residual could be prepared and tested against the normal distribution. Because this cannot be done, the only practical way to test for normality is to test the distribution of the collective residuals with the understanding that each residual should actually relate to a separate distribution. The STAR Program performs such a test and alerts the auditor to the presence of apparent *abnormality* (also known in statistical literature as *nonnormality*) in the base-period residuals.

The STAR Program describes the type of abnormality that has been encountered as *left skewness, right skewness,* or *kurtosis.* Skewness means that the distribution of the residuals is asymmetrical rather than symmetrical like the normal bell-shaped curve. In left skewness, the mean occurs to the left of the mode, or distribution peak. It is ordinarily caused by one or more extreme negative residuals. In right skewness, the mean occurs to the right of the mode, ordinarily because of one or more extreme positive residuals.

Kurtosis means that the distribution is either unusually peaked or unusually flat. (The latter case is rare, in our experience.) A peaked distribution may be caused by one or more large residuals on one side or on each side of the mean. These large residuals tend to inflate the standard error of the regression estimate to the extent that the other residuals appear unusually small in relative terms and appear to cluster tightly around the regression line, creating the appearance of a peaked distribution.

Table 4.6 contains cross-sectional PRODUCTION QUANTITIES and HOURS WORKED data for Paranormal Productions Inc. Figure 4.10 shows a plot of the residuals that result from regressing production against hours. The figure also shows a frequency distribution of the residuals and, for comparative purposes, an approximately normal distribution. A complete STAR Program printout for this application is included as Printout B.5.

Table 4.6 Paranormal Productions Inc. cross-sectional production quantities and hours worked data

Obs#	Prod. Y	Hours X	Obs#	Prod. Y	Hours X
1	31	39	21	52	70
2	32	39	22	51	83
3	32	42	23	55	72
4	36	49	24	62	81
5	41	72	25	41	58
6	33	47	26	53	61
7	39	57	27	100	134
8	19	26	28	70	85
9	53	68	29	82	106
10	40	48	30	65	79
11	38	50	31	67	86
12	38	50	32	61	92
13	56	74	33	71	84
14	45	60	34	72	91
15	62	79	35	66	83
16	45	64	36	62	76
17	55	73	37	82	97
18	53	65	38	60	72
19	61	82	39	60	73
20	37	47	40	37	47

Abnormality, as we have noted, generally results from the presence of outliers in the residuals. Sometimes, however, the underlying distribution of the disturbance terms may be genuinely non-normal. In such cases it may be difficult, if not impossible, to modify the model in order to deal with the abnormality. A more fruitful approach may be to abandon the assumption that the disturbances are basically normal in favor of an alter-

```
         RECORDED   REGRESSION            RESIDUALS GRAPHED IN UNITS
 OBS#     AMOUNT     ESTIMATE   RESIDUAL  OF 1 STD. ERROR ( 4.62120)   OBS#
         --------   ----------  --------
                                          -4 -3 -2 -1  0  1  2  3  4
                                          -I—I—I—I—I—I—I—I—I-
   1        31         30          1 -I        I      I*     I     I-    1
   2        32         30          2 -I        I      I*     I     I-    2
   3        32         32         -0 -I        I       *     I     I-    3
   4        36         38         -2 -I        I      *I     I     I-    4
   5        41         55        -14 -I   *    I       I     I     I-    5
   6        33         36         -3 -I        I    *  I     I     I-    6
   7        39         44         -5 -I        I  *    I     I     I-    7
   8        19         20         -1 -I        I      *I     I     I-    8
   9        53         52          1 -I        I      I*     I     I-    9
  10        40         37          3 -I        I      I  *   I     I-   10
  11        38         38         -0 -I        I       *     I     I-   11
  12        38         38         -0 -I        I       *     I     I-   12
  13        56         57         -1 -I        I       *     I     I-   13
  14        45         46         -1 -I        I      *I     I     I-   14
  15        62         61          1 -I        I      I*     I     I-   15
  16        45         49         -4 -I        I  *    I     I     I-   16
  17        55         56         -1 -I        I      *I     I     I-   17
  18        53         50          3 -I        I      I  *   I     I-   18
  19        61         63         -2 -I        I      *I     I     I-   19
  20        37         36          1 -I        I      I*     I     I-   20
  21        52         54         -2 -I        I      *I     I     I-   21
  22        51         64        -13 -I    *   I       I     I     I-   22
  23        55         55         -0 -I        I       *     I     I-   23
  24        62         62         -0 -I        I       *     I     I-   24
  25        41         44         -3 -I        I    *  I     I     I-   25
  26        53         47          6 -I        I       I   *  I    I-   26
  27       100        103         -3 -I        I  *    I     I     I-   27
  28        70         65          5 -I        I       I  *  I     I-   28
  29        82         81          1 -I        I       I*    I     I-   29
  30        65         61          4 -I        I       I *   I     I-   30
  31        67         66          1 -I        I       I*    I     I-   31
  32        61         70         -9 -I    *          I      I     I-   32
  33        71         64          7 -I        I       I   * I     I-   33
  34        72         70          2 -I        I       I*    I     I-   34
  35        66         64          2 -I        I       I *   I     I-   35
  36        62         58          4 -I        I       I *   I     I-   36
  37        82         74          8 -I        I       I     *I    I-   37
  38        60         55          5 -I        I       I  *  I     I-   38
  39        60         56          4 -I        I       I *   I     I-   39
  40        37         36          1 -I        I      I*     I     I-   40
                                          -I—I—I—I—I—I—I—I—I-
                  Approximately             Frequency of Residuals
                  Normal Distribution       00110100236694421000000
        9-I       of 40 Residuals     9-I          *
        8-I                           8-I          *
        7-I                           7-I          *
        6-I           *               6-I         ***
        5-I          ***              5-I         ***
        4-I        *******            4-I         *****
        3-I        *******            3-I         ******
        2-I       *********           2-I         ********
        1-I      *************        1-I  * * *  *********
        -I—I—I—I—I—I—I—I—I-       0-I—I—I—I—I—I—I—I—I-
        -4 -3 -2 -1  0  1  2  3  4    -4 -3 -2 -1  0  1  2  3  4
```

Figure 4.10 Paranormal Productions, Inc. Plot of residuals from the regression function $\hat{Y}_t = -0.0131 + 0.7662X_t$. The large negative residuals in periods, 5, 22, and 32 have caused the apparent left skewness and kurtosis in the residuals.

native method that requires no assumption about their distribution. Such an approach changes the mathematics of the audit interface, including the calculation of excesses to be investigated (dealt with in Chapter 5). Methods for dealing with an underlying non-normal distribution are discussed in Section 8.6 and a numerical example that uses the data in Table 4.6 is given for one of the methods.

4.4.5 Multicollinearity

Multicollinearity, a high correlation between two or more independent variables, is a condition that is significant in many applications of regression analysis. The principal effect of multicollinearity is to increase the standard error of the regression coefficients of those variables that are highly correlated. In practical terms, multicollinearity makes it difficult to disentangle the effects of those variables to arrive at reliable separate estimates of their coefficients.

In auditing applications of regression analysis, regression estimates of the dependent variable usually are more important than estimates of the coefficients of the independent variables. In such applications, therefore, multicollinearity is seldom a problem even when it occurs. In addition, where a set of independent variables is multicollinear, the stepwise selection procedure used by the STAR Program (see Section 4.3) will usually ensure that significant multicollinearity is not present within the set of selected variables. For these reasons no specific test for multicollinearity has been included in the STAR Program.

General References

S. Chatterjee, *Regression Analysis by Example.* New York: Wiley, 1977.

N. R. Draper and H. Smith, *Applied Regression Analysis.* New York: Wiley, 1981.

M. Ezekiel and K. A. Fox, *Methods of Correlation and Regression Analysis,* 3rd ed. New York: Wiley, 1959.

A. Koutsoyiannis, *Theory of Econometrics,* 2nd ed. London: Macmillan, 1977.

M. S. Lewis-Beck, *Applied Regression: An Introduction.* Beverly Hills, CA: Sage Publications, 1980.

J. Neper, *Applied Linear Regression Models.* Homewood, IL: R. D. Irwin, 1983.

K. W. Smillie, *An Introduction to Regression and Correlation.* New York: Academic Press, 1966.

5

THE AUDIT INTERFACE

5.1 Introduction

In this chapter we explain the technique that the STAR Program uses to detect significant fluctuations from the ULR by the dependent variable. This technique, which blends statistics and quantified audit judgments, represents the *audit interface*. The three audit parameters that the auditor must provide in the audit interface are the monetary precision (MP), the reliability factor (R), and the direction of test (i.e., overstatement or understatement). These parameters are discussed in Chapters 1 and 6.

5.2 Basic Concepts

The primary purpose of the audit interface is to achieve a specified level of reliability that one or more observations containing errors will be identified for investigation if the amount of accounting errors affecting the recorded total of the dependent variable in a specified direction is at least as much as the monetary precision. As used here and later in this book, *errors* includes both intentional irregularities and unintentional mistakes in the amounts or in the application of accounting principles.

The basic concept underlying the audit interface is that the recorded amounts of the dependent variable in the projection period may have been materially affected by accounting errors, while the estimates projected from the regression model should not be so affected (because the model is based on observations that have been audited or obtained from sources considered reliable). Residuals in the audit period therefore are expected to have been caused by:

- The random variation that is inherent in business operations and in estimates made by using a regression model
- Errors or unusual events that affect the recorded amount of the dependent variable in the projection period

STAR sets a *cut-off point* for each residual in the projection period. If the residual exceeds the cut-off point, the excess is treated as an excess to be investigated. This is illustrated in Figure 5.1. The computation of the cut-off point involves the quantified audit parameters and certain statistics, in particular the standard error of the residual (see Section 3.5).

The computation of the cut-off point is complicated by the fact that the way in which material error might be spread among the values of the de-

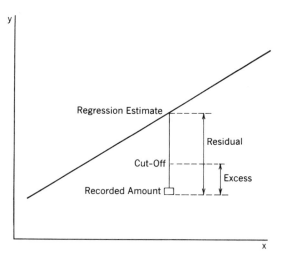

Figure 5.1   Excess to be investigated. This diagram shows that the excess to be investigated is the difference between the recorded amount and the cut-off point.

pendent variable is unknown. For example, it could all be bunched in 1 month or it could be spread throughout 12 months. Fortunately, there is always a certain spread of error that is *most adverse* in the sense that it is the most difficult to detect. STAR computes this most adverse spread of error and uses it in the calculation of the cut-off point. This results in cut-off points that are conservative if the error is not spread in the most adverse way.

If STAR identifies an excess to be investigated, then, until further audit work is performed, the auditor's level of reliability will be less than required. If a satisfactory explanation of the excess cannot be obtained, the auditor would ordinarily need to increase the extent of the tests of details of the affected observation. The STAR Program calculates how many extra items should be sampled to bring the auditor's reliability back to the required level. In Section 5.3 we will explain how this sample size is calculated.

In Chapter 3 we introduced the concept of the standard error of the residual, the standardized residual (the residual divided by its standard error), and the t distribution. We calculated the standard error of the residual for period 48 for the Gamma Company application. It is 214.4970, and the standardized residual is

$$\frac{e_{48}}{s(e_{48})} = \frac{-266}{214.4970} = -1.24$$

This statistic is distributed as t with 34 degrees of freedom. We will use these concepts and statistics in this chapter. We will also use the fact that the monetary precision, MP, has been set at \$600,000 (shown as \$600 on the STAR printout in Figure 2.4, since the dependent variable is in thousands of dollars), the reliability factor, R, has been set at 3.0, and the direction of test is *understatement*.

5.3 Identifying Excess to be Investigated

In this section we will explain how cut-off points and excesses to be investigated are calculated. We will also illustrate the principles involved, using as an example the period-48 data for the Gamma Company, since we used this example in previous sections and many of the factors have already been calculated.

An important factor in the calculation of a cut-off point is the most adverse spread of error between individual observations. That such a thing as the most adverse spread of error should exist may not be immediately obvious. The key to understanding why it does exist is to recognize that there are two opposing factors that determine the probability of detecting error:

- The size of the individual error taintings. The smaller the error tainting of a particular observation, the less probable it is that the observation will be identified.
- The number of error-tainted observations. The more error-tainted observations there are, the more likely it is that at least one will be identified.

It can be shown that the interaction of these two opposing factors ensures that a certain spread of error will result in the tightest cut-off requirement. This spread is the most adverse spread of error because any other will allow a cut-off point that is less stringent.

The most adverse spread of error is dependent on two main factors: the size of the MP relative to the standard error of the residual and the required reliability level. The greater the relative MP, and the lower the required reliability level, the greater the most adverse spread of error.

In the analysis that follows, all of the calculations will be expressed in terms of "standardized" dollars. That is, dollar amounts will be divided by the standard error of the residual for period 48. This will make it unnecessary to flip back and forth between standardized dollars (which are needed for t distribution calculations) and real dollars. At any point, standardized dollars can be translated back into real dollars by multiplying by the standard error. The symbol "s$" will be used to denote standardized dollar amounts. The standardized residual is $-s\$1.24$, as shown in Section 5.2. The standardized MP is $\$600/214.497 = s\$2.80$.

We will now show how cut-off points could be set for successively thinner spreads of error if those spreads were known. The important thing is that the cut-off points will get closer to the regression line for a few iterations, and then begin to move further away. The most conservative cut-off point, the one closest to the regression line in this example, will be the one used by the STAR Program. (In Section 5.5 we discuss a relatively unusual condition where the cut-off point may not be the one closest to the regression line.)

In the following analysis it will be assumed that such error as exists will be spread equally throughout those observations that contain errors. While there is no basis for this assumption, it can be show.. that it results in the most conservative cut-off point for the given number of error-tainted observations.

Because the reliability factor set for the exercise is R = 3.0, the reliability level required is 95% (see Table A.1). In other words, 5% is the maximum risk that the auditor is prepared to accept that no error-tainted observations will be identified if the total understatement is s$2.80 or more.

5.3.1 Spread of one

If it is assumed that the total error of s$2.80 (if it exists) will taint only one observation, then the cut-off point must be set such that there is only a 5% risk that the error-tainted observation will not be identified.

The first step is to establish a *risk point* such that 95% of all *correct* Y values (standardized) will fall below it (i.e., 95% of the residuals will fall below it on the hypothesis that there is no error in the data). Then the cut-off point is simply set at a distance of s$2.80 below the risk point. If 95% of all *correct* Y values fall below the risk point, then 95% of all *recorded* values that understate the correct Y value by s$2.80 or more must fall below the cut-off point. Thus any observation with an understatement of s$2.80 or more will be identified with 95% reliability.

Determining the risk point is equivalent to determining that point on the *t* distribution (the one with 34 degrees of freedom) such that 95% of all *t* values fall below it. The STAR Program uses a formula to calculate *t* values. Certain of these are shown in Table A.2 for illustrative purposes. The *t* value is 1.69. The cut-off point is therefore

$$s\$1.69 - s\$2.80 = -s\$1.11$$

The complete process is illustrated in Figure 5.2. Thus residuals that are larger than −s$1.11 in the negative direction (i.e., −s$1.11 × 214.497 = −$238 or larger, in real dollars) will be treated as excessive.

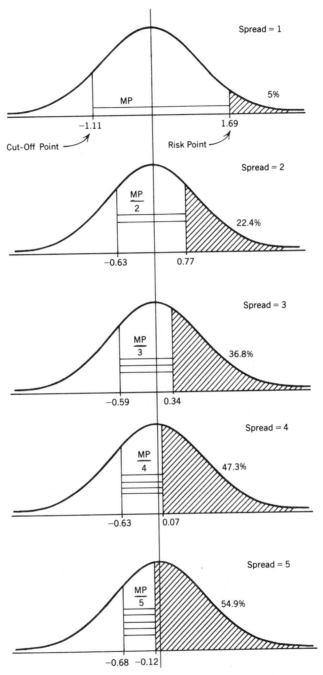

Figure 5.2 Finding the most adverse spread of error. Cut-off points for successively thinner spreads of error get closer to the regression line to start with and then get further away. This example shows how the calculations are made for the Gamma Company data, period 48. In this case, the most adverse spread of error is 3, since that spread results in the most conservative cut-off point: −0.59 in standardized dollars.

5.3.2   Spread of two

If it is assumed that the total understatement of s$2.80 (if it exists) will affect two separate observations by s$1.40 each, then the cut-off point must be set so that, with 95% reliability, at least one of those observations will be identified. Put differently, the auditor can accept a maximum 5% risk that both error-tainted observations will escape identification. The risk that both of such observations escape identification is the product of the risks that each escapes. Because 22.4% × 22.4% = 5%, 22.4% is the acceptable risk that a particular error-tainted observation is not identified.

The risk point must be set such that 77.6% (100% − 22.4%) of all correct standardized Y values will fall below it, and the cut-off point must be set at a distance of s$1.40 (one-half standardized MP) below it. If 77.6% of all *correct* Y values fall below the risk point, then 77.6% of all *recorded* values that understate the correct Y value by s$1.40 or more will fall below the cut-off point. Thus given any error of understatement of s$1.40 or more, the risk is not more than 22.4% that the error-tainted observation will not be detected.

The t value that corresponds to a risk of 22.4% is 0.77. The cut-off point is therefore

$$s\$0.77 - s\$1.40 = -s\$0.63$$

This is illustrated in Figure 5.2.

5.3.3   Spread of three

If it is assumed that the total understatement of s$2.80 (if it exists), will affect three separate observations by s$0.93 each, then, because 36.8% × 36.8% × 36.8% = 5%, 36.8% is the acceptable risk that a particular error-tainted observation will not be identified.

The t value that corresponds to a risk of 36.8% is 0.34. The cut-off point is therefore

$$s\$0.34 - s\$0.93 = -s\$0.59$$

This is illustrated in Figure 5.2.

5.3.4   Spreads of four, five, and more

If the error is assumed to affect four observations equally by one-fourth of MP (i.e., s$0.70), the acceptable risk of not identifying a particular error-tainted observation is 47.3% (47.3% × 47.3% × 47.3% × 47.3% = 5%).

The *t* value that corresponds to a risk of 47.3% is 0.07. The cut-off point is therefore

$$s\$0.07 - s\$0.70 = -s\$0.63$$

For a spread of five, the individual risk is 54.9%, the *t* value is − s$0.12, and the cut-off is

$$-s\$0.12 - s\$0.56 = -s\$0.68$$

These are illustrated in Figure 5.2.

5.3.5   Most adverse spread of error

Table 5.1 is a summary of the cut-off points that would be required for various known spreads of error. It is clear from this summary that the most conservative cut-off point is − s$0.59, the one that corresponds to three error-tainted observations. The cutoffs that correspond to one or two, or to four or five such observations are all further away. If this exercise were to be continued for even more thinly spread error, the trend would continue. Accordingly, three is the most adverse spread of error, and − s$0.59 is the most conservative cut-off point.

Initially it might seem that the maximum number of observations over

Table 5.1   Gamma Company setting the cut-off point for observation 48

Spread	Risk Point	t Value	Error Tainting	Cut-Off Point
1	5.0%	1.69	2.80	−1.11
2	22.4%	0.77	1.40	−0.63
==> 3	36.8%	0.34	0.93	−0.59 <==
4	47.3%	0.07	0.70	−0.63
5	54.9%	−0.12	0.56	−0.68

which a material error might be spread should be limited by the number of observations in the accounting period. For example, if the application uses monthly data, the need to consider the risk of spreading a material error over more than 12 observations might appear doubtful. The STAR Program, nevertheless, does not place any upper limit on the most adverse spread of error, and the calculation is performed separately for each observation. Spreads ranging into the thousands are possible.

This approach to calculating the most adverse distribution helps to ensure that the statistical assurance provided by STAR is not diluted over multiple STAR applications. For example, if the calculation did not consider the possibility that a material error could be spread over 60 observations, the risk that material error could be spread over five different STAR applications that use monthly data might be higher than the nominal level. Another consequence of the way in which the most adverse spread of error is calculated is that the monetary precisions specified for designing multiple STAR applications may be considered noncumulative with respect to the combined applications.

Table 5.1 shows how the cut-off point gets closer to the regression line as the error affects more observations. However, if it affects more than three observations, the cut-off point can be relaxed. An error exactly equal to MP is most adversely spread when it affects three observations equally. The error, the risk points, and the cut-off points are expressed in standardized dollars. Standardized dollars can be translated into normal dollars by multiplying by the standard error which, in this case, is 214.497.

5.3.6 Excess to be investigated

As we explained previously, the cut-off point that will be most conservative for the period-48 residual for Gamma Company is $-$s$0.59. This translates to

$$-s\$0.59 \times 214.497 = -\$127$$

in real dollars (expressed in thousands). Accordingly, the residual of $-\$266$ is excessive by $\$139$. The more accurate amount, shown on the STAR printout of Figure 2.3, is $\$138$. The difference is due to the fact that the calculations shown have been performed with numbers that are more rounded than those that STAR uses.

5.4   Optional Sample Data

Besides identifying excesses to be investigated, the audit interface module of the STAR Program also designs supplementary statistical samples that may be used to test details of those recorded amounts of the dependent variable that have been determined to contain excesses. Such samples are appropriate when no adequate explanation of an "excess to be investigated" can be obtained. Their purpose is to "close the gap" between the specified reliability level and the achieved reliability level.

We will demonstrate how the STAR Program calculates the optional sample data for the excess to be investigated that was discussed in the previous section. The observed residual in that case was −s$1.24. The auditor's concern is that the true residual (i.e., the residual excluding any error component) might be understated by s$0.93 or more. Put another way, the auditor is concerned that the true residual might fall above −s$0.31. Thus −s$0.31 is called the *effective risk point*. The risk that the true residual is above −s$0.31 (the *effective risk*) can be calculated from the *t* distribution. It is 61.9%, as illustrated in Figure 5.3. It exceeds the *target risk* level for the observation, which is 36.8% (see Section 5.3.3).

The optional sample must be designed so as to reduce the effective risk to the target risk for the observation. Thus the appropriate risk level for the optional sample is 36.8%/61.9% = 59.5%. Put another way, the product of the effective risk and the optional sample risk must equal the target risk.

A reliability factor of $R = .52$ (see Table A.1) is equivalent to a reliability

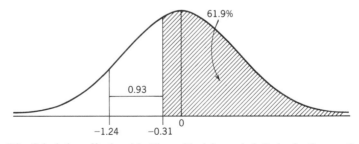

Figure 5.3   Calculating effective risk. The residual for period 48, in the Gamma Company example, is −s$1.24. There is a 61.9% probability that the correct residual for this observation will be more than one-third of MP (s$0.93) above this amount. Since the cut-off point has been set to detect errors of one-third MP, 61.9% is the effective risk associated with the result.

level of 40.5% (the complement of the optional sample risk, 59.5%). Based on the implied precision limit and reliability factor, the STAR Program determines a maximum sample size and a selection interval, and generates a random starting point for the selection of the sample items to test the recorded amount for that observation. The sampling approach contemplated by the STAR Program in designing this sample is a probability-proportional-to-size technique, which is embodied in an audit sampling plan widely used in DH&S as a companion technique to the STAR Program. (See Section 7.4.2.)

In terms of this sampling plan, an appropriate monetary sampling interval for the tests of details can be calculated by dividing the reliability factor into the required precision. The precision limit is s$0.93, or $200 (MP divided by 3, the most adverse spread of error). Hence the sampling interval (rounded down for conservatism) is $200/0.52 = $384.

As will be discussed further in Chapter 7, the population to be sampled depends on the direction of the test. The recorded value of the dependent variable itself may be sampled if the audit objective relates to overstatement errors. If that were the case, the maximum sample size would be the recorded value of the dependent variable divided by the selection interval (2993/384 = 8). As it is, because the audit objective relates to understatement errors, the sample should be taken from a population that could reveal understatements or omissions in the recorded amounts of the dependent variable. Because the best estimate of the dependent variable for period 48 is $3259 (Figure 2.3), the regression estimate, the best estimate of the maximum extra sample required, is $3259/$384 = 8 items.

5.5   Excesses Greater than Residuals

Under some circumstances the STAR Program will indicate an excess to be investigated that is larger than the residual. At first this might seem contrary to common sense—after all, the residual is the difference between the recorded value and the best estimate of the dependent variable. Clearly such an excess is unlikely to be identified in a conventional analytical review. Such excesses are referred to as "paradoxical excesses."

To understand how paradoxical excesses arise, it is necessary to remember that the STAR Program sets cut-off points on the basis of the monetary precision, the reliability level, the direction of test, and the statistical characteristics of the regression function (the standard error of the residual, in particular). In general, the more stringent the audit requirements, the tighter the cut-off points and the greater the excesses to be investigated. At a certain point, the auditor's requirements may become so demanding relative to the statistical characteristics of the regression function that cut-off points cross to the opposite side of the regression estimates and paradoxical excesses might be identified.

For example, if a regression model with a standard error of $1000 were to be used to obtain 95% assurance that sales are not understated by more than $100, then, because the audit objectives are so demanding in relation to the predictive ability of the regression model, it is likely that paradoxical excesses would be identified.

Paradoxical excesses occur infrequently, and their presence suggests that the precision and reliability that have been specified are relatively difficult to achieve through analytical review. The related regression model should be assessed to determine if it is the best model practicable under the circumstances. As statistical objectives become more demanding, the auditor should be prepared to invest more effort in developing a model of sufficient quality to achieve those objectives efficiently. In a figurative sense, paradoxical excesses indicate that the auditor may be trying to "squeeze blood from a turnip."

The audit response to paradoxical excesses is, in theory, no different from that for other excesses to be investigated. However, because an analytical explanation is ordinarily not feasible for the entire excess, the usual response should be to increase the tests of details by the size of the optional sample designed by the STAR Program. If part of the excess can be explained analytically, the Program should be rerun with the explained part removed from the recorded amount. The revised optional sample would then be the appropriate one to use.

AUDITING APPLICATIONS OF REGRESSION ANALYSIS

6

DESIGNING AUDIT MODELS

6.1 Introduction

Use of the STAR Program for an audit application consists of the following steps:

- Designing the audit model
- Running the STAR Program
- Reviewing the audit model
- Investigating unusual fluctuations
- Evaluating the audit results

We discuss the auditing decisions to be made in designing an audit model in this chapter, and we discuss the remaining steps in Chapter 7.

The decisions involved in designing effective and efficient audit models require a blend of audit judgment and statistical techniques. Such decisions should be based on the general and specific audit objectives in the circumstances, the related statistical considerations, and the data available for use as variables. In the next section we discuss the audit and statistical objectives that apply to all audit applications, and in the remainder of the chapter we discuss the specific objectives and other elements of audit models for individual applications.

6.2   General Audit and Statistical Objectives

The auditing objective of analytical review will be accomplished most effectively by a model that provides the best fit that is practicable in the circumstances. Achievement of this objective requires a clear understanding of the factors affecting the operations of the organization being audited and perceptiveness in recognizing potential relationships among the variables that are available for use. Experimentation in specifying the variables and the data profile to develop a model that best achieves the audit purpose of an application is appropriate and should be encouraged, both in the initial design of the model and, as discussed in Chapter 7, after its review.

6.2.1   Statistical best fit

In analytical review applications, the auditor's purpose ordinarily will be to develop a model that will provide the best estimates of the dependent variable and, consequently, the lowest residuals. As explained in Section 3.4.2, "best" is measured by the standard error of the regression function or, equivalently, by the coefficient of residual variation. For any given set of observations of a dependent variable, the regression function that results in the lowest coefficient of residual variation will also result in the highest coefficients of correlation and regression improvement. Thus the respective coefficients will present consistent indications of the statistical "goodness of fit" in typical analytical review applications.

6.2.2   Practical constraints

There are two practical constraints on the statistical degree of fit that can be obtained in an audit model for any particular application. First are the inherent characteristics of the operations of the business or organization being audited. Some operations are relatively stable, while others are highly volatile in relation to any set of variables that can reasonably be identified. Refinements in the model will not, and indeed should not, obscure real volatility in the underlying operations.

Second is the practical inevitability of imperfections to some degree in any audit model. Such imperfections may arise from limitations in the auditor's knowledge or in the available data or from cost–benefit considerations relating to the audit purpose of the application. We use the term *im-*

perfections here to mean matters that frequently are described in regression literature as *specification errors* and *measurement errors.* In that context, specification errors usually refer to the omission of significant independent variables or to the use of a less appropriate form of functional relationship (e.g., the use of a linear function when a nonlinear function would be more appropriate); measurement errors refer to inaccuracies in the data used as the observed values of the variables.

Practical means for reducing imperfections in audit models are discussed in this and later chapters. General criteria for selecting significant and reliable independent variables are provided in Section 6.5, and suggestions for dealing with common sources of potential imperfections that are unique to accounting data are discussed in Section 6.6.

Although perfection in an audit model is unlikely to be achieved, we think that a combination of statistical tests and informed audit judgment provides ample precaution against the risk of significant imperfections. As a practical matter, the quality of an audit model must be judged against the quality of the available alternatives rather than against some imaginary perfection. Under this criterion, it seems evident that the imperfections remaining in audit models generated by the STAR Program should not be greater, and probably are much less, than those that are present (even if not recognized) in the implicit models used in subjective analytical review procedures. We have been surprised at times to observe that some auditors, who have been content for years to use subjective techniques with no apparent concern for the imperfections inherent in them, tend to become hypersensitive about imperfections in regression models. We hope this book will help in placing such concerns in perspective.

6.2.3   Correlation criteria

We do not recommend any minimum value for the coefficient of correlation or any maximum value for the coefficient of residual variation as a requirement for use of an audit model in an analytical review application, for two reasons. The first is that these statistics are recognized through the standard error, which is used to compute the cut-off point for excesses to be investigated, as explained in Chapter 5; the compensatory effect of lower correlation or higher residual variation is that it tends to require more audit investigation.

The second reason is that we believe the statistical discipline and measurements obtained through regression analysis, regardless of the residual variation or correlation, will ordinarily result in a better analytical review than subjective techniques applied to the same data. In our view, this is also true in those situations in which no significant variable is identified. In such situations, the auditor typically and logically would revert to the mean of the dependent variable as the most reasonable measure of expected results. For this reason, the STAR Program computes mean estimates in such situations, and uses the standard error of the mean in lieu of the standard error of the regression estimate in identifying excesses to be investigated. We think that the extension of the rationale incorporated in the audit interface to these extreme situations permits them to be dealt with more effectively than could be done by use of subjective techniques.

6.2.4   Correlation and causation

The distinction between correlation and causation needs to be understood in considering the audit and statistical objectives of audit models. This distinction applies in any application of regression analysis and thus is not limited to those for analytical review.

Statistical correlation may, but does not necessarily, imply a cause-and-effect relationship between variables. For example, a high correlation might be shown between rainfall and floods. Such correlation would provide a reasonable basis for inferring that rainfall causes floods, but obviously not that floods cause rainfall. As another example, a high correlation has been found between teachers' salaries and sales of alcoholic beverages. In this case it seems clear that there is no cause-and-effect relationship, regardless of which of the variables is treated as dependent, but that both of the variables are influenced similarly by other socioeconomic independent variables.

In many cases the distinction correlation and causation may be more complex and less apparent, and possibly less relevant for the purpose of the application, than the simple but extreme examples just given. For instance, increases in the physical volume of sales alone would increase total sales and cost of sales; increases in unit costs, on the other hand, might decrease the physical volume of sales but increase the unit sales prices and either increase or decrease total sales and cost of sales. The ramifications of cost–price–volume relationships may be a fertile field for regression analysis for management and other economic purposes. It may suffice for the auditor's analytical review purposes, however, to establish that management has been able to maintain a relatively stable relationship between certain variables (e.g., sales and costs) throughout relevant periods, without detailed analysis of the causes of changes in each of the variables unless such analysis is necessary to explain unusual fluctuations.

6.3 Specific Objectives of an Audit Application

The auditor defines the specific objectives of an application by making decisions about the following matters, and entering these decisions in the form of specifications for the STAR Program:

- The dependent variable
- The type and number of observations in the data profile
- The direction of the audit test
- The statistical reliability and precision desired

6.3.1 Dependent variable

The specific account, class of transactions, or financial statement component to be tested and the audit purpose of the application determine the dependent variable to be specified. The audit purpose of an application may be to review fluctuations in operating accounts or to review the reasonableness of balances in balance-sheet accounts. In either case the purpose may relate to accounts at one operating location or at multiple locations.

If the audit purpose is to review fluctuations in operating accounts at a single location, the dependent variable might be the monthly amounts of sales, the cost of sales, or the major classifications of operating expenses.

Audit tests of balance-sheet accounts at a single location often include tests of details at some interim date, supplemented by tests or a review of transactions for the intervening period from that date to the end of the year being audited. In such situations, the audit purpose of an application might be to review certain components of the transactions during the intervening period, and the dependent variable might be the monthly amounts of transactions (e.g., collections on receivables or credits to inventory accounts for cost of sales). The purpose of such review would be to consider the cumulative effect of any unusual fluctuations in such transactions on the ending balance of the related account. The STAR Program achieves this purpose by using the regression estimates of the dependent variable during the intervening period to project an ending balance and by comparing the projected balance with the recorded balance to determine any excess to be investigated. This type of application is described as an *ending balance projection*. An example of an ending balance projection is included as Printout B.6.

In audits of companies that operate in multiple locations, the base profile might consist of certain locations that have been, or will be, audited for the current year by other procedures, and the projection profile might include all other locations. The audit purpose of such an application might be to review fluctuations in the yearly total of operating accounts or ending balances in balance-sheet accounts in the projection profile to identify locations to be visited or otherwise investigated because of unusual fluctuations. In such applications, the yearly total or ending balance of a specific account or component would be the dependent variable.

In specifying the dependent variable, the auditor must also make decisions about the following matters relating to the audit purpose of the application:

- The accounting unit for which the application is to be made
- The level of detail of the accounts to be used

The accounting unit for a particular application might be the consolidated group, one particular company, an operating division, a branch, or some other subdivision of the entity. The level of detail of the accounts might be, for example, total cost of sales or the separate material, labor, and overhead components. In determining the accounting unit and level of detail to be used, the objective should be to achieve the maximum practicable audit effectiveness and efficiency.

To be effective for audit purposes, the accounting unit used should be no larger than the smallest unit on whose financial statements the auditor is to express an opinion. If, for example, the auditor is to express an opinion on the financial statements of each subsidiary company, the accounting unit could be each such company or some subdivision of it, but should not be the consolidated entity.

A similar limitation need not be applied to the level of detail of accounts to be used unless the auditor is to issue a special report on a particular account. In the usual situation, the auditor expresses an opinion on financial statements in which amounts are stated in broad financial statement components (e.g., cost of sales, selling expenses, and administrative and general expenses). In such cases these components or subdivisions of them may be used as the dependent variable in applications to test the respective components. If further details of these components are presented as supplementary information, which the auditor does not consider necessary for fair presentation of the financial statements, such details are comprehended in the standard form of opinion only as they relate to those statements taken as a whole. In such circumstances, the auditor may conclude that it is not necessary to use, as a separate dependent variable, each level of detail that is presented as supplementary information. If an unqualified opinion is to be expressed in a special report on a particular component of the financial statements, however, that component should be used as the dependent variable in any application that is to be relied on by the auditor for that purpose.

Subject to the limitations in the preceding two paragraphs, both audit effectiveness and efficiency will be improved by specifying an accounting unit and level of detail of accounts that result in the best statistical fit, as discussed in Section 6.2. For this reason it ordinarily is desirable to exclude from an application any accounting units for which there is a known diversity in operating conditions that would be expected to adversely affect the correlation between the variables to be used. Similarly, the level of detail of variables to be used should exclude accounts that would be expected to adversely affect the correlation. For example, operating locations that have been affected by strikes or other disruptions and accounts that have been affected by a change in accounting principles generally should be excluded. Any units or accounts that are excluded should be covered by other STAR applications or by other auditing procedures. Consequently, excessive refinement in making exclusions to improve the correlation in one or more applications may decrease the overall audit efficiency with little, if any, improvement in effectiveness. Thus audit judgment and an understanding of the business operations are needed in deciding on the accounting unit and level of detail to be used in specifying the dependent variable.

6.3.2   Type and number of observations in the data profile

As discussed in the preceding section, the type of data profile to be specified depends on the audit purpose of the application. The two basic types of data profiles are *time-series* and *cross-sectional* data profiles. These terms were defined in Section 2.4.2. In a cross-sectional profile, the units might be subdivisions (e.g., operating locations) of the accounting unit for which the application is being made. In some applications, a data profile that includes both time-series and cross-sectional observations may be useful; such a combination may be described as a *cross-time* profile. Such a profile might, for example, include monthly observations from several locations.

As discussed in Section 2.4.2, the data profile consists of two parts: the base profile and the projection profile. The base profile includes the set of observations that is used in computing the regression function and other regression statistics; the projection profile includes the set that is used in computing the regression estimates and excesses to be investigated in the current audit period. For time-series applications, the base profile includes observations from prior periods that ordinarily will have been audited in those periods. For cross-sectional applications, the base profile ordinarily should consist of selected units that have or will be audited by other procedures during the current period to validate them for use as the base, or should consist of prior audited amounts.

The number of observations to be included in the base profile is influenced by two conflicting considerations. The general effect of a larger number of observations is to increase the degrees of freedom and thereby to decrease the standard error of the regression estimates. A contrary effect may result, however, from adding earlier periods in a time-series profile, or from adding more units in a cross-sectional profile, either of which may have been affected by different operating conditions that would increase the standard error.

For a time-series profile, it ordinarily is desirable to eliminate the oldest observations if operating conditions have changed in more recent periods, because this will help to reduce the standard error. For a cross-sectional profile, it may be appropriate to subdivide or stratify the units into two or more profiles on the basis of size or some other characteristic that reduces the standard error.

Because of the conflicting considerations and variety of circumstances the auditor is likely to encounter, we do not suggest specific guidelines for the number of observations to be included in the base profile. We have found, however, that 36 monthly or 20 quarterly observations usually are reasonable for time-series profiles, and that 20 observations usually are reasonable for cross-sectional profiles.

The projection profile for time-series applications generally should include observations for all periods of the year being audited, although it may be desirable to run the STAR Program separately for periods preceding and following an interim examination date. For cross-sectional applications, the projection profile should include all units being audited in the STAR application.

6.3.3   Direction of the audit test

The direction of the audit test to be specified is either overstatement or understatement. As explained in Chapter 5, this specification is used in the audit interface computation of the cut-off point for determining whether there are excesses to be investigated. If the audit purpose of the application is to test the dependent variable for possible overstatement, the relevant residuals usually will be those arising from excesses of the recorded amounts over the related regression estimates. In tests for understatement, the relevant residuals usually will be those in the opposite direction. Exceptions to this rule arise in some situations (paradoxical excesses), which are explained in Section 5.5. The STAR Program can test in either direction.

Decisions about the direction of test and the types and combinations of auditing procedures that are necessary to accomplish reasonable tests of financial statement components in both directions are matters of audit judgment that are not unique to STAR applications; they are matters about which different auditors may have different views. Further discussion of this topic per se is beyond the scope of this book, but some of the examples that we cite throughout the book are indicative of our general views on appropriate types and combinations of auditing procedures.

6.3.4   Statistical reliability and precision

The concepts of statistical reliability and precision and their role in auditing were introduced in Chapter 1, and their application to the audit interface was explained in Chapter 5. As indicated earlier, the reliability level (a probability percentage) desired for an application of the STAR Program is specified through a reliability factor. The relationship between reliability levels and reliability factors is shown in Table A.1. The monetary precision limit is specified directly as a monetary amount in the same units as the dependent variable.

These parameters are the connecting link between statistical techniques and audit judgment. The culmination of an auditor's judgment about the ultimate objectives of auditing procedures can be expressed by specifying these parameters for use in designing either an audit model for analytical review or a statistical sample for an audit test of details. For either of these purposes, reliability should be related to the auditor's judgment about audit risks, and precision should be related to his or her judgment about materiality.

The matters to be considered in making these judgments are discussed in SAS 39 [1] and SAS 47 [2]. The appendix to SAS No. 39 discusses and illustrates the combination of risks relating to internal accounting control, analytical review, and tests of details. The material in this appendix is as relevant to analytical review applications as it is to audit sampling applications. The following features of Table 2 in the appendix to SAS 39 relate to the discussion in this book:

- The percentages shown in the table are in terms of "risk," which is the complement of "reliability" as used in this book.
- The column headings in the table show the assumed risk assigned to analytical review (AR), while the percentages in the body of the table are the computed risks for tests of details (TD) for the respective assumed levels of internal accounting control risk (IC). For the purposes of this book, the positions of AR and TD in the table could be reversed so that the percentages in the body of the table would become the risks for analytical review applications.

6.4   Classification and Source of Independent Variables

Independent variables can be classified as either *real* or *dummy* variables.

6.4.1   Real variables

Real variables consist of monetary or other quantitative measures of size, and they can be classified by source as either *internal* or *external* variables.

Internal variables.   These variables consist of values that originate within the organization being audited. They include accounting and operating data expressed in monetary terms or in other quantitative units (e.g., the number of hours worked, the quantity of products shipped, or the number of employees). Accounting and operating reports are the primary source of internal variables.

External variables.   These consist of values that originate outside the company being audited. Examples of external variables include gross national product, price indices, employment statistics, prime interest rates, population data, and specific industry statistics. Government agencies, industry associations, and private research organizations are the primary sources for external variables.

6.4.2   Dummy variables

Dummy variables are those that are used to differentiate between the absence or the presence of some condition or event not otherwise quantified as a real variable. They may be used, for example, to differentiate between observations affected or not affected by unusual events (e.g., acquisitions, disposals, fires, and strikes) or by holidays, which are reasonably expected to have an effect on the dependent variable. Dummy variables typically are expressed in terms of the binary numbers 0 and 1, but they may be in terms of any other set of numbers that serve to distinguish one observation from another, based on some characteristic that may be significant in a particular application.

The STAR Program includes options to generate seasonal variables, which are a special type of variable. If these options are specified, the Program tests to determine whether there is a significant seasonal pattern in the dependent variable. STAR can also generate a trend variable (not strictly a dummy variable, but dealt with here for convenience) that the Program can use to adjust for significant time-related trends.

6.5   General Criteria for Independent Variables

Once the audit objectives of a STAR application have been defined (as discussed in Section 6.3), the remaining step in designing the audit model is the selection of the independent variables to be specified. This can be viewed as a three-stage process: (1) the initial selection of the variables, (2) possible refinements of the variables before running the Program, and (3) possible improvements in the audit model after reviewing it and other results shown on the Program printouts. The first of these stages is discussed in this section, the second is discussed in Section 6.6, and the third is discussed in Chapter 7.

Audit judgment and knowledge of the business being audited are particularly important in specifying the independent variables, because the correlation and other results of an application depend largely on the identification of significant variables. As explained in Chapter 4, the STAR Program will eliminate any specified variables that are not statistically significant, but it obviously cannot include significant variables unless they have been specified by the auditor. Although this creates a general incentive to specify more rather than fewer variables, certain restrictive criteria for variables are necessary for an application to serve its audit purposes. These criteria are *plausibility, relevance,* and *audit independence.*

6.5.1   Plausibility and relevance

A relationship between an independent variable and the dependent variable should be both plausible and relevant for the audit purpose of an application. These two criteria are discussed together for convenience in dealing with their similarities and differences. A *plausible* relationship is one that the auditor may reasonably expect to exist based on his or her understanding of the business and its accounting procedures. The relationship should be plausible with regard to the base profile and to the projection profile.

A relationship that is logically very tenuous or remote would not be plausible, even though the correlation might be high, because the auditor would be unable to explain it on the basis of knowledge of the business. This kind of correlation is known as *spurious correlation.* A corollary effect of spurious correlation is that the auditor would not have a reasonable basis for expecting the relationship to continue to apply to the projection profile of audit interest. A *relevant* relationship is one that affords evidence that is meaningful for the purpose of the application and which, therefore, can be expected to provide projections that will be useful in identifying observations that contain errors or irregularities.

Plausibility and relevance are not quite the same thing, although they have similarities. For example, a relationship between gross profit as a dependent variable and sales and cost of sales as independent variables obviously is plausible, because gross profit is determined by deducting cost from sales. It is equally obvious, however, that a regression function derived from these variables would not be relevant for audit purposes, because it would only provide evidence of arithmetic accuracy.

Similarly, a relationship between sales and cost of sales is inherently plausible but would not be relevant for audit purposes if (1) there is only one product and it has a known constant cost and selling price or (2) there are several products but periodic cost of sales is determined as a constant estimated percentage of sales. However, the relationship would be relevant if known or estimated costs vary among products.

A relationship between sales and cost of sales is plausible, whether these variables are expressed as gross or net amounts. Some deductions in determining net amounts may, however, affect these variables differently. For example, sales allowances or customer deductions may not involve returned goods that are deducted from cost of sales. Similarly, cash discounts or retroactive quantity discounts may be recorded during accounting periods later than those in which the gross sales and corresponding costs were recorded. If such deductions and the relevant time lag are material, the gross amounts may be more relevant for use as variables. In this case the deductions should be tested separately by analytical review or otherwise.

If cost of sales is determined at standard costs, and variances from actual cost are recorded when purchases and production occur rather than when sales occur, the relationship of sales to standard costs may be more relevant than the relationship to actual costs because of the timing difference in recognizing the variances. The relationship of sales to standard costs may also be more relevant when separate tests of the cost variances are feasible. In such applications, basic raw material prices or indexes, labor rates, and production or sales volume would be plausible and relevant variables.

A relationship between sales and inventory purchases or production is also plausible and may be relevant for some audit purposes. Such a relationship, however, ordinarily would require use of observations of purchases or production of earlier periods to reflect the usual inventory turnover experience. Variations from the latter, resulting from strikes or other interruptions in the operations of the client, may be useful as real or dummy variables.

A relationship between sales and selling expenses is also plausible and relevant, even though the expenses may include relatively fixed components that do not vary significantly with sales. Such components will be comprehended in the constant in the regression function when selling expenses are the dependent variable. The preceding comments concerning selling expenses apply also to administrative and general expenses, although the latter may include a larger proportion of relatively fixed expenses.

In considering the plausibility of relationships between variables, the possibility of time lags in such relationships should be recognized. For example, a time lag may be expected between sales and collections on receivables, depending on the credit terms of the sales. If monthly collections are the dependent variable, sales for the current and one or more preceding months may be more plausible as the independent variables than sales for the current month alone.

The plausibility of dummy variables for trend and seasonality depends on whether the auditor thinks such variables may identify changes that might occur in the dependent variable, either gradually over time (trend) or systematically within each year (seasonality), which are not reflected in any other independent variable. For example, the relationship between sales and cost of sales may change gradually because of competitive pressures, or periodically in a pattern that corresponds with the seasons of the year. On the other hand, the relationship may remain relatively stable, although both variables are increasing because of inflation or expanding physical volume, or because of a seasonal pattern that affects both somewhat equally.

Because the effects of trend or seasonality may be too subtle to identify subjectively, we think these variables ordinarily should be specified if the auditor has any reason to believe that they may be significant and no real variables are available that might provide a better measure of the effects of these factors. If the dummy variables are not significant, they will simply be excluded from the audit model by the automatic tests performed by the Program. Examples of real variables that might provide better measures include an index of specific prices or of general inflation (if increases in unit prices are changing the relationship between physical volume and total sales) or statistics relating to weather conditions (if such conditions are likely to affect the relationship between sales and costs).

The discussion in this section is merely illustrative of the kinds of factors to be considered in applying the general criteria of plausibility and relevance, and does not purport to be exhaustive or definitive. In specifying the independent variables, there is no substitute for a clear understanding of the business operations and the audit purpose of the application.

6.5.2   Audit independence

The audit independence criterion requires that variables specified as independent variables for statistical purposes should be either (1) obtained from independent sources or (2) tested through other auditing procedures. This criterion encompasses the dual objectives of assuring reasonable accuracy in the data used as observations and avoiding circularity in the logic of applications. It applies to observations in both the base profile and the projection profile.

External variables, by definition, originate from sources outside the company being audited and ordinarily would satisfy the audit independence criterion. Tables of statistics published by government agencies or industry associations should not, however, be used uncritically. The auditor should read any explanations that accompany such a table to understand what it purports to show and to decide whether it is relevant for the intended application. If the company being audited has a dominant effect in the compilation of industry statistics, the auditor should recognize this in considering the relevance of such statistics to the application.

Dummy variables should be based on conditions known to the auditor, and thus ordinarily would satisfy the audit independence criterion.

Internal variables that may be treated as being from independent sources are those derived from records that are maintained by persons who are not in a position to manipulate, directly or indirectly, the records of the dependent variable being tested. Application of this criterion requires a study and evaluation of the internal accounting control with respect to the particular records being considered. Further discussion of this subject, however, is beyond the scope of this book. In addition to the basic accounting records and periodic financial statements, other possible internal sources of independent variables include auxiliary records of production, shipments, number of employees, and other quantitative operating data.

Tests to establish the independence of internal variables through other auditing procedures ordinarily should be for misstatement in the direction that is properly related to the direction of test specified for the dependent variable. If, for example, sales is the independent variable and cost of sales is the dependent variable in an application to test cost of sales for overstatement, the test to establish the independence of sales should also be for overstatement. In this situation, any errors of overstatement in sales would have the effect of increasing the regression estimates of cost of sales. This would tend to obscure errors of overstatement in the cost of sales by reducing the probability of identifying excesses to be investigated or by reducing the amount of the excesses that are identified.

Tests to establish the independence of internal variables need not be performed separately, but can be accomplished through appropriate application and coordination of other auditing procedures. In performing these tests, the auditor must be careful to avoid the problem of circularity. An example of circularity in this context would be the use of A as the independent variable in an application to test a dependent variable B for overstatement, and the use of B as the independent variable in another application to test A for overstatement, without any other tests for overstatement of either variable. In the following paragraphs we provide several examples that show how circularity can be avoided by practical combinations of typical auditing procedures.

Confirmation of accounts receivable from customers, combined with tests for overstatement of credits to such receivables from cash-receipts records and other sources, such as sales returns and allowances records, constitute corollary tests for overstatement of sales. Consequently, sales through the confirmation date could appropriately be used as an independent variable in applications to test for overstatement of such dependent variables as cost of sales, selling expenses and administrative and general expenses.

Tests for overstatement of inventories, through observation and tests of the compilation of physical inventories, combined with tests of cutoffs and of transactions charged to inventory accounts, constitute corollary tests for understatement of cost of sales. Consequently, cost of sales through the physical inventory date could appropriately be used as an independent variable in applications to test for understatement of sales.

If sales for the current year are tested for understatement without cost of sales being used as an independent variable, sales may be used as an independent variable in applications to test for understatement of cost of sales. Such applications, following tests of a physical inventory at an interim date, combined with tests for overstatement of charges to inventory during the intervening period, would provide a corollary test for overstatement of inventory at the balance-sheet date. If cost of sales for the current year is tested for overstatement without sales being used as an independent variable, cost of sales may be used as an independent variable in applications to test for overstatement of sales. Such applications, following confirmation of accounts receivable at an interim date, combined with the use of sales as an independent variable to test for understatement of collections and other credits to receivables during the intervening period, would provide a corollary test for overstatement of receivables at the balance-sheet date.

6.6 Possible Improvements in Audit Models

The variables selected initially should be considered further to decide whether refinements of them might improve the audit model. Certain factors that sometimes are present in accounting records may provide an opportunity for such refinements. These factors can be classified generally as (1) errors in variables, (2) unusual transactions or events, and (3) changes in conditions. Before discussing these factors further, we first consider the general forms of possible refinements and their statistical effect on audit models.

6.6.1 General forms and effects of refinements of variables

Possible refinements of the initial variables may take the form of (1) adjustment of the observations to eliminate the actual or estimated effects of a factor that has been identified, (2) use of such effects as a separate variable, or (3) use of a dummy variable as a surrogate for the unknown effects.

The general order of preference among these forms of refinement is that actual amounts are preferable to estimates, and adjustment of the observations to eliminate the actual effects is preferable to use of such effects as a separate variable. The choice between estimates and dummy variables, however, depends generally on the availability and expected reliability of the estimates.

The preferability of actual amounts over estimates is obvious. The preferability of adjustment of the observations affected over use of the actual amounts as a separate variable arises from the statistical effects of the latter option. Because of the likelihood of some degree of partial correlation between the new variable and other variables and the loss of 1 degree of freedom in the computations, the results of using a separate variable are likely to approximate reasonably well, but not be equal to, the actual effects of the factor identified.

To compare the use of estimated and dummy variables, we consider the latter option first. If an identified factor affects only one observation of the variable involved, using a dummy value of 1 for the observation affected is equivalent to using an estimate of any amount (with zeros being used for the other observations in either case). Although the values of the variables and their coefficients obviously will differ in the two cases, their products will be equal, and therefore the other relevant regression results will be identical.

If more than one observation is affected, the regression results will be the same, whether a dummy value of 1 or some other uniform estimate is used for each affected observation. Nonuniform estimates will either improve or impair the model, depending on how well they approximate the actual factors. In choosing between the use of estimated or dummy variables the auditor should consider other conditions that affect the application, particularly the availability or difficulty of obtaining estimates. A dummy variable may be as effective as and easier to obtain than more completely quantified estimates.

6.6.2 Errors in variables

Although the objective of analytical review is to detect errors in the projection profile that would materially affect the financial statements, we are also concerned with possible errors in the base profile used to develop the audit model. Since the data in the base profile ordinarily will have been audited (previously in time-series applications, or currently by other means in cross-sectional applications), any errors that would materially affect the financial statements presumably would have been identified and corrected by adjustments. In that event, the adjustments should also be recognized in the data used in the base profile. If previously identified errors were not adjusted because their effects were not considered material to the financial statements, it nevertheless will ordinarily be worthwhile to adjust the data in the base profile to correct such errors unless their effect is negligible.

In addition to the possible errors already discussed, there may be errors in the recording or allocation of amounts between months or quarters that do not affect the aggregate amounts included in the annual financial statements. These may be regarded as *intraperiod timing errors,* in contrast to *interperiod timing differences* (as that term is used in accounting with reference to income tax allocations and certain other matters). For brevity in the remainder of this chapter, we refer to such errors simply as *timing errors*. These errors ordinarily would be systematic, in the sense that they arise from the system or process for recording transactions and periodic allocations. Typical examples include the system or process used for establishing cutoffs for monthly sales and purchase transactions, for recording cost of sales, and for periodic accruals and amortization.

At one extreme, systems may be found in which periodic recording is quite accurate, with only minor (if any) adjustments being required at the end of the year. At the other extreme, systems may be found—especially in smaller businesses—in which little if any effort is made to achieve proper periodic recording, with the result that substantial adjustments are required to prepare financial statements at the end of the year. Between these extremes are intermediate variations in degree, including systems that are designed to provide proper periodic recordings by quarters, but not by months. The auditor's general knowledge of the client's systems should be adequate for the purpose of deciding whether refinements of variables are needed because of systematic timing errors.

Probably the most common situations requiring consideration in this respect are the systems for making cutoffs in the recording of accounts payable and purchases and for recording inventories and cost of sales.

Accounts payable and purchases.   In some systems, purchases may be recorded through a voucher system or similar record that provides a continuous balance of accounts payable. In other systems, the primary recording of purchases may be through the cash disbursements records, with accounts payable being recorded only from lists of unpaid invoices at the end of a month, quarter, or year.

If the listing of unpaid invoices is recorded monthly, there would be no systematic differences between the continuous and periodic systems. The results under both systems, however, depend on the accuracy of the monthly cutoffs, and this accuracy may vary if more careful attention is given to cutoffs for the last month in each quarter or year. The effect of more careful attention at such dates ordinarily would be difficult to quantify, but the use of a dummy variable to reflect that effect may improve the model.

If accounts payable are recorded only from quarterly or annual listings of unpaid invoices, the model is likely to be improved by eliminating, from the observations involved, the net effect of recording the current balance and reversing the preceding balance.

Inventories and cost of sales.   Systems for recording inventories and cost of sales can be classified broadly as perpetual inventory systems and periodic inventory systems. For simplicity in this section, we ignore the flow of inventory from raw materials through work in process to finished goods or to other accounts, and confine our comments to purchases and cost of sales.

In a perpetual system, as its name implies, inventory accounts are continuously charged for the cost of inventory acquired and credited for the cost of sales or other dispositions. These accounts show perpetual balances that purport to represent inventory on hand. Perpetual inventory records ordinarily show the transactions and balances in detail, by reference to descriptions, part numbers, or other identification of inventory items, and the perpetual balances ordinarily are adjusted at least annually to agree with actual balances based on physical inventories.

If the amount of an inventory adjustment is significant, the audit model can be improved by eliminating the effect of that adjustment. Ordinarily this adjustment will be made in the period in which it is recorded. If the periods to which the adjustment applies are known, however, it is better to adjust those periods.

In a periodic inventory system, the inventory balances are determined solely by periodic physical inventories, and cost of sales is determined from purchases and the changes in the physical inventories. If physical inventories are taken at the end of each month or other period to be used as an observation in a data profile, the results for such periods should be the same as they would be under a perpetual inventory system. In a periodic inventory system, if physical inventories are not taken at the ends of such periods, systematic timing errors are almost certain to exist. The effect of such errors is that recorded cost of sales is the same as purchases for all periods except the one in which an inventory adjustment is recorded, and the recorded costs for that period include both current purchases and the change in inventory that occurred during all periods since the preceding physical inventory.

If the amount of a periodic inventory adjustment is not significant in relation to the aggregate cost of sales for the periods since the last similar adjustment, and if there is no reason to believe that the actual (but unknown) inventories have fluctuated significantly within the intervening periods, the audit model can be improved by eliminating the effect of the inventory adjustment, as explained previously.

The conditions described in the preceding paragraph imply that purchases can reasonably be used as a surrogate for cost of sales in the audit model. Our experience indicates that these conditions are present in many cases. Whether they are present in a particular case depends largely on the client's operating policies and practices with respect to matters such as the lead time for purchases, the basis used for determining purchasing requirements, the policy concerning production for inventory versus specific orders, the typical inventory levels and turnover rates, and seasonal factors affecting production and sales.

If the factors just mentioned or any other factors cause the auditor to expect significant fluctuations in the actual (but unknown) inventories at the end of any of the periods between the physical inventory dates, or if the recorded inventory adjustment is significant in relation to the aggregate cost of sales in the intervening period, the auditor should consider additional possibilities for improving the model. In addition to any other improvements that might be suggested by the circumstances in a particular case, these possibilities include the use of seasonal variables, sales backlogs, sales forecasts, or lagged actual sales as variables.

If sales backlogs or forecasts are to be used, the lead time required for purchasing and production should be recognized in order to achieve an appropriate matching of these variables with purchases by periods. If neither of those variables are available, actual sales lagged by the lead time can be used as a variable on the premise that this is a surrogate for management's expectations that generated the inventory purchases.

6.6.3   Unusual transactions or events

Unusual transactions or events are those that differ in some significant way from the client's recurring business operations. When unusual transactions are identified and their amounts are known, such amounts should be eliminated from the observations in which they are included. The amounts that are eliminated should be audited as appropriate by other procedures, since they would be effectively excluded from investigation as a part of the analytical review procedures.

For our purpose here, unusual events are distinguished from unusual transactions because their effects ordinarily are not readily determinable. Typical examples of unusual events include disruptions of operations resulting from causes such as strikes, equipment failures, severe weather conditions, and fires or other physical disasters. If an unusual event affects more than one period and reasonable estimates of its effects can be made, the estimates should be eliminated from the observations affected. Otherwise the event should be treated as a dummy variable.

If the unusual event affected only one observation, the dummy variable should be 1 for that observation and 0 for the others. If the unusual event affected more than one observation, the dummy variable could also be 1 for each observation affected, which would imply that the event affected each observation approximately equally. If there is some basis for assuming that the relative effects on the observations were different, some reasonable surrogate for the relative effects should be used instead of a constant 1. For example, the number of days a plant was closed during each period because of a strike might be a reasonable surrogate for the relative effects of such an event.

6.6.4   Changes in conditions

In this section we are concerned with changes in conditions that have a continuing effect on the business operations or the accounting records after the date of the change. Examples of changes that affect operations include the acquisition or disposal of subsidiaries; the introduction or discontinuance of product lines or major products; the enactment of laws or regulations affecting matters such as sales prices, product quality, production methods, or marketing arrangements; and major changes in competitive conditions. Examples of changes that affect accounting records include those relating to methods of accounting for matters such as inventory, depreciation, pensions and fringe benefits, leasing transactions, and capitalization of interest.

For the purpose of specifying an audit model, the treatment of changes in conditions should generally be similar to that of unusual transactions or events, as discussed previously. If new subsidiaries, operating locations, or products involve operations under significantly different conditions, the results of such operations should be segregated, if feasible, and audited through separate applications of the STAR Program or by other procedures. Changes in volume alone need not be treated as changes in conditions unless the operating relationships being considered are particularly sensitive to volume. If it is not appropriate or feasible to segregate the effects of changes in conditions so that they can be audited by other applications or procedures, the use of reasonable estimates as a separate quantitative variable or of a dummy variable to reflect the effect of such changes ordinarily will improve the audit model.

6.7   Experience from Typical Applications

We present Table 6.1 to provide some indication of the range of statistical results that may reasonably be expected from typical audit applications of the STAR Program. The table shows the number of significant variables and the principal other statistical results from slighty over 9000 actual audit applications. These results, which were obtained for use in an internal study, were accumulated concurrently and consecutively as the applications were being processed in our firm's timesharing system, and accordingly they are a good cross section of actual experience.

Table 6.1   Statistical results from typical applications

Number of significant variables	Percent of applications
0 (Mean used)	6
1	42
2	31
3	12
4	5
5 or more	4
	100

Coefficient of correlation	Percent of applications
$\geq 0.98 < 1.00$	32
.95 0.98	19
.85 0.95	23
.70 0.85	13
.50 0.70	8
.00 0.50	5
	100

Table 6.1   (*continued*)

Coefficient of regression improvement	
≥ 0.90 < 1.00	13
.80 0.90	19
.65 0.80	22
.50 0.65	17
.30 0.50	15
.00 0.30	14
	100

Coefficient of residual variation	
≥ 0.00 < 0.03	15
.03 0.08	38
.08 0.15	27
.15 0.30	15
.30 0.50	3
.50 or more	2
	100

References

1. American Institute of Certified Public Accountants, "Audit Sampling." *Statement on Auditing Standards* 39, 1981.
2. American Institute of Certified Public Accountants, "Audit Risk and Materiality in Conducting an Audit." *Statement on Auditing Standards* 47, 1983.

7

COMPLETING AUDIT APPLICATIONS

7.1 Introduction

After the audit model has been designed and the observations to be used in the data profile have been obtained, the auditor's next steps are to (1) run the STAR Program, (2) review the Program printouts (and possibly revise the model), (3) investigate any unusual fluctuations identified by the Program, and (4) evaluate any errors discovered through such investigation. Running the STAR Program (step 1) was discussed in Chapter 2 and is explained in detail in the STAR Program User Guide. Steps 2, 3, and 4 are the subject of this chapter.

7.2 Reviewing the Program Printout

The auditor should review the STAR Program printout before proceeding with the investigation of any excesses identified for that purpose. As further explained in the following, however, some of the information shown in the printout may not require any further action by the auditor.

7.2.1 Specifications and observations

The specifications should be reviewed to determine that they were entered as intended. Depending on the printout option selected, the input data may

147

or may not be printed. In either case, however, the totals for each variable will have been determined by the Program and compared with hash totals that the Program requires the user to enter. Of course, if any errors are detected in the input, they should be corrected and the Program should be run again.

7.2.2   Regression function and other regression statistics

The section of the printout that displays the results of the regression analysis of the variables in the base profile shows the regression function and other regression statistics. Some of the statistics that are shown, and others that are not, are used in the audit interface segment of the Program to accomplish its purposes. They are included on the printout primarily for audit documentation, for use in possible applications of the Program for nonauditing purposes, and because it is customary statistical practice to do so. From an audit point of view, it is not essential that they be evaluated, although a review of them may suggest possible improvements in the model that could lead to greater audit efficiency. The meaning and computation of these results was explained in Chapter 3.

Ideally, all possibilities for improvement in the audit model should have been exhausted when the model was specified originally. Realistically, however, a review of the regression results may suggest possible improvements that were not apparent originally. The development of an audit model, therefore, can be regarded as an iterative process in which the auditor specifies an audit model, runs the Program, reviews the regression results for possible improvements in the model, and if necessary makes those improvements and reruns the Program. At a certain point, preferably early in the process, the model is deemed to be good enough for its intended purpose. For typical audit applications, the review for possible improvements should focus on the coefficient of residual variation and on the pattern of the residuals.

7.2.3   Coefficient of residual variation

Although the statistical validity of the regression results does not depend on the magnitude of the coefficient of residual variation, larger coefficients are likely to be accompanied by more and greater excesses to be investigated, which will reduce audit efficiency. Possible improvements in the audit model should therefore be considered if the coefficient of residual variation is greater than expected from experience with similar applications (e.g., applications in prior years or on other audit engagements). Possibilities for improving the model were discussed in Chapter 6.

7.2.4   Residuals

One of the most useful printouts that the STAR Program produces is a plot of the residuals. In a time-series application, it shows how the residuals behave over time. In a cross-sectional application, it shows how the residuals relate to operating units. A review of this graph can sometimes give the auditor insights into the nature of the data and ideas for improving the model that are not otherwise easily obtained. The pattern may suggest a trend or seasonal factor, an omitted variable, an unusual transaction or event, or a change in conditions.

A pattern in which a sequence of predominately positive (or negative) residuals for earlier observations is followed by a sequence of residuals predominately of the opposite sign could indicate a trend that could be represented by a real or dummy variable. A pattern that recurs with some regularity might indicate seasonality. An unusually large individual residual could suggest an unusual transaction or event. A sequence of somewhat random positive and negative residuals, followed by a sequence with predominately one sign, might indicate a change in conditions. Other possibilities may be suggested by the pattern of residuals in a particular application.

An example of a pattern caused by changes in conditions occurred in an application that related sales in a hotel restaurant to cost of sales during the period of high inflation in the late 1970s. In this case the residual plot displayed a jagged pattern in the residuals. Further investigation revealed that the pattern resulted from the fact that menu prices were only increased every few months, while costs kept rising steadily. The gradual decline in the gross profit ratio would be halted abruptly when the menu prices were increased, and then start declining again. As a result of the review of residuals, the model was improved by use of an index of menu prices as an additional variable.

7.3   Investigating Unusual Fluctuations

Unusual fluctuations identified by the STAR Program are designated on the printout as *excesses to be investigated*. How they are calculated by the STAR Program was explained in Chapter 5. Where the Program has identified an excess to be investigated, the recorded amount of the dependent variable should be tested for possible misstatement in the direction of test specified for the application. An excess to be investigated may be caused by:

- An error in the recorded amount of the dependent variable
- An unusual transaction or event, or a change in conditions
- An error in an independent variable, some imperfection in the audit model, or an extreme random fluctuation

A particular excess may be investigated by either (1) obtaining a satisfactory analytical explanation for the excess or (2) testing additional details of the recorded amount of the dependent variable. Generally, an analytical explanation is preferable and is more likely to be obtainable if the amount of the excess is substantial in relation to the recorded amount. Otherwise, a satisfactory analytical explanation is less likely and therefore additional tests of details may be the more feasible alternative.

7.3.1   Analytical approach

When the analytical approach is used, the excess should be satisfactorily explained as being attributable to some specific cause. Reasonable approximations of amounts attributable to such causes are satisfactory, but unquantified vague explanations are not.

The auditor should maintain a healthy degree of skepticism in accepting explanations of excesses. Before accepting an explanation, the auditor should be satisfied that (1) it is reasonable and could account for at least the amount of the excess and (2) it is not based on some factor that has already been reflected in the model. To illustrate the latter, a change in sales volume ordinarily would not be a valid explanation for an excess if sales or cost of sales was used in the model as an independent variable.

Inevitably there is a large element of judgment in a decision to accept an explanation of an excess, and an associated risk that the judgment may be incorrect. However, this is no different from the risk inherent in use of subjective techniques for analytical review or in evaluation of evidence obtained by other auditing procedures.

The working papers documenting the investigation of excesses should indicate the evidential matter examined and the computations made to corroborate representations by management or any other explanations obtained.

7.3.2   Tests of details

While ordinarily it is preferable to obtain a satisfactory analytical explanation of an excess to be investigated, often it is not possible to do so, particularly if the excess is small in relation to the recorded amount of the dependent variable. If the analytical approach has been used but no satisfactory explanation has been found, the investigation should simply be regarded as inconclusive. The fact that no error was found does not mean that none exists; conversely, the failure to find the cause of an excess does not mean that the cause is error. In these circumstances the auditor has not obtained sufficient evidence from analytical review to support a conclusion at the reliability level specified for the application. Therefore, additional tests of details are needed as an alternative. If the excess is relatively small, the auditor may decide initially that an analytical explanation is unlikely and elect to perform additional tests of details as the first alternative.

When additional tests of details are to be performed, the tests should be made from records that are pertinent to the recorded amounts of the dependent variable and appropriate for the direction of test. Because an excess may have been caused by errors at any stage, from initial recording through final summarization in the general ledger, the tests of details should encompass all of those functions.

The STAR Program designs a statistical sample that should be used to perform the additional tests of details. The design of the sample is based on the DH&S Audit Sampling Plan. As explained in Chapter 5, the sample design is integrated with the results of the STAR Program to preserve the level of assurance that was specified for the application. The sample should be selected through the sampling technique known variously as *cumulative monetary amounts* (CMA) sampling, *dollar unit sampling* (DUS), *monetary attribute sampling* (MAS), and sampling with *probability proportional to size* (PPS).

The records to be treated as the population for the additional tests of details depend on the direction of test specified for the STAR application. If the test is for overstatement, the population consists of the records that support the observations of the dependent variable. These records are referred to as the *primary population*. Any errors of overstatement obviously will be included in this population.

Because errors of understatement can arise from the omission of transactions that should have been recorded (as well as from errors in recorded transactions) the auditor should test some source of information that can reasonably be expected to indicate transactions that should have been recorded. Such a source of information is referred to as a *reciprocal population*. The use of reciprocal populations for tests of details is common in auditing, although the descriptive term may not be. Typical examples include the use of disbursement checks and vendors' invoices recorded after the end of the year in tests for unrecorded costs, expenses, and payables at the balance-sheet date; and the use of sales orders or shipping documents in tests for unrecorded sales and receivables. In this last example, and in some other reciprocal populations, the records may not show monetary amounts. In such cases the test of details necessarily must be made from a numerical sample, rather than a monetary sample.

To facilitate the selection of sample items, the STAR Program printout shows the following information for each observation that includes an excess to be investigated: (1) a random starting number, (2) a selection interval, and (3) the maximum number of sample items to be selected. The starting number and selection interval are expressed in monetary amounts and in the same units as the dependent variable (e.g., $1000s). This information can be used to select a monetary sample from either a primary or a reciprocal population. The simplest procedure for this purpose, which results in *systematic* selection with a random start, is as follows:

1. Enter the random starting number (which must be no greater than the selection interval) as a negative amount in an adding machine, calculator, or computer.

2. Enter the population items as positive amounts until the cumulative amount equals or exceeds zero. Select the last item entered as a sample item.

3. Enter the selection interval as a negative amount. If the cumulative amount is not negative repeat this step until it is negative.

4. Repeat the process described in steps 2 and 3 until all population items have been entered.

A *systematic-random* selection for a monetary sample can be made as follows:

1. Obtain a set of random numbers from a table, or a computer program. Each random number should be less than or equal to the selection interval, and the set should include as many numbers as the maximum sample items shown on the printout. The first random number is the initial *target*.

2. Enter the population items as positive amounts in an adding machine or computer until the cumulative amount equals or exceeds the target. Select the last item entered as a sample item.

3. Subtract the selection interval from the cumulative amount. If the cumulative amount is not negative repeat this step until it is negative. The next random number becomes the target.

4. Repeat the process described in steps 2 and 3 until all population intervals have been entered.

If a *numerical* or *attribute* sample is required because a reciprocal population does not include monetary amounts, the sample can be selected as follows:

1. Determine the number of items in the population.

2. Divide that number by the maximum number of sample items shown on the printout to obtain a numerical selection interval.

3. Use the computed numerical interval, in lieu of the monetary interval shown on the printout, and follow either of the selection procedures just described for monetary samples. For this purpose, use item counts, number of items per page, sequential document numbers, or similar data to accumulate the number of items, instead of adding monetary amounts.

7.4   Evaluating Audit Results

The final step in a STAR application is the evaluation of the audit results. If the STAR Program does not identify any excesses to be investigated, the objective of the application will have been achieved, and therefore no further evaluation is necessary. If excesses are identified, the need for further evaluation depends on whether any errors are found through the audit investigation, and this may depend on the auditor's definition of "error." If errors are found, the nature, cause, and effect of the errors should be considered in evaluating their qualitative and quantitative implications.

7.4.1   Definition of errors

The definition of errors to be used depends on the auditor's objective for the particular application, which is indicated by the decisions made in specifying the audit model. As discussed in Chapter 6, the auditor's objective is related to the level of detail of accounts or accounting units to be presented in the financial statements or other information being audited. Therefore, any condition that causes the amount of an item presented in such information to be incorrect should be regarded as an error to be evaluated.

This definition excludes misclassifications of entries within groups of accounts that are combined in the financial information being audited. Such misclassifications are excluded because they would not affect the auditor's opinion on the basic financial information presented, although they might be the subject of comments or suggestions to management. The size of errors is not an element in their definition but should be considered in their evaluation, as discussed later.

Other matters to be considered in applying this definition include the distinction between errors, changes in accounting estimates, differences in judgment, and unauthorized transactions. The considerations concerning these matters in STAR applications are the same as those in applying any other auditing procedures and, therefore, are not dealt with here.

7.4.2   Evaluation of errors

The nature, cause, and effect of errors may affect either their qualitative or quantitative implications. Errors may arise, for example, because accounting principles or policies are incorrectly applied, or because the incorrect principles or policies were adopted in the first place. Errors may be intentional or unintentional. They may result from weaknesses in the design of the system of internal accounting control, from the limitations that are inherent in such systems, or from lack of compliance with the system.

The qualitative characteristics of errors may influence the auditor's judgment about their materiality, the need for their disclosure in the financial statements, or about comments or suggestions to be made to management. These considerations, however, are the same whether errors are detected in STAR applications or by other auditing procedures and, therefore, are not discussed further in the book.

In determining the quantitative implications of errors, the auditor should consider the nature and cause of the errors that have been detected. Depending on these characteristics, the auditor may conclude that such implications (1) are restricted to the isolated transactions or events that gave rise to the errors or to an identifiable category of similar transactions or events, or (2) extend to the entire set of observations used in the application. The auditor should exercise careful professional judgment and healthy skepticism in deciding whether the quantitative implications of errors detected can reasonably be regarded as isolated.

The statistical evaluation of a STAR application for analytical review is analogous to that of a statistical sample for a test of details. For both types of auditing procedures the evaluation should be based on the sample items or the regression observations in which the errors were detected, and it should include an estimate and an upper precision limit with respect to the total errors in the population or projection profile being audited.

The audit decisions made in designing the sample or regression model determine the probability of selection desired for both procedures, but the means by which those decisions are implemented are different. For an audit sample the probability desired is achieved by computing the required sample size or selection interval, and this computation is based on the variability in the results that could be obtained from all possible samples of a given size. For a STAR application the probability desired is achieved by computing the required cut-off point for identifying excesses to be investigated (as explained in Chapter 5), and this computation is based on the variability in the underlying process that generates the observations of the dependent variable. Therefore it is evident that the cut-off computations can also be used to determine the probabilities needed for a statistical evaluation of the audit results of a STAR application.

We present below a simple method that we believe is conservative but ordinarily satisfactory for computing the estimate of the total error in the projection profile.* The basic formula for this purpose follows:

$$E = \sum_{t=1}^{n'} E_t m_t$$

where E = Estimated total errors in the projection profile.

n' = Number of observations in which errors were detected.

E_t = Amount of errors detected analytically in an observation t, or estimated from an optional sample by use of the next formula.

m_t = Error estimation multiplier for the applicable observation t, which is $1 / (1 -$ Most Adverse Risk for the observation).

The most adverse risk is the risk associated with the "risk point" (as illustrated in Chapter 5). It can be found for a particular application by obtaining a printout in the form illustrated in Printout B.7. The complement of the most adverse risk is the probability of selection (identification of an excess to be investigated) of the applicable observation. The reciprocal of this probability is the multiplier m_t to be used in extrapolating errors detected.

If errors are detected in an observation through use of an optional sample of details as indicated on the STAR Printout, rather than through an analytical investigation, an estimate of the total errors in the observation

---

*To the best of the authors' knowledge the first public presentation of this method of estimation was made at a conference at the University of North Carolina in May 1982. The method was described by Gary Holstrum (a DH&S partner at that time) in his comments as a discussant on a paper by W. R. Kinney Jr. and G. L. Salamon, "Regression Analysis in Auditing: A Comparison of Alternative Investigation Rules." During the evening preceding the conference, Gary Holstrum and Kenneth W. Stringer learned from Stephen J. Aldersley that he had independently developed a similar method. That method, together with a refinement of it, was described in a draft of a paper that he furnished to Holstrum and Stringer at that time and revised in June 1982. The refinement of that method was described briefly in a paper by S. J. Aldersley and D. A. Leslie on "Models for Multilocation Audits," which was presented at a symposium at the University of Illinois on November 9–10, 1984. The authors of this book have benefitted from discussions with those individuals about their observations in the course of the study and use of the STAR Program by Clarkson Gordon.

should be made from the sample and used as indicated in the preceding formula. The formula for this estimate follows:

$$E_t = \sum_{i=1}^{j} E_{ti} \left(\frac{I_t}{A_{ti}} \right)$$

where E_t = Estimated total errors in the observation t.

j = Number of sample items in which errors were detected.

E_{ti} = Amount of error detected in a sample item i from observation t.

I_t = Selection interval for the optional sample from observation t (shown on the STAR Printout).

A_{ti} = Recorded amount of the sample item in which the error was detected.

To maintain the reliability level specified for a STAR application, the upper precision limit specified initially must be adjusted to include both the estimated total errors and their incremental effect on the precision limit. A simple method that we think is conservative and ordinarily satisfactory for this purpose is given in the following formulas:

$$MP' = MP + E'$$

$$E' = \sum_{t=1}^{n'} E_t m_t P_t$$

where MP' = Adjusted upper monetary precision limit.

MP = Specified upper precision limit.

E' = Precision-adjusted estimate of errors.

P_t = Precision adjustment factor for the applicable observation (as shown in Table A.7).

and other notations are as shown previously.

The relationship between the initial precision limit specified, the effects of errors detected, and the final evaluation of the results of an application can be summarized as follows:

	Precision Limit Specified	Effects of Errors Detected	Final Evaluation of Results
Estimated errors	None	E	E
Precision limit	MP	$(E' - E)$	$MP + (E' - E)$
Total	MP	E'	MP'

There is an important distinction between the two components of the adjusted precision limit. The estimate of the errors is a statistical measure of the condition of the records comprising the projection profile, and this estimate is not affected by the reliability level specified for the application. In contrast, the precision limit is not related to the condition of the records but is a measure of the statistical assurance that can be attributed to the results of the application, and this is affected directly by the reliability level specified. Thus the estimate of errors relates to the financial statements being audited, while the reliability and precision relate to the basis for the auditor's opinion on those statements. For further discussion of the consideration to be given by an auditor to the estimate of total errors and the risk that actual errors may exceed that estimate, readers are referred to SAS 39 and 47.

The methods presented above are simply the regression analogue of the monetary sample evaluation methods used in the DH&S Audit Sampling Plan [1]. Certain refinements or variations are possible in applying the basic concept underlying these methods. One possible refinement is to revise all of the audit interface computations to give effect to the errors detected. The net effect of this revision would be revised values for the error estimation multipliers m_t, and these could then be used as indicated in the formulas given previously. Another possible refinement would be to use binomial probabilities for computing the precision adjustment factors p_t, instead of the Poisson probabilities used for computing those shown in Table A.7. A third variation would be to use the method known as DUS cell evaluation [2]. We have omitted further discussion of these alternatives because we think they involve significant complications or other considerations and are unlikely to alter the audit decisions that would be made on the basis of the simpler methods presented here.

Since the method developed for computing monetary precision limits under the DH&S Audit Sampling Plan was a new statistical method, it has been the subject of extensive research by academicians and practitioners. The upper limit computed by this method is often referred to in that context as the Stringer bound or limit. Most of this research has dealt with the known conservatism of the method under some conditions, and with possibilities for reducing such conservatism without sacrificing the mathematical rigor that the method was designed to achieve. A review of this reseach literature or further exposition of the underlying method is beyond the scope of this book, but references to selected portions of this literature are included [3].

In contrast to the research mentioned above we are aware of relatively little work by others, except that referred to in the footnote on page 156. that deals specifically with evaluation of the results of using regression analysis for analytical review. Consequently we encourage further research concerning possible improvement in the methods presented here or the development of alternative methods.

References

1. (a) Deloitte Haskins & Sells, "Audit Sample Routine," *Auditape System Manual,* 1967.
   (b) Deloitte Haskins & Sells, *Audit Sampling: A Programmed Instruction Course,* 1970.
2. D. A. Leslie, A. D. Teitlebaum, and R. J. Anderson, *Dollar-Unit Sampling: A Practical Guide for Auditors,* Toronto: Copp Clark Pitman, 1979.
3. (a) R. J. Anderson and A. D. Teitlebaum, "Dollar-Unit Sampling: A Solution to the Audit Sampling Dilemma," *CA Magazine,* April 1973.
   (b) S. E. Fienberg, J. Neter, and R. A. Leitch, "Estimating the Total Overstatement Error in Accounting Populations," *Journal of the American Statistical Association,* June 1977.
   (c) W. R. Kinney Jr. "Integrating Audit Tests: Regression Analysis and Partitioned Dollar-Unit Sampling," CICA Auditing Research Symposium, 1977.
   (d) J. H. McCray, "Evaluating Dollar Unit Sampling Upper Bounds," unpublished manuscript, 1981.
   (e) G. R. Meikle, "Example of a Sampling Plan," *Statistical Sampling in an Audit Context, an Audit Technique Study.* Toronto: Canadian Institute of Chartered Accountants, 1972.
   (f) J. Neter and J. K. Loebbecke, *Behavior of Major Statistical Estimators in Sampling Populations—An Empirical Study.* American Institute of Certified Public Accountants, 1975.
   (g) J. Neter, R. A. Leitch, and S. E. Fienberg, "Dollar Unit Sampling: Multinomial Bounds for Total Overstatement and Understatement Errors," *The Accounting Review,* January 1978.

(h) J. Neter, H. S. Kim, and L. E. Graham, "On Combining Stringer Bounds for Independent Monetary Unit Samples from Several Populations," *Auditing: A Journal of Practice and Theory,* Fall 1984.

(i) F. F. Stephan, "Some Statistical Problems Involved in Auditing and Inspection," *Proceedings of the American Statistical Association,* 1963.

(j) K. W. Stringer, "Practical Aspects of Statistical Sampling in Auditing," *Proceedings of the American Statistical Association,* 1963.

MORE ADVANCED STATISTICAL CONCEPTS AND TECHNIQUES

8

STATISTICAL TESTS AND TRANSFORMATIONS

8.1 Introduction

In this chapter we deal with some of the mathematical and computational aspects of the material that was covered in Chapter 4. We start by discussing the concepts of statistical inference and statistical significance. We then show how tests of significance of independent variables are applied in the stepwise regression algorithm used in the STAR Program. Next we explain and illustrate the statistical tests for discontinuity, autocorrelation, heteroscedasticity, and abnormality.

The tests that we will describe all follow a common pattern. First, a *test statistic* is computed that measures the condition being tested (e.g., the degree of autocorrelation). The formula for the test statistic is designed in such a way that it is possible to determine what range of values is plausible for the statistic, under the hypothesis that the condition is *not* present. (The hypothesis that the condition is not present is often called the *null hypothesis*.) The endpoints of the range of plausible values are called *critical values*. If the value of the test statistic falls outside the range of plausible values, the implication is that the null hypothesis is incorrect. In other words, there is prima facie evidence that the condition being tested for is present.

The critical values for a test statistic are determined from the probability distribution of the statistic (this distribution is known from statistical theory) and the tester's decision about what constitutes a *significant* level of improbability. In statistical work, 5% and 1% are two often-used *significance levels*. To say that "the test statistic is significant at the 5% level" means that the probability is 5% or less that the value that has been calculated for the test statistic could occur if the null hypothesis were correct. The STAR Program applies its test at certain preset levels of significance. These levels can, however, be modified by the user.

A number of different probability distributions are used to describe the behavior of test statistics. The test statistics that are of principal interest in this chapter are so-called *F statistics* that follow the *F distribution* (both named after Sir Ronald Fisher, a great British statistician). *F* statistics are ordinarily expressed as a ratio of two other statistic (and, for that reason are sometimes also called *F ratios*). Both the numerator and the denominator of the ratio have degrees of freedom associated with them, and those two parameters determine the shape of the particular *F* distribution that applies. An example of the *F* distribution and a typical critical value is shown in Figure 8.1. Tables, such as Table A.3 and Table A.4, are available to determine the critical value for *F*, given its two parameters and the required significance level.

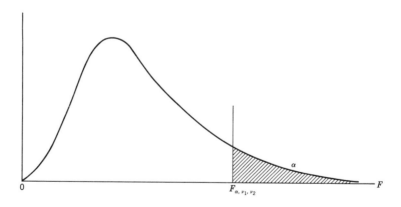

Figure 8.1   *F* distribution with ν_1 and ν_2 degrees of freedom. A critical value corresponding to a significance level of α is also shown.

8.2   Significance of Independent Variables

The statistic that is used to test for the statistical significance of an independent variable is the ratio of the sum of squares explained by the new variable to the mean of the residual (unexplained) sum of squares.

$$F = \frac{\text{sum of squares explained by new variable}/1}{\text{residual sum of squares}/(n - k - 1)}$$

The greater this F ratio, the more significant the variable being tested. It can be shown that F behaves according to the F distribution. Thus the variable is judged to be significant when the F ratio exceeds a critical value determined by the F distribution and the level of significance at which the test is conducted. The numerator of this statistic has one degree of freedom, the denominator has $n - k - 1$ degrees of freedom. Therefore, the statistic has an F distribution with 1 and $n - k - 1$ degrees of freedom. To illustrate the significance test, we will assume a 5% significance level, because that is the level that the STAR Program uses (unless it is preset to use another level).

The F ratio depends on two things:

1. The ratio of the variation explained by the new variable to the residual variation. The greater this ratio, the greater the F ratio.
2. The degrees of freedom associated with the residual variation ($n - k - 1$). The greater the degrees of freedom, the greater the F ratio.

The calculations for testing TIME AT STANDARD for significance in the Gamma Company application are shown in Table 8.1. This is an example of an *analysis-of-variance* table. The statistics in the table come from Section 3.4.1.

The test statistic for the admission of X_1 is

$$F = \frac{3,912,198\ 1}{1,332,340/(36-1-1)} = 99.84$$

The critical value for a ratio with 1 degree of freedom for the numerator and 34 for the denominator is 4.13 at the 5% significance level (this can be

Table 8.1   Gamma Company analysis of variance—one independent variable

Type of Variation	Sum of Squares	Degrees of Freedom	Mean Square	F Ratio
Explained	3,912,198	1	3,912,198	99.84
Unexplained	1,332,340	34	39,186	
Total	5,244,538	35		

interpolated from Table A.4). Because the computed ratio of 99.84 exceeds this critical value, the independent variable is significant at the 5% level. This means that the risk that the variable is not really significant, but through a random occurrence appears to be so, is 5% or less (much less than 5% in this case, since the ratio is very high).

The F test can easily be extended to test the significance of the marginal effect of using one or more additional independent variables. When used for this purpose, the test is applied progressively to each new variable being considered for admission to the regression function. This is illustrated in Table 8.2, which is based on the Gamma Company statistics that were developed in Section 4.2.2. In that section we showed that the residual sum of squares after the admission of X_2 is 762,905 and that the explained sum of squares is 4,481,633. Since the explained sum of squares after the admission of X_1 was 3,912,198 (see Table 8.1), the marginal improvement

Table 8.2   Gamma Company analysis of variance—two independent variables

Type of Variation	Sum of Squares	Degrees of Freedom	Mean Square	F Ratio
Explained				
Effect of X_1	3,912,198	1	3,912,198	99.84
Marginal effect of X_2	569,435	1	569,435	24.63
Joint effect	4,481,633	2	2,240,817	
Unexplained	762,905	33	23,118	
Total	5,244,538	35		

brought about by the admission of X_2 is $4,481,633 - 3,912,198 = 569,435$. The test statistic is therefore

$$F = \frac{569,435/1}{762,905/(36 - 2 - 1)} = 24.63$$

The critical F value at the 5% level for a ratio with 1 and 33 degrees of freedom is 4.14. Because the computed ratio of 24.63 exceeds the critical value, the marginal effect of X_2 may be accepted as significant at the 5% level.

Just as the F test can be used to test whether a variable should be admitted to the regression function, it can also be used to test the significance of a variable that is already in the regression function. Thus it can be used to test whether a variable that is in should remain in or be eliminated.

The F ratio can also be expressed in terms of partial correlation coefficients (see Section 4.2.1, where the concept was introduced). The partial correlation coefficient between a dependent variable Y and an independent variable X represents the marginal contribution of X to explaining Y. To calculate this coefficient, it is necessary to exclude the combined effect of all the other variables from both X and Y. This is done by separately regressing both X and Y against all of the other independent variables and taking the residuals. The partial correlation coefficient between X and Y is obtained by correlating the two sets of residuals.

If the residuals that result from regressing Y against $X_2, X_3, \ldots, X_k$ are denoted by e_t, and the residuals that result from regressing X_1 against $X_2, X_3, \ldots, X_k$ are denoted by f_t, then the partial correlation coefficient between Y and X_1 after removing the influence of $X_2, X_3, \ldots, X_k$ is denoted by

$$R_{Y1\cdot23\ldots k} = \frac{\Sigma e_t f_t}{\sqrt{\Sigma e_t^2}\sqrt{\Sigma f_t^2}}$$

Note that, in $R_{Y1\cdot23\ldots k}$, the symbol "$Y1$" indicates that the correlation is between Y and X_1. The symbol "$23\ldots k$" that follows the period indicates that the influence of the variables $X_2, X_3, \ldots, X_k$ has been removed. In general, the partial correlation between Y and X_i, after both have been adjusted for the other variables, is

$$R_{Yi\cdot12\ldots(i-1)(i+1)\ldots k}$$

The F ratio for testing the significance of X_1 given that $X_2 \ldots X_k$ are in the regression function can be expressed in terms of the partial correlation coefficient as

$$F = \frac{R^2_{Y1\cdot23\ldots k}/1}{(1 - R^2_{Y1\cdot23\ldots k})/(n - k - 1)}$$

where $n - k - 1$ is the number of degrees of freedom that the regression function will have if the new variable is admitted. This formula is equivalent to the original one previously introduced, and therefore F has an F distribution with 1 and $n - k - 1$ degrees of freedom.

8.2.1   Stepwise regression

As we explained in Chapter 4, the STAR Program uses a stepwise regression algorithm that employs a forward selection procedure coupled to a backward elimination procedure. The steps are as follows:

1. Calculate the coefficient of correlation between Y and each of the specified X variables. Find the X variable with the highest coefficient. This is the first candidate for admission.

2. Calculate an F ratio and see if it is significant. If it is, admit the candidate variable to the function. If it is not, stop the procedure and proceed on the basis that there are no significant variables. Go to step 7.

3. If all of the specified variables are in the regression, stop the procedure and go to step 7. Otherwise calculate the partial correlation coefficient between Y and each of the remaining X variables after removing the influence of the admitted variables. Find the X variable with the highest coefficient. This is the next candidate for admission.

4. Calculate an F ratio and see if it is significant. If it is, admit the candidate variable to the function. If it is not, stop the procedure and go to step 7.

5. If more than two independent variables are in the regression, the

backward elimination procedure comes into play. Otherwise, the program continues with the forward selection procedure in Step 3.

6. Backward elimination procedure: Calculate the partial coefficient of correlation between Y and each X variable in the regression after removing the influence of the other X variables in the regression. Find the X variable with the lowest coefficient. Form an F ratio and test it for significance. If it is significant, go to step 3 and flip back into the forward-selection mode. If it is not, the variable has evidently been made redundant by the admission of the other variables. Eliminate it. Go to step 5 to see if any other variables need to be eliminated at this point.

7. The stepwise procedure ends when all redundant variables have been eliminated from the function and any variables that have not been admitted are insignificant.

A detailed account of the computations that are necessary to implement the stepwise regression algorithm is given in Chapter 9.

8.3 Discontinuity of the Regression Function

In Chapter 4 we introduced the concepts of discontinuity in the base period and discontinuity between the base and audit periods. In this section we use the Universal Chemicals example to show how the calculations are made to test for discontinuity in the base. The calculations for discontinuity between the base and audit periods are fairly similar and a specific example of the calculations is not included.

8.3.1 Discontinuity within the base period

The calculations for the test (which was introduced in Section 4.5) for discontinuity within the base period proceed as follows:

1. Divide the observations for the base period into two subperiods—the last year and all preceding years.

2. Use the stepwise regression procedure to generate an overall regression function from the entire base.

3. Compute separate regression functions for each of the two subperiods using the independent variables used in step 2.

4. Calculate the residual sum of squares for the overall regression and for both of the separate regressions.

If there is no discontinuity in the data, all three regression functions will more or less coincide. In that case, the combined residual sum of squares for the two separate regressions will about equal the residual sum of squares for the overall regression. Conversely, if the data are discontinuous, the regression functions will not all coincide and the combined separate functions will provide a tighter fit than the overall function. The combined residual sum of squares for the separate regressions will be significantly less than the residual sum of squares for the overall function.

The statistic that is used to test for discontinuity is

$$F = \frac{[\text{SUMOVERALL} - (\text{SUM}_1 + \text{SUM}_2)]/(k + 1)}{(\text{SUM}_1 + \text{SUM}_2)/(n_1 + n_2 - 2k - 2)}$$

where SUMOVERALL is the residual sum of squares for the overall function, SUM_1 and SUM_2 are the residual sums of squares for the two separate regressions, n_1 and n_2 are the number of base observations in each of the separate subsets, and k is the number of independent variables.

Because the regression functions that are fitted separately to the two subparts of the base must always fit at least as well as the overall function, F can never be negative. In the ideal situation, the three functions will be identical, SUMOVERALL will equal $\text{SUM}_1 + \text{SUM}_2$, and consequently F will be zero. When the data are significantly discontinuous, the two separately fitted regression functions will fit better than the overall function; SUMOVERALL will be significantly larger than $\text{SUM}_1 + \text{SUM}_2$ and therefore F will be a large positive number. F therefore is a measure of the discontinuity of the data.

It can be shown that F has an F distribution with $(k + 1)$ and $(n_1 + n_2 - 2k - 2)$ degrees of freedom. This means that discontinuity can be tested by comparing F with a percentage point of the appropriate F distribution. The STAR Program tests for discontinuity at the 1% level (unless it has been preset to test at a different level). This means that, if there is no discontinuity in the base, the probability is only 1% that the actual observations and resulting F statistic will lead to a conclusion that the data are discontinuous. The test for discontinuity was developed and published by Chow [1]. (See also Fisher [2].)

For the data shown in Table 4.3, the overall function, based on 36 observations, is

$$Y_t = -67.9933 + 0.9266X_t + e_t$$

and the sum of the squared residuals is

$$SUMOVERALL = 146,584$$

The function for the first 24 base observations is

$$Y_t = 3.7545 + 0.7489X_t + e_t$$

and the sum of the squared residuals as

$$SUM_1 = 9,631$$

The function for the last 12 base observations is

$$Y_t = 42.0620 + 0.8717X_t + e_t$$

and the sum of the squared residuals is

$$SUM_2 = 31,029$$

The three regression lines that correspond to these three functions are shown in Figure 4.4. The F ratio is

$$F = \frac{[146,584 - (9,631 + 31,029)]/(1 + 1)}{(9,631 + 31,029)/(24 + 12 - 2 - 2)}$$

$$= 41.68$$

The 1% significance point for a variable having an F distribution with 2 and 32 degrees of freedom is 5.35 (Table A.3). Since F is greater than this, the data are judged to be significantly discontinuous.

8.3.2   Discontinuity between base and audit periods

The test for discontinuity between the base period and the audit period is applied as follows:

1.   Compute the regression function from the base data.

2.   Using the same independent variables as in step 1, compute a regression function based on an *augmented* set of data consisting of the base data plus the audit period data.

3.   Compare the sum of the squared residuals from the regression functions computed in steps 1 and 2. If they are significantly different, this suggests that there has been a shift away from the original function during the audit period.

The F ratio used for this test is

$$F = \frac{(\text{SUM}_A - \text{SUMOVERALL})/(n_A - n)}{\text{SUMOVERALL}/(n - k - 1)}$$

where SUM_A and n_A are the sum of the squared residuals and the number of observations, respectively, in the augmented set, and the other statistics are as defined in Section 8.3.1. This statistic has an F distribution with $n_A - n$ and $n - k - 1$ degrees of freedom.

8.4   Autocorrelation

As explained in Section 4.4, a first-order autoregressive scheme is one in which the disturbance in period t consists of a part that depends on the disturbance in period $t - 1$ and a part that is random and independent. This can be expressed in terms of the disturbances from the ULR as

$$u_t = \rho u_{t-1} + v_t$$

where ρ (rho) is the *coefficient of autocorrelation,* or the *autoregressive parameter;* u_t is $Y_t - (\alpha + \beta X_t)$; and v_t is the random independent disturbance.

In practice, an estimate r of ρ is calculated from the residuals from the regression function. Thus

$$e_t = re_{t-1} + f_t$$

expresses the autoregressive scheme in terms of the observable residuals. The coefficient r measures the extent to which residuals depend on their previous value and is an estimate of ρ. If r is close to zero, there is little autocorrelation and no pattern will be noticeable. If r is close to 1 (say 0.9), the autocorrelation will be high and a time graph of the residuals will reveal a marked pattern. This is apparent from the graphs in Figure 4.6.

When significant first-order autocorrelation is present, the correct underlying model (assuming just one independent variable) is

$$Y_t = \alpha + \beta X_t + \rho u_{t-1} + v_t$$

This is called a *generalized linear model,* in contrast to an ordinary linear model, because it incorporates a more general assumption about the behavior of the residuals. In fact, the ordinary linear model is just a special case of the generalized model in which $\rho = 0$.

8.4.1 Estimating the coefficient of autocorrelation

The estimated coefficient of autocorrelation, r, is the coefficient that relates e_t to e_{t-1} in the equation

$$e_t = re_{t-1} + f_t$$

In this equation, r plays the same role the coefficient b plays in the regression function $Y_t = a + bX_t + e_t$. Thus the formula for calculating r is similar to the least squares formula used for the calculation of b. It is

$$r = \frac{\sum_{t=2}^{n} e_t e_{t-1}}{\sum_{t=2}^{n} e_t^2}$$

8.4.2   Test for autocorrelation

The test that the STAR Program applies for autocorrelation is known as the Durbin–Watson test. It is based on the relative size of the sum of the squared differences between successive residuals. When positive autocorrelation is present, the Durbin–Watson statistic is small, indicating that successive residuals tend to be significantly closer together than they would be were they independent. The statistic developed by Durbin and Watson [3] to test for first-order autocorrelation is

$$ d = \frac{\sum\limits_{t=2}^{n} (e_t - e_{t-1})^2}{\sum\limits_{t=1}^{n} e_t^2} $$

The value of the d statistic ranges between 0 and 4. Ideally its value should be 2, which indicates no autocorrelation. The closer it gets to 0, the stronger the positive autocorrelation; the closer it gets to 4, the stronger the negative autocorrelation. This can be demonstrated quite easily for the situation where d is based on a large number of observations, but not so easily for where n is small. We will demonstrate the simpler case.

The numerator in the formula for d can be expanded to give the expression

$$ d = \frac{\sum\limits_{t=2}^{n} e_t^2 - 2 \sum\limits_{t=2}^{n} e_t e_{t-1} + \sum\limits_{t=2}^{n} e_{t-1}^2}{\sum\limits_{t=1}^{n} e_t^2} $$

When the number of observations is large, one observation more or less makes very little difference to the sum of the squared residuals. So the three sums of squares that appear in the expression are approximately equal. Therefore

$$ d \approx \frac{\sum\limits_{t=2}^{n} e_t^2 - 2 \sum\limits_{t=2}^{n} e_t e_{t-1} + \sum\limits_{t=2}^{n} e_t^2}{\sum\limits_{t=2}^{n} e_t^2} $$

$$\simeq \frac{2 \sum\limits_{t=2}^{n} e_t^2}{\sum\limits_{t=2}^{n} e_t^2} - \frac{2 \sum\limits_{t=2}^{n} e_t e_{t-1}}{\sum\limits_{t=2}^{n} e_t^2}$$

Hence

$$d \simeq 2 \left(1 - \frac{\sum\limits_{t=2}^{n} e_t e_{t-1}}{\sum\limits_{t=2}^{n} e_t^2} \right)$$

So by definition of r

$$d \simeq 2(1 - r)$$

Because r varies between -1 and $+1$, d varies between 0 and 4. Furthermore, when

$$r = 1, \quad d = 0$$
$$r = 0, \quad d = 2$$
$$r = -1, \quad d = 4$$

Because only positive autocorrelation is likely in accounting data, the range 0 to 2 is important and the situation in which d lies between 2 and 4 can be ignored. The particular point between 0 and 2 at which the value of d will be judged to indicate serious positive autocorrelation depends on the significance level at which the test is to be conducted and on the degrees of freedom associated with the d statistic. STAR, for example, tests at the 1% level (unless it has been preset to test at a different level). The d statistic is closely related to the F statistic and, like F, has two parameters. The degrees of freedom for the numerator and the denominator of d are k and n, respectively.

Although the exact distribution of d is not known, Durbin and Watson established that it lies between the known distributions of two other statistics, d_L (lower limit) and d_U (upper limit). They tabulated the values for these two statistics at the 5% and 1% levels of significance for various values of n and k. Positive autocorrelation is clearly significant if d is less than d_L and not significant if d is greater than or equal to d_U. If d falls between d_L and d_U, however, the test is inconclusive. STAR conservatively regards d less than d_U as a significant indication of positive autocorrelation. Tables A.5 and A.6 show critical values of d_U and d_L suitable for performing tests at the 1% and 5% levels of significance respectively.

8.4.3 Generalized regression

Just as ordinary regression analysis is used to estimate the parameters of the ordinary linear model, generalized regression analysis is used to estimate the generalized linear model. The generalized regression function (also called a *generalized least squares,* or GLS, function) is

$$Y_t = a + bX_t + re_{t-1} + f_t$$

This is an estimate of the ULR

$$Y_t = \alpha + \beta X_t + \rho u_{t-1} + v_t$$

Because by definition

$$e_{t-1} = Y_{t-1} - (a + bX_{t-1})$$

the GLS function can (after some rearrangement of the terms) be expressed as

$$Y_t - rY_{t-1} = a(1 - r) + b(X_t - rX_{t-1}) + f_t$$

This can be written as

$$Y_t^* = a^* + bX_t^* + f_t$$

where it is understood that

$$Y_t^* = Y_t - rY_{t-1}$$
$$X_t^* = X_t - rX_{t-1}$$

and

$$a^* = a(1 - r)$$

When the function is written in this way, it looks just like an ordinary regression function, except that it involves Y^* and X^* rather than Y and X. In fact, this suggests the method that STAR uses to calculate a generalized regression function.

The first step is to calculate a set of transformed variables

$$
\begin{aligned}
Y_1^* &= \sqrt{1 - r^2}\, Y_1 & X_1^* &= \sqrt{1 - r^2}\, X_1 \\
Y_2^* &= Y_2 - r\, Y_1 & X_2^* &= X_2 - r\, X_1 \\
Y_3^* &= Y_3 - r\, Y_2 & X_3^* &= X_3 - r\, X_2 \\
Y_4^* &= Y_4 - r\, Y_3 & X_4^* &= X_4 - r\, X_3 \\
&\quad\cdot & &\quad\cdot \\
&\quad\cdot & &\quad\cdot \\
&\quad\cdot & &\quad\cdot \\
Y_n^* &= Y_n - r\, Y_{n-1} & X_n^* &= X_n - r\, X_{n-1}
\end{aligned}
$$

The first observation is transformed differently from the rest because there is no preceding observation. An alternative is simply to drop the first observation. That approach, however, would reduce the degrees of freedom by one. It can be shown that the transformation applied by the STAR Program in period 1 maintains the degrees of freedom (see Kadiyala [4]).

The next step is to use ordinary regression analysis to calculate a regression function

$$Y_t^* = a^* + bX_t^* + f_t$$

based on the transformed variables.

Finally, the generalized function is computed. The regression coefficient b is the same as the coefficient of the ordinary function that relates the transformed variables. The constant is calculated from the formula

$$a = \frac{a^*}{1 - r}$$

and a term is added to include the previous residual. The GLS function is therefore

$$\hat{Y}_t = a + bX_t + re_{t-1}$$

in periods $t = 2,3,4, \ldots$, and

$$\hat{Y}_1 = a + bX_1 + \sqrt{1 - r^2}\, e_1$$

in period 1. In all periods ($t = 1,2,3,4, \ldots$), $e_t = Y_t - (a + bX_t)$.

Because the generalized regression function includes a factor to take account of the pattern in the original residuals, the residuals from that generalized function should not show a pattern. That is, they should not be autocorrelated. In practice, however, they may be, either because the form of the autocorrelation has been misspecified (it is more complex than first-order autocorrelation) or because r, the estimated coefficient of autocorrelation, underestimates the true coefficient, ρ. The latter situation is quite common, because r has to be calculated on the basis of the observed residuals rather than the disturbances from the ULR.

The estimate of the coefficient of autocorrelation can be improved by treating it as a first approximation and repeating the process. More specifically, the STAR Program works as follows:

1. Calculate r and a generalized regression function

$$Y_t = a + bX_t + re_{t-1} + f_t$$

2. Test the residuals f_t for autocorrelation. If they are not significantly autocorrelated, the function is satisfactory. Stop here.

3. If the residuals are autocorrelated, r is probably not a good estimate. Treat the generalized function as if it were the original ordinary function (i.e., just use the $\hat{Y}_t = a + bX_t$ part) and return to step 1.

It can be shown that this procedure yields values of r that get successively closer to the value of the true parameter ρ. As a practical matter, the approximations do not get significantly better after the first few iterations. STAR stops the process after three. If after three iterations the residuals are still autocorrelated, the presumption is that the form of the autocorrelation is not first order, as was originally assumed. The STAR Program gives a warning message that the function is not usable for audit purposes.

8.4.4 Illustrative calculations

We will illustrate the tests and transformations using the Autocorp application of Section 4.4. The following factors can be derived from the residuals shown in Figure 4.7. They will be needed in the calculations that follow:

$$\sum_{t=2}^{n} (e_t - e_{t-1})^2 = 63,101$$

$$\sum_{t=1}^{n} e_t^2 = 95,514$$

$$\sum_{t=2}^{n} e_t e_{t-1} = 45,300$$

$$\sum_{t=2}^{n} e_t^2 = 95,248$$

The coefficient of autocorrelation is

$$r = \frac{\sum_{t=2}^{n} e_t e_{t-1}}{\sum_{t=2}^{n} e_t^2} = \frac{45,300}{95,248} = 0.4756$$

Therefore the estimated autoregressive scheme is

$$e_t = 0.4756 e_{t-1} + f_t$$

The d statistic that is used to test the significance of the autocorrelation is

$$d = \frac{\sum_{t=2}^{n} (e_t - e_{t-1})^2}{\sum_{t=1}^{n} e_t^2} = \frac{63,101}{95,514} = 0.66$$

The parameters of this d statistic are $k = 1$ and $n = 36$. Table A.5 shows $d_U = 1.32$. Because $d < d_U$, the conclusion is that the residuals are auto-correlated.

The next step is to transform the variables using the coefficient of auto-correlation ($r = 0.4756$). The Y variables are transformed as follows

$$Y_1^* = \sqrt{1 - 0.4756^2}\ 649 = 571$$
$$Y_2^* = 660 - 0.4756 \times 649 = 351$$
$$Y_3^* = 766 - 0.4756 \times 660 = 452$$
$$\cdot$$
$$\cdot$$
$$\cdot$$
$$Y_{36}^* = 805 - 0.4756 \times 786 = 431$$

The X variables are transformed similarly

$$X_1^* = \sqrt{1 - 0.4756^2}\ 287 = 252$$
$$X_2^* = 303 - 0.4756 \times 287 = 167$$
$$X_3^* = 355 - 0.4756 \times 303 = 211$$
$$\cdot$$
$$\cdot$$
$$\cdot$$
$$X_{36}^* = 417 - 0.4756 \times 360 = 246$$

When ordinary least squares regression is applied to the transformed variables, the regression function that results is

$$\hat{Y}_t^* = a^* + bX_t^* = 55.0259 + 2.0796X_t^*$$

The standard error of this regression function is

$$s_v^* = 41.871$$

The constant of the GLS function is

$$a = \frac{55.0259}{1 - 0.4756} = 104.9319$$

The function is therefore

$$Y_t = 104.9319 + 2.0796X_t + 0.4756e_{t-1} + f_t$$

This can be compared with the original ordinary least squares function

$$Y_t = -68.0789 + 2.5554X_t + e_t$$

shown in Figure 4.7.

It can be seen from the preceding discussion that the original ordinary least squares function can be regarded as a GLS function in which $\rho = 0$. This original function can be denoted by GLS⁰. So far GLS⁰ has been transformed to GLS′. It is now necessary to consider whether GLS′ needs to be transformed into GLS″, and GLS″ in turn to GLS‴. As we indicated earlier, the STAR Program does not look beyond GLS‴ because in practice this is seldom worthwhile.

To test whether GLS′ successfully circumvents the problem of autocorrelation, it is necessary to test whether the new residuals f_t are autocorrelated. Once again the Durbin–Watson test is used. The calculations are similar to those that were made in the first iteration. The factors that are required are

$$\sum_{t=2}^{n} (f_t - f_{t-1})^2 = 69,432$$

$$\sum_{t=1}^{n} f_t^2 = 59,608$$

where the residuals are those from GLS′. The Durbin–Watson statistic is therefore

$$d = \frac{\sum_{t=2}^{n} (f_t - f_{t-1})^2}{\sum_{t=1}^{n} f_t^2} = \frac{69,432}{59,608} = 1.16$$

Because the 1% critical value is $d_U = 1.32$, as before, and $d < d_U$, the autocorrelation is significant at the 1% level.

The GLS′ function has evidently not overcome the problem of auto-correlation. However, it can be regarded as a first approximation to GLS″. The next step is refinement of the estimate of the coefficient of autocorrelation. This is done by calculating a new coefficient based on GLS′. The required factors are

$$\sum_{t=2}^{n} e_t e_{t-1} = 63{,}713$$

$$\sum_{t=2}^{n} e_t^2 = 102{,}607$$

where the residuals are formed from the GLS′ function by treating it as if it were the OLS function. That is

$$e_t = Y_t - (104.9319 + 2.0796X_t)$$

Therefore the coefficient of autocorrelation is

$$r' = \frac{\displaystyle\sum_{t=2}^{n} e_t e_{t-1}}{\displaystyle\sum_{t=2}^{n} e_t^2} = \frac{63{,}713}{102{,}607} = 0.6209$$

This is a better approximation to the true coefficient of autocorrelation than the first approximation. The new coefficient of autocorrelation is now used to transform the original variables in the same way as before. The application of OLS to these new transformed variables gives

$$\hat{Y}_t^* = a^* + bX_t^* = 45.0505 + 2.0386X_t^*$$

The standard error of this function is

$$s_v^* = 39.5844$$

The constant for the generalized function is

$$a = \frac{45.0505}{1 - 0.6209} = 118.8505$$

(The calculation does not work out exactly as shown because the coefficient of autocorrelation shown here has been rounded to 4 decimal places.) Therefore the new generalized least squares regression function GLS″ is

$$Y_t = 118.8505 + 2.0386X_t + 0.6209e_{t-1} + f_t$$

Once again, autocorrelation is tested for by applying the Durbin–Watson test. The factors are

$$\sum_{t=2}^{n} (f_t - f_{t-1})^2 = 78,671$$

$$\sum_{t=1}^{n} f_t^2 = 53,276$$

Therefore

$$d = \frac{\sum_{t=2}^{n} (f_t - f_{t-1})^2}{\sum_{t=1}^{n} f_t^2} = \frac{78,671}{53,276} = 1.48$$

Because this exceeds the critical value of 1.32, the conclusion is that the autocorrelation is not significant at the 1% level, that the function GLS″ has successfully circumvented the problem of autocorrelation, and that the final generalized least squares regression function is

$$Y_t = 118.8505 + 2.0386X_t + 0.6209e_{t-1} + f_t$$

This is the GLS function shown in Figure 4.7. If GLS″ had not worked, STAR would have gone through one more iteration using GLS″ as an approximation to GLS‴. If GLS‴ had not worked, the Program would have regarded the autocorrelation as fatal for audit purposes.

The standard error of the residual in a projection period is the same as the standard error of the residual from the OLS function that relates the transformed variables. This is the same as the standard error of f_t from the GLS function. Thus

$$s(f_t) = s_v^* \sqrt{1 + \frac{1}{n} + \frac{(X_t^* - \bar{X}^*)^2}{\Sigma x_t^{*2}}}$$

For example, in period 39 for the Autocorp example

$$s(f_{39}) = 39.5844 \sqrt{1 + \frac{1}{36} + 0.2774} = 45.224$$

The remaining audit interface calculations are the same as for the nonautocorrelated case.

8.5   Heteroscedasticity

A reasonable assumption for most audit applications of regression analysis (and the one that is built into the STAR Program) is that, where heteroscedasticity exists, the standard error of the disturbances in period t is proportionate to one of the independent variables. That is

$$\sigma_t = \sigma_u X_t$$

where σ_u is some constant, X is one of the independent variables, and σ_t is the standard error of the disturbance for observation t.

In this situation, large values of X tend to have proportionately larger values of u associated with them than do small values of X. Therefore a model that is weighted by the reciprocal of X will tend to have disturbances with a constant standard error. For example, if in the ordinary linear model

$$Y_t = \alpha + \beta_1 X_{1t} + \beta_2 X_{2t} + u_t$$

it is reasonable to assume that $\sigma_t = \sigma_u X_{1t}$, then the model

$$\frac{Y_t}{X_{1t}} = \alpha \left(\frac{1}{X_{1t}} \right) + \beta_1 + \beta_2 \left(\frac{X_{2t}}{X_{1t}} \right) + \frac{u_t}{X_{1t}}$$

will have a constant standard error. The theory behind the tests for, and treatment of, heteroscedasticity is dealt with by Johnston [7, Chapter 7] and by Koutsoyiannis [6, Chapter 9].

We will use the Heteroco application, which was introduced in Section 4.5.3, to illustrate the test for heteroscedasticity and the use of weighted least squares regression to overcome the problem. In that application, the ordinary least squares function is

$$\hat{Y}_t = 29.6635 + 2.945X_{1t} + 0.8393X_{2t}$$

8.5.1 Test for heteroscedasticity

The STAR Program tests for heteroscedasticity by calculating the coefficient of correlation between the size (absolute value) of the residuals and each independent variable and testing whether the highest of those coefficients is significant. The coefficient of correlation will be insignificant if the residuals are homoscedastic, because their size will then not be related to the independent variable. On the other hand, finding a significant coefficient of correlation is prima facie evidence that the disturbances are heteroscedastic.

The absolute residuals are denoted by $|e_t|$. The coefficient of correlation between $|e_t|$ and X is

$$R_{|e|X} = \frac{\Sigma(X_t - \bar{X})(|e_t| - \overline{|e|})}{\sqrt{\Sigma(X_t - \bar{X})^2}\sqrt{\Sigma(|e_t| - \overline{|e|})^2}}$$

In this case X_1 is most highly correlated with a coefficient of correlation of .7739.

To test the significance of the correlation coefficient between $|e|$ and X is to test the null hypothesis that $R_{|e|X} = 0$. The F ratio for testing this hypothesis is

$$F = \frac{R_{|e|X}^2}{(1 - R_{|e|X}^2) \, / \, (n - 2)}$$

It has an F distribution with 1 and $n - 2$ degrees of freedom.

A strong correlation between the absolute residuals and X_1 in the Heteroco example is apparent from the scatter diagram shown in Figure 4.9. Since $R_{|e|X1} = .7739$, the F statistic is

$$F = \frac{.7739^2}{(1 - .7739^2)(30 - 2)} = 41.8$$

This statistic has an F distribution with 1 and 28 degrees of freedom. Its critical value at the 1% level (the default level at which the STAR Program tests) is 7.64. Therefore the correlation coefficient is significant at the 1% level and, as a result, the residuals are assumed to be heteroscedastic. Furthermore, the pattern of heteroscedasticity is assumed to be

$$\sigma_t = \sigma_u X_{1t}$$

8.5.2 Weighted least squares

The first step in weighted regression for the Heteroco application is to transform the variables by dividing them by X_1. Thus

$$Y^* = \frac{Y}{X_1}$$

$$X_1^* = \frac{1}{X_1}$$

$$X_2^* = \frac{X_2}{X_1}$$

The next step is to use ordinary regression to fit a regression function to the transformed variables Y^*, X_1^*, and X_2^*. This function is called the *transformed function,* and its standard error is a constant. In the Heteroco application, the function is

$$Y_t^* = 2.0701 - 97.5193X_{1t}^* + 0.8987X_{2t}^* + e_t^*$$

and its standard error is 0.0863.

The final step in weighted least squares is to multiply the transformed function by X_1. This retransforms it into familiar terms and means that the regression estimate for observation t is

$$\hat{Y}_t = Y_t^* X_{1t}$$

The end result is a familiar-looking function

$$Y_t = a + b_1X_{1t} + b_2X_{2t} + e_t$$

which is the *weighted least squares* (or WLS) function. For the Heteroco application it is

$$Y_t = -97.5193 + 2.9701X_{1t} + 0.8987X_{2t} + e_t$$

The standard error of the WLS function is variable and can be calculated for any observation by multiplying the standard error of the transformed function by the value of X_1. Thus if s_u^* is the standard error of the transformed function, then $s_t = X_{1t}s_u^*$ is the standard error of the WLS function for observation t.

The standard error of an individual residual from a WLS function is calculated in a similar way. It is

$$s(e_t) = X_{1t}s(e_t^*)$$

where $s(e_t^*)$ is the standard error of an individual residual from the transformed function. For example, in period 31 in the Heteroco application, it can be shown that, following the formulas of Section 3.5, $s(e_{31}^*) = 0.08754$. Because $X_{1,31} = 300$, the standard error for the weighted residual is

$$s(e_{31}) = 300 \times 0.08754 = 26.3$$

The remaining audit interface calculations are the same as in the homoscedastic case.

8.6 Abnormality

In this section we use the Paranormal Productions Inc. application (introduced in Chapter 4) to illustrate the mathematics of the tests for abnormality that are applied by the STAR Program. We also discuss methods of dealing with cases in which the underlying distribution of the disturbances is genuinely non-normal.

8.6.1   Sample moments and cumulants

The statistics that are used to test for abnormality of the residuals are derived from various sample moments and cumulants. The second, third, and fourth sample moments are

$$m_2 = \frac{\Sigma e_t^2}{n}$$

$$m_3 = \frac{\Sigma e_t^3}{n}$$

$$m_4 = \frac{\Sigma e_t^4}{n}$$

In the example, these work out as

$$m_2 = 20$$

$$m_3 = -110$$

$$m_4 = 2091$$

The sample cumulants, assuming v degrees of freedom, are

$$k_2 = \frac{v}{v - 1} m_2$$

$$k_3 = \frac{v^2}{(v - 1)(v - 2)} m_3$$

$$k_4 = \frac{v^2}{(v - 1)(v - 2)(v - 3)} [(v + 1)m_4 - 3(v - 1)m_2^2]$$

(For more on sample cumulants, see Kendall and Stuart [5].)

Notice that, because $v - 3$ is a divisor in the calculation of k_4, at least 4 degrees of freedom are required before k_4 can be calculated and the following tests applied. In the example, there are 38 (40 − 2) degrees of freedom and the sample cumulants are

$$k_2 = \frac{38}{37} \times 20 = 21$$

$$k_3 = \frac{38^2}{37 \times 36} \times (-110) = -119$$

$$k_4 = \frac{38^2}{37 \times 36 \times 35} \times 39 \times 2091 - 3 \times 37 \times 20^2 = 1110$$

The calculations of the sample cumulants do not work out exactly as shown, because the sample moments have been rounded.

8.6.2 Test for skewness

The test for skewness that is applied by the STAR Program (described by Kendall and Stuart [5] on page 297) uses the statistic

$$G = \sqrt{\frac{(v-1)(v-2)}{6v}} \times \frac{k_3}{k_2^{3/2}}$$

G has an expected value of zero if the residuals are symmetrically distributed (for example, if they are normal) and a variance of approximately

$$\text{var}(G) = 1 - \frac{6}{v} + \frac{22}{v^2} - \frac{70}{v^3}$$

The probability distribution of G is not known. When v tends to infinity, however, var(G) tends to 1 and the fourth moment of G tends to 3, which is in conformity with a tendency to normality. But the tendency is by no means very rapid. The test value used by STAR is $2.576\sqrt{\text{var}(G)}$, which is the value suggested by the normal distribution. The null hypothesis that the e_t are not skew is rejected at the 1% level when

$$|G| > 2.576\sqrt{\text{var}(G)}$$

in favor of the alternative hypothesis that they are skew. Positive G indicates right skewness, negative G indicates left skewness.

In the example, the test statistic for skewness is

$$G = \sqrt{\frac{37 \times 36}{6 \times 38}} \times \frac{-119}{21^{3/2}} = -3.0$$

The variance of G is

$$\text{var}(G) = 1 - \frac{6}{38} + \frac{22}{38^2} - \frac{70}{38^3} = 0.8561$$

The critical value for skewness is

$$2.576\sqrt{0.8561} = 2.4$$

Because $|G| = 3.0 > 2.4$ and G is negative, left skewness is indicated at the 1% significance level.

8.6.3   Test for kurtosis

The test for kurtosis applied by the STAR Program (described by Kendall and Stuart [5] on page 305) uses the statistic

$$H = \sqrt{\frac{(v - 1)(v - 2)(v - 3)}{24v(v + 1)}} \times \frac{k_4}{k_2^2}$$

which has an expected value of zero and a variance of approximately

$$\text{var}(H) = 1 - \frac{12}{v} + \frac{88}{v^2} - \frac{532}{v^3}$$

if the distribution is normal. The null hypothesis that the distribution is not kurtic ($H = 0$) is rejected in favor of the alternative that it is kurtic when

$$H > 2.576\sqrt{\text{var}(H)}$$

In the example, the test statistic for kurtosis is

$$H = \sqrt{\frac{37 \times 36 \times 35}{24 \times 38 \times 39}} \times \frac{1110}{21^2} = 2.9$$

Its variance is

$$\text{var}(H) = 1 - \frac{12}{38} + \frac{88}{38^2} - \frac{532}{38^3} = 0.7355$$

The critical value for kurtosis is

$$2.576\sqrt{0.7355} = 2.2$$

Because $H = 2.9 > 2.2$, the frequency distribution is judged to be significantly kurtic at the 1% level.

8.6.4 Audit interface considerations

The audit interface calculations in Chapter 5 are based on the assumption that disturbances from the ULR are normally distributed. If there is an indication that the cause of abnormality in the residuals is not simply the presence of explainable outliers but an underlying non-normal distribution of the disturbances then an alternative approach to the audit interface calculations may be appropriate.

One way to deal with residuals that are not normally distributed is to find some other probability distribution that is a better approximation than the normal distribution. The approximating distribution should reflect degrees of skewness and kurtosis that are consistent with those found in the base data. This can be an attractive alternative although non-normal distributions are generally more complex and less tractable than the normal distribution. Kendall and Stuart [5] deal with methods for finding such probability distributions in their Chapter 12.

A second approach is to transform the residuals into a variable that is approximately normal. This has the advantage of making it possible to deal with the audit interface in familiar, normal distribution terms. For the transformed residuals to be usable, they must be put through an inverse transformation and expressed in terms of the original data. Both the underlying rationale and the calculations required for these transformations are quite complex. Kendall and Stuart [5] discuss such transformations in their Chapter 6.

A third method for dealing with abnormality is based on well established results in the field of nonparametric statistics, which is concerned with statistical inferences that do not depend on any assumptions about the mathematical form of the underlying distribution. The distribution of interest for our purpose is described generally in nonparametric literature as the *empirical distribution* or sometimes as the *statistical image* of the population [8–10]. For our purposes, the empirical distribution is the distribution of the residuals in the regression base. It can be shown that the empirical distribution function can be used as an estimate of the probability distribution. We will use the data from the Paranormal Productions example introduced in Chapter 4 to illustrate how the empirical distribution function can be used in the audit interface calculations.

The first step for this purpose is to tabulate the cumulative empirical distribution (generally known as the *empirical distribution function*) as shown in Table 8.3. The residuals are the same as those shown in Figure 4.10, except that they are given to 2 decimal places here for convenience in the following discussion and they have been sorted into ascending order from largest negative to largest positive. The cumulative distribution column shows the proportion of residuals that are less than or equal to the corresponding residual. For example, 75% of the residuals are less than or equal to 2.42. Because there are 40 residuals in the example, the cumulative distribution rises in steps of 1/40 or 2.5%.

A graph of the cumulative empirical distribution is shown in Figure 8.2. The graph is rather uneven because it is based on a limited number of residuals. If thousands of residuals had been observed the graph would have been much smoother. A cumulative normal distribution for the same range of residuals is also shown in Figure 8.2. A comparison of the two graphs shows clearly the effect of left skewness and kurtosis. The long left hand tail (skewness) and the steep rise in the cumulative distribution around 0 (kurtosis) are evident.

To illustrate the use of the cumulative distribution in the audit interface calculations we assume that the monetary precision is $25, the desired reliability level is 95%, and the test is for overstatement. Just as in the normal case, cut-off points are calculated after taking the most adverse spread of error into account.

Table 8.3 Paranormal Productions.
Cumulative Empirical Distribution

Obs #	Rank	Residual	Cumulative Distribution
5	1	-14.15	2.5
22	2	-12.58	5.0
32	3	-9.48	7.5
7	4	-4.66	10.0
16	5	-4.02	12.5
25	6	-3.43	15.0
6	7	-3.00	17.5
27	8	-2.66	20.0
19	9	-1.82	22.5
21	10	-1.62	25.0
4	11	-1.53	27.5
14	12	-0.96	30.0
17	13	-0.92	32.5
8	14	-0.91	35.0
13	15	-0.69	37.5
11	16	-0.30	40.0
12	17	-0.30	42.5
3	18	-0.17	45.0
23	19	-0.15	47.5
24	20	-0.05	50.0
29	21	0.80	52.5
9	22	0.91	55.0
40	23	1.00	57.5
20	24	1.00	60.0
31	25	1.12	62.5
1	26	1.13	65.0
15	27	1.48	67.5
2	28	2.13	70.0
34	29	2.29	72.5
35	30	2.42	75.0
18	31	3.21	77.5
10	32	3.24	80.0
36	33	3.78	82.5
39	34	4.08	85.0
30	35	4.48	87.5
38	36	4.85	90.0
28	37	4.89	92.5
26	38	6.27	95.0
33	39	6.65	97.5
37	40	7.69	100.0

The process is similar to that explained in Chapter 5. For example, suppose we want to determine how to set the cut-off point on the assumption that the total error (if it equals $25) will affect three observations. First we note that the acceptable risk of not identifying a particular one of the three observation is 36.8% (because 36.8% × 36.8% × 36.8% = 5%). Table 8.3 is used to determine the point in the cumulative distribution that in-

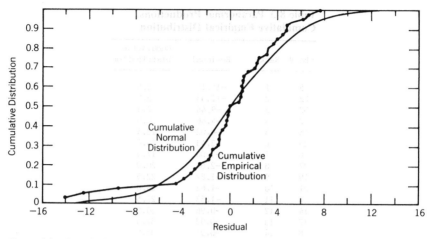

Figure 8.2 Cumulative empirical distribution of the residuals shown in Table 8.3 and cumulative normal distribution.

cludes the 36.8% point. It occurs at the 15th ranked residual (observation number 13) at which point the cumulative distribution is 37.5%. The risk point is the amount of the residual, that is, -0.69. The cut-off point is $-0.69 + 25/3 = 7.64$.

The cut-off points corresponding to spreads through 16 are shown in

Table 8.4

Spread	Risk %	Cumulative Distribution	Residual Rank	Risk Point	Cut-Off
1	5.0	5.0	2	-12.58	12.42
2	22.4	22.5	9	-1.82	10.68
3	36.8	37.5	15	-0.69	7.64
4	47.3	47.5	19	-0.15	6.10
5	54.9	55.0	22	0.91	5.91
6	60.7	62.5	25	1.12	5.29
7	65.2	67.5	27	1.48	5.05
8	68.8	70.0	28	2.13	5.26
9	71.7	72.5	29	2.29	5.07
10	74.1	75.0	30	2.42	4.92
11	76.2	77.5	31	3.21	5.48
12	77.9	80.0	32	3.24	5.32
13	79.4	80.0	32	3.24	5.16
14	80.7	82.5	33	3.78	5.57
15	81.9	82.5	33	3.78	5.45
16	82.9	85.0	34	4.08	5.64

Table 8.4. It can be seen from this table that the most adverse spread of error is 10, the target risk is 74.1%, and the most conservative cut-off point is 4.92. If the residual for a projection observation were 7.00, for example, the excess to be investigated would be $7.00 - 4.92 = 2.08$.

Like the calculation of the excess to be investigated, the calculation of the optional sample data parallels the calculations performed in the normal case (see Section 5.4). In the example just given, in which the residual for a projection observation is 7.00, the effective risk point is $7.00 - 25/10 = 4.5$. The effective risk that corresponds to this can be read from Table 8.3. It is 90%. The target risk is 74.1% and therefore the appropriate risk level for the optional sample is $74.1\% / 90\% = 82.3\%$. This translates to a reliability factor of 0.195 and a sampling interval (rounded down) of $(25/10) / 0.195 = 12$.

References

1. G. C. Chow, "Tests of Equality between Sets of Coefficients in Two Linear Regressions." *Econometrica,* vol. 28, pp. 591–605, 1960.
2. F. M. Fisher, "Tests of Equality between Sets of Coefficients in Two Linear Regressions: An Expository Note." *Econometrica,* vol. 38, pp. 361–366, 1970.
3. J. Durbin and G. S. Watson, "Testing for Serial Correlation in Least-Squares Regression." *Biometrika,* vol. 27, pp. 409–428, 1950, and vol. 38, pp. 157–178, 1951.
4. K. R. Kadiyala, "A Transformation Used to Circumvent the Problem of Autocorrelation." *Econometrica,* vol. 36, pp. 93–96, 1968.
5. Kendall and Stuart, *The Advanced Theory of Statistics.* Vol. 1, 3rd ed. London: Charles Griffin, 1969.
6. A. Koutsoyiannis, *Theory of Econometrics.* London: Macmillan, 1973.
7. J. Johnston, *Econometric Methods,* 2nd ed. New York: McGraw-Hill, 1972.
8. G. E. Noether, *Elements of Nonparametric Statistics.* New York: Wiley, 1969.
9. J. D. Gibbons, *Nonparametric Statistical Inference.* New York: McGraw-Hill, 1971.
10. P. G. Hoel, *Introduction to Mathematical Statistics.* New York: Wiley, 1984.

General References

S. Chatterjee, *Regression Analysis by Example.* New York: Wiley, 1977.

N. R. Draper and H. Smith, *Applied Regression Analysis.* New York: Wiley, 1981.

M. Ezekiel and K. A. Fox, *Methods of Correlation and Regression Analysis,* 3rd ed. New York: Wiley, 1959.

A. Koutsoyiannis, *Theory of Econometrics,* 2nd ed. London: Macmillan, 1977.

M. S. Lewis-Beck, *Applied Regression: An Introduction.* Beverly Hills, CA: Sage Publications, 1980.

J. Neper, *Applied Linear Regression Models.* Homewood, IL: R. D. Irwin, 1983.

K. W. Smillie, *An Introduction to Regression and Correlation.* New York: Academic Press, 1966.

9

MULTIVARIATE REGRESSION COMPUTATIONS

9.1 INTRODUCTION

In Chapter 5 we introduced formulas that deal with two independent variables. These were quite satisfactory for that purpose, but they only apply to functions with two independent variables. New formulas are needed for three-variable regression, four-variable regression, and so on. These can all be developed fairly easily, but they are cumbersome and tend to obscure the fact that there really is not much difference in concept between two-variable, three-variable, and k-variable regression.

Fortunately, *matrix algebra* provides a compact and powerful means of representing and manipulating what are essentially arrays of numbers and symbols. Furthermore, matrix formulas generally do not depend on the number of variables or the number of observations. They apply to one-, two-, three-, or k-variable regression on n observations.

As an example of how matrix notation can be used to express an idea in regression analysis, consider the two-variable linear model for Gamma Company that was discussed in Chapter 4. In this example, there are 36 observations on three variables: X_1, X_2, and Y. The regression equation holds that for each observation

$$Y_t = a + b_1 X_{1t} + b_2 X_{2t} + e_t$$

For convenience (because it eliminates the constant term), the equation can be expressed in terms of deviations from the mean. If the 36 equations were written out for each observation, they would look something like

$$y_1 = b_1 x_{11} + b_2 x_{21} + e_1$$
$$y_2 = b_1 x_{12} + b_2 x_{22} + e_2$$

$$\cdot$$
$$\cdot$$
$$\cdot$$

$$y_{36} = b_1 x_{1,36} + b_2 x_{2,36} + e_{36}$$

If the actual observations rather than symbols are used, these equations become

$$-395 = -258b_1 - 109b_2 + e_1$$
$$-587 = -329b_1 - 126b_2 + e_2$$

$$\cdot$$
$$\cdot$$
$$\cdot$$

$$653 = 251b_1 + 151b_2 + e_{36}$$

Without any loss of information, this system of 36 equations can be written as

$$
\begin{bmatrix} -395 \\ -587 \\ \cdot \\ \cdot \\ \cdot \\ 653 \end{bmatrix}
=
\begin{bmatrix} -258b_1 - 109b_2 \\ -329b_1 - 126b_2 \\ \cdot \\ \cdot \\ \cdot \\ 251b_1 + 151b_2 \end{bmatrix}
+
\begin{bmatrix} e_1 \\ e_2 \\ \cdot \\ \cdot \\ \cdot \\ e_{36} \end{bmatrix}
$$

or as

$$
\begin{bmatrix} -395 \\ -587 \\ \cdot \\ \cdot \\ \cdot \\ 653 \end{bmatrix}
=
\begin{bmatrix} -258 & -109 \\ -329 & -126 \\ \cdot & \cdot \\ \cdot & \cdot \\ \cdot & \cdot \\ 251 & 151 \end{bmatrix}
\begin{bmatrix} b_1 \\ b_2 \end{bmatrix}
+
\begin{bmatrix} e_1 \\ e_2 \\ \cdot \\ \cdot \\ \cdot \\ e_{36} \end{bmatrix}
$$

where it is understood that

$$
\begin{bmatrix}
-258 & -109 \\
-329 & -126 \\
\cdot & \cdot \\
\cdot & \cdot \\
\cdot & \cdot \\
251 & 151
\end{bmatrix}
\begin{bmatrix}
b_1 \\
b_2
\end{bmatrix}
=
\begin{bmatrix}
-258b_1 - 109b_2 \\
-329b_1 - 126b_2 \\
\cdot \\
\cdot \\
\cdot \\
251b_1 + 151b_2
\end{bmatrix}
$$

These arrays can be represented by symbols such as

$$\mathbf{Y} = \mathbf{Xb} + \mathbf{e}$$

where the symbols are in bold type to indicate that they refer to arrays of numbers. As long as it is remembered that

$$
\mathbf{Y} =
\begin{bmatrix}
y_1 \\
y_2 \\
\cdot \\
\cdot \\
\cdot \\
y_{36}
\end{bmatrix}
\quad
\mathbf{X} =
\begin{bmatrix}
x_{11} & x_{21} \\
x_{12} & x_{22} \\
\cdot & \cdot \\
\cdot & \cdot \\
\cdot & \cdot \\
x_{1,36} & x_{2,36}
\end{bmatrix}
\quad
\mathbf{b} =
\begin{bmatrix}
b_1 \\
b_2
\end{bmatrix}
\quad
\mathbf{e} =
\begin{bmatrix}
e_1 \\
e_2 \\
\cdot \\
\cdot \\
\cdot \\
e_{36}
\end{bmatrix}
$$

none of the original information has been lost, and the entire system of 36 equations is expressed in a neat, compact notation. The advantage of this notation is that exactly the same symbols can be used, no matter how many variables are included in the model. For example, if there were four independent variables in the model, the system of 36 equations would be

$$
\begin{aligned}
y_1 &= b_1x_{11} + b_2x_{21} + b_3x_{31} + b_4x_{41} + e_1 \\
y_2 &= b_1x_{12} + b_2x_{22} + b_3x_{32} + b_4x_{42} + e_2 \\
&\quad\cdot\quad\cdot\qquad\cdot \\
&\quad\cdot\quad\cdot\qquad\cdot \\
&\quad\cdot\quad\cdot\qquad\cdot \\
y_{36} &= b_1x_{1,36} + b_2x_{2,36} + b_3x_{3,36} + b_4x_{4,36} + e_{36}
\end{aligned}
$$

This system can also be written as

$$\mathbf{Y} = \mathbf{Xb} + \mathbf{e}$$

exactly as before, where

$$
Y = \begin{bmatrix} y_1 \\ y_2 \\ . \\ . \\ . \\ y_{36} \end{bmatrix}
\qquad
X = \begin{bmatrix} x_{11} & x_{21} & x_{31} & x_{41} \\ x_{12} & x_{22} & x_{32} & x_{42} \\ . & . & . & . \\ . & . & . & . \\ . & . & . & . \\ x_{1,36} & x_{2,36} & x_{3,36} & x_{4,36} \end{bmatrix}
$$

$$
b = \begin{bmatrix} b_1 \\ b_2 \\ b_3 \\ b_4 \end{bmatrix}
\qquad
e = \begin{bmatrix} e_1 \\ e_2 \\ . \\ . \\ . \\ . \\ e_{36} \end{bmatrix}
$$

The symbols **Y, X, b,** and **e** each represent an array or *matrix* of numbers (or symbols representing numbers). Matrices can be manipulated in various ways. For example, they can be added together, subtracted from one another, multiplied together, or "inverted." Just as the ordinary rules of algebra determine what can and cannot be done with ordinary numbers, so there are rules of matrix algebra that determine how matrices can be manipulated.

9.2 Elements of Matrix Algebra

A matrix with n rows and k columns such as

$$
A = \begin{bmatrix} A_{11} & A_{12} & \cdots & A_{1k} \\ A_{21} & A_{22} & \cdots & A_{2k} \\ . & . & & . \\ . & . & & . \\ . & . & & . \\ A_{n1} & A_{n2} & \cdots & A_{nk} \end{bmatrix}
$$

is called a *matrix of order n by k*. It consists of nk elements (numbers or symbols). A matrix may consist of only one row or column, in which case it is sometimes called a *vector*. If, like the vector

$$\mathbf{e} = \begin{bmatrix} e_1 \\ e_2 \\ \cdot \\ \cdot \\ \cdot \\ e_n \end{bmatrix}$$

it consists of only one column of elements, it is called a *column vector*. If, like the vector

$$\mathbf{e} = [e_1 \ e_2 \ \cdots \ e_n]$$

it consists of only one row, it is called a *row vector*.

Two matrices **A** and **B** of order $n \times k$ are said to be *equal* if both contain exactly the same elements in the same positions. Two $n \times k$ matrices can be *added* to produce a third matrix by adding together elements in similar positions. Thus if

$$\mathbf{A} = \begin{bmatrix} 5 & 0 \\ 7 & -3 \end{bmatrix} \qquad \mathbf{B} = \begin{bmatrix} 2 & -4 \\ -8 & 6 \end{bmatrix}$$

then

$$\mathbf{C} = \mathbf{A} + \mathbf{B} = \begin{bmatrix} 7 & -4 \\ -1 & 3 \end{bmatrix}$$

Similarly, matrices can be *subtracted*, thus

$$\mathbf{C} = \mathbf{A} - \mathbf{B} = \begin{bmatrix} 3 & 4 \\ 15 & -9 \end{bmatrix}$$

A matrix can be *multiplied by a number* (or *scalar*, as such numbers are known in matrix terminology). Thus

$$2\mathbf{A} = \begin{bmatrix} 10 & 0 \\ 14 & -6 \end{bmatrix}$$

Matrices can be *multiplied* together following a rather special multiplication rule. Suppose

$$\mathbf{A} = \begin{bmatrix} A_{11} & A_{12} & A_{13} \\ A_{21} & A_{22} & A_{23} \end{bmatrix} \qquad \mathbf{B} = \begin{bmatrix} B_{11} & B_{12} \\ B_{21} & B_{22} \\ B_{31} & B_{32} \end{bmatrix}$$

Then

$$\mathbf{C} = \mathbf{AB} = \begin{bmatrix} C_{11} & C_{12} \\ C_{21} & C_{22} \end{bmatrix}$$

where

$$C_{11} = A_{11}B_{11} + A_{12}B_{21} + A_{13}B_{31}$$
$$C_{12} = A_{11}B_{12} + A_{12}B_{22} + A_{13}B_{32}$$
$$C_{21} = A_{21}B_{11} + A_{22}B_{21} + A_{23}B_{31}$$
$$C_{22} = A_{21}B_{12} + A_{22}B_{22} + A_{23}B_{32}$$

For example, if

$$\mathbf{X} = \begin{bmatrix} 2 & -3 & 0 \\ 1 & 4 & -6 \end{bmatrix} \qquad \mathbf{Y} = \begin{bmatrix} 4 & 1 \\ 2 & 7 \\ 3 & 0 \end{bmatrix}$$

then

$$\mathbf{Z} = \mathbf{XY} = \begin{bmatrix} 8-6+0 & 2-21+0 \\ 4+8-18 & 1+28+0 \end{bmatrix} = \begin{bmatrix} 2 & -19 \\ -6 & 29 \end{bmatrix}$$

Two matrices can be multiplied together only if they are *conformable*. This means that the matrix on the left-hand side of the multiplication must have as many columns as the matrix on the right-hand side has rows. Thus for example, a 2×3 matrix like $\mathbf{X}$ may be multiplied by a 3×2 matrix like $\mathbf{Y}$. The result is a matrix of order 2×2. In general, a matrix of order $n \times k$ may be multiplied by a matrix of order $k \times m$ to give a matrix of order $n \times m$.

In the example, $\mathbf{Y}$ can also be multiplied by $\mathbf{X}$, but the result is not the same as multiplying $\mathbf{X}$ by $\mathbf{Y}$. Thus

$$\mathbf{YX} = \begin{bmatrix} 8+1 & -12+4 & 0-6 \\ 4+7 & -6+28 & 0-42 \\ 6+0 & -9+0 & 0+0 \end{bmatrix} = \begin{bmatrix} 9 & -8 & -6 \\ 11 & 22 & -42 \\ 6 & -9 & 0 \end{bmatrix}$$

Because $\mathbf{Y}$ is 3×2 and $\mathbf{X}$ is 2×3, the resulting 3×3 matrix is $\mathbf{YX}$, which is different from the 2×2 matrix $\mathbf{XY}$. This *noncommutative* property of matrix multiplication is one way in which matrix algebra differs from ordinary arithmetic.

Certain types of matrices play an important role in matrix algebra. A *square matrix* is a matrix with as many columns as rows (a 2×2 matrix, for example). The *unit* or *identity matrix* of order n is the $n \times n$ matrix with 1's in the main diagonal and zeros elsewhere. It is usually written as $\mathbf{I}_n$. For example

$$\mathbf{I}_5 = \begin{bmatrix} 1 & 0 & 0 & 0 & 0 \\ 0 & 1 & 0 & 0 & 0 \\ 0 & 0 & 1 & 0 & 0 \\ 0 & 0 & 0 & 1 & 0 \\ 0 & 0 & 0 & 0 & 1 \end{bmatrix}$$

The identity matrix is important because it plays a role in matrix algebra similar to that played by the number 1 in ordinary arithmetic. If a matrix of suitable order is multiplied by the identity matrix of suitable order, the resulting matrix is the same as the original matrix. For example, if

$$\mathbf{A} = \begin{bmatrix} 3 & 1 \\ -2 & 5 \\ 1 & 0 \\ 6 & 9 \\ 2 & -3 \end{bmatrix}$$

then

$$\mathbf{AI}_2 = \begin{bmatrix} 3 & 1 \\ -2 & 5 \\ 1 & 0 \\ 6 & 9 \\ 2 & -3 \end{bmatrix} \begin{bmatrix} 1 & 0 \\ 0 & 1 \end{bmatrix} = \begin{bmatrix} 3+0 & 0+1 \\ -2+0 & 0+5 \\ 1+0 & 0+0 \\ 6+0 & 0+9 \\ 2+0 & 0-3 \end{bmatrix} = \mathbf{A}$$

Also

$$\mathbf{I}_5\mathbf{A} = \begin{bmatrix} 1 & 0 & 0 & 0 & 0 \\ 0 & 1 & 0 & 0 & 0 \\ 0 & 0 & 1 & 0 & 0 \\ 0 & 0 & 0 & 1 & 0 \\ 0 & 0 & 0 & 0 & 1 \end{bmatrix} \begin{bmatrix} 3 & 1 \\ -2 & 5 \\ 1 & 0 \\ 6 & 9 \\ 2 & -3 \end{bmatrix} = \begin{bmatrix} 3 & 1 \\ -2 & 5 \\ 1 & 0 \\ 6 & 9 \\ 2 & -3 \end{bmatrix} = \mathbf{A}$$

The *transpose* of a matrix $\mathbf{A}$ is written $\mathbf{A}'$ and is the matrix that is obtained by interchanging columns and rows. Thus if

$$\mathbf{A} = \begin{bmatrix} 3 & 1 \\ -2 & 5 \\ 1 & 0 \\ 6 & 9 \\ 2 & -3 \end{bmatrix} \text{ then } \mathbf{A}' = \begin{bmatrix} 3 & -2 & 1 & 6 & 2 \\ 1 & 5 & 0 & 9 & -3 \end{bmatrix}$$

There are some useful rules for dealing with transposed matrices.

$(A + B)' = A' + B'$. The transpose of the sum of two matrices equals the sum of the transposed matrices.

$(A - B)' = A' - B'$.

$(AB)' = B'A'$. The transpose of the product AB equals the transpose of B times the transpose of A.

A matrix A is *symmetric* if its rows and columns are interchangeable, that is, if $A = A'$. Clearly only a square matrix can be symmetric. An example of a symmetric matrix is

$$A = \begin{bmatrix} 5 & 4 & 7 & 0 \\ 4 & 19 & -2 & 6 \\ 7 & -2 & 3 & 5 \\ 0 & 6 & 5 & -5 \end{bmatrix}$$

In regression analysis, a particular symmetric matrix is especially important. It arises from a matrix of observations on the independent variables, such as the following

$$X = \begin{bmatrix} x_{11} & x_{21} \\ x_{11} & x_{21} \\ \cdot & \cdot \\ \cdot & \cdot \\ \cdot & \cdot \\ x_{1,36} & x_{2,36} \end{bmatrix}$$

where the x's represent deviations from the means for the two variables X_1 and X_2. The symmetric matrix that arises out of this X matrix is $X'X$, that is

$$X'X = \begin{bmatrix} \Sigma x_1^2 & \Sigma x_1 x_2 \\ \Sigma x_2 x_1 & \Sigma x_2^2 \end{bmatrix}$$

$\mathbf{X'X}$ is the matrix equivalent to squaring a number. The importance of this matrix is that it contains all the sums of squares and cross products for the independent variables.

9.2.1   Matrix inversion

In ordinary arithmetic, the laws of algebra permit one number to be divided by another, provided that the divisor is not equal to 0. Thus if A, x, and y are ordinary numbers, the equation $Ax = y$ can be solved for x quite simply by dividing both sides of the equation by A (providing that A is not zero). Thus $x = y/A$ is the solution. Dividing both sides of the equation by A is the same as multiplying both sides by the number A^{-1}. Thus $A^{-1}Ax = A^{-1}y$ or $1x = A^{-1}y$. For example, if the equation is $3x = 6$, it is solved by multiplying each side by 3^{-1}. Thus $x = 3^{-1}6 = 2$ is the solution. The number A^{-1} is called the *inverse* of A.

In matrix algebra, the main problem in solving an equation $\mathbf{Ax = y}$ consists of finding a matrix, called the *inverse of* $\mathbf{A}$ and usually denoted by the symbol $\mathbf{A}^{-1}$, such that $\mathbf{A}^{-1}\mathbf{Ax} = \mathbf{x} = \mathbf{A}^{-1}\mathbf{y}$. Note that $\mathbf{A}^{-1}\mathbf{A} = \mathbf{I}$, the identity matrix, just as in ordinary arithmetic $A^{-1}A = 1$.

As an example of how the inverse of a matrix can be used, consider the problem of solving the simultaneous equations

$$7x_1 + 3x_2 = 36$$

$$6x_1 - x_2 = 13$$

These equations can be written in matrix terms as

$$\begin{bmatrix} 7 & 3 \\ 6 & -1 \end{bmatrix} \begin{bmatrix} x_1 \\ x_2 \end{bmatrix} = \begin{bmatrix} 36 \\ 13 \end{bmatrix}$$

which is a matrix equation of the form $\mathbf{Ax = y}$. It is clear that (however it is calculated) the inverse of $\mathbf{A}$ is

$$\mathbf{A}^{-1} = \begin{bmatrix} 0.04 & 0.12 \\ 0.24 & -0.28 \end{bmatrix}$$

because

$$A^{-1}A = \begin{bmatrix} 0.04 & 0.12 \\ 0.24 & -0.28 \end{bmatrix} \begin{bmatrix} 7 & 3 \\ 6 & -1 \end{bmatrix} = \begin{bmatrix} 1 & 0 \\ 0 & 1 \end{bmatrix}$$

Hence the solution to the equation is

$$A^{-1}y = \begin{bmatrix} 0.04 & 0.12 \\ 0.24 & -0.28 \end{bmatrix} \begin{bmatrix} 36 \\ 13 \end{bmatrix} = \begin{bmatrix} 3 \\ 5 \end{bmatrix}$$

The solution $x_1 = 3$, $x_2 = 5$ may be verified by substituting these values in the original equations. The problem of solving the matrix equation $Ax = y$ is essentially the problem of inverting A to get A^{-1}.

Over the years, many ways have been developed to invert matrices. The method we will illustrate is called the Gauss–Jordan method. For the manual inversion of small matrices such as the one just shown, it is not the easiest method to use. It is efficient, however, in computer terms and can be applied to very large matrices. Certain of the precomputer, manual methods, while fine for small matrices, are hopelessly inefficient for large ones. A further advantage of the Gauss–Jordan method is that, when applied to the main inversion problem of multiple regression analysis, it provides some very useful statistics along the way.

As an introduction to the Gauss–Jordan method of matrix inversion, we will demonstrate first how a simple algebraic method can be applied to solve simultaneous equations. The equations are

$$7x_1 + 3x_2 = 36$$
$$6x_1 - 1x_2 = 13$$

In step 1, the first equation is divided by 7. This gives

$$1x_1 + \tfrac{3}{7}x_2 = \tfrac{36}{7}$$
$$6x_1 - 1x_2 = 13$$

Then 6 times the first equation is subtracted from the second equation. This gives

$$1x_1 + \tfrac{3}{7}x_2 = \tfrac{36}{7}$$
$$0x_1 - \tfrac{25}{7}x_2 = -\tfrac{125}{7}$$

In step 2 the second equation is divided by $-\tfrac{25}{7}$

$$1x_1 + \tfrac{3}{7}x_2 = \tfrac{36}{7}$$
$$0 + 1x_2 = 5$$

Then $\tfrac{3}{7}$ times the second equation is subtracted from the first equation. This gives

$$1x_1 + 0 = 3$$
$$0 + 1x_2 = 5$$

The solution, $x_1 = 3$ and $x_2 = 5$, is on the right-hand side of the equations.

In matrix terms, the original equation was

$$\begin{bmatrix} 7 & 3 \\ 6 & -1 \end{bmatrix} \begin{bmatrix} x_1 \\ x_2 \end{bmatrix} = \begin{bmatrix} 36 \\ 13 \end{bmatrix}$$

Then in steps 1 and 2, the left-hand side and the right-hand side of the equation were transformed. (This is the same as multiplying both sides by some matrix). The ending equation was

$$\begin{bmatrix} 1 & 0 \\ 0 & 1 \end{bmatrix} \begin{bmatrix} x_1 \\ x_2 \end{bmatrix} = \begin{bmatrix} 3 \\ 5 \end{bmatrix}$$

Because the matrix on the left-hand side of the original equation has been transformed into the identity matrix, the transforming matrix must be the inverse of that matrix.

We can now demonstrate the Gauss–Jordan method. First an *augmented* matrix is set up. This is the original **A** matrix, the **Y** matrix and the identity matrix written side by side. Thus

$$\left[\begin{array}{rr|r|rr} 7 & 3 & 36 & 1 & 0 \\ 6 & -1 & 13 & 0 & 1 \end{array}\right]$$

The method consists of applying the same transformation to the three components of the augmented matrix so that what started as the **A** component is transformed into the identity matrix, what started as the **Y** component is transformed into the solution vector, and what started as the identity matrix is transformed into **A**$^{-1}$, the inverse of **A**.

In step 1, row one is divided by 7 and then 6 times row one is subtracted from row two. This gives

$$\left[\begin{array}{rr|r|rr} 1 & \frac{3}{7} & \frac{36}{7} & \frac{1}{7} & 0 \\ 0 & -\frac{25}{7} & -\frac{125}{7} & -\frac{6}{7} & 1 \end{array}\right]$$

The element used for the transformation (7, in this first step) is called the *pivotal* element. In step 2, row two is divided by $-\frac{25}{7}$, the new pivotal element, and then $\frac{3}{7}$ times row two is subtracted from row one. This gives

$$\left[\begin{array}{rr|r|rr} 1 & 0 & 3 & \frac{1}{25} & \frac{3}{25} \\ 0 & 1 & 5 & \frac{6}{25} & -\frac{7}{25} \end{array}\right]$$

which can also be written as

$$\left[\begin{array}{rr|r|rr} 1 & 0 & 3 & 0.04 & 0.12 \\ 0 & 1 & 5 & 0.24 & -0.28 \end{array}\right]$$

The result of the Gauss–Jordan method is that the left-hand matrix is now the 2 × 2 identity matrix, the middle two-element vector is the solution vector **x,** and the right-hand matrix is the inverse matrix. The order in which the pivotal elements are chosen makes no difference to the result. The reader might wish to prove this point by reworking the example beginning with -1 as the first pivotal element rather than with the 7.

For a matrix to be inverted, it must be what is called a *nonsingular* matrix. Trying to invert a singular matrix is the matrix equivalent of trying to divide an ordinary number by zero. Singularity is not dealt with further in this text, because the way in which matrices are used for stepwise regression ensures that only nonsingular matrices, or at least only the nonsingular parts of them, are inverted. Any standard text on matrices discusses this subject.

The Gauss–Jordan method can be explained in a somewhat more general framework in relation to the problem of solving the 3×3 equation

$$\begin{bmatrix} A_{11} & A_{12} & A_{13} \\ A_{21} & A_{22} & A_{23} \\ A_{31} & A_{32} & A_{33} \end{bmatrix} \begin{bmatrix} x_1 \\ x_2 \\ x_3 \end{bmatrix} = \begin{bmatrix} y_1 \\ y_2 \\ y_3 \end{bmatrix}$$

The generalization of the method to a $k \times k$ matrix will be obvious. As before, the first step is formation of the augmented matrix.

$$\mathbf{A}_0 = \begin{bmatrix} A_{11} & A_{12} & A_{13} & y_1 & 1 & 0 & 0 \\ A_{21} & A_{22} & A_{23} & y_2 & 0 & 1 & 0 \\ A_{31} & A_{32} & A_{33} & y_3 & 0 & 0 & 1 \end{bmatrix}$$

Three transformations are performed on the augmented matrix to generate a new matrix in which:

The 3×3 matrix on the left-hand side is $\mathbf{I}_3$, the 3×3 identity matrix.
The 3×1 column vector in the middle is the solution to the original equation.
The 3×3 matrix on the right hand side is $\mathbf{A}^{-1}$, the inverse of $\mathbf{A}$.

The pivotal elements can be taken in any order, but for illustrative purposes we will start with A_{11}.

In step 1, row one is transformed by dividing it by the pivotal element A_{11}. Each succeeding row is then transformed by deducting from it the first element in the row times the newly transformed first row. After step 1, therefore, the new augmented matrix is

$$\mathbf{A}_1 = \left[\begin{array}{ccc|c|ccc} 1 & B_{12} & B_{13} & v_1 & E_{11} & 0 & 0 \\ 0 & B_{22} & B_{23} & v_2 & E_{21} & 1 & 0 \\ 0 & B_{32} & B_{33} & v_3 & E_{31} & 0 & 1 \end{array}\right]$$

where

$$B_{12} = \frac{A_{12}}{A_{11}}$$

$$B_{13} = \frac{A_{13}}{A_{11}}$$

$$v_1 = \frac{y_1}{A_{11}}$$

$$E_{11} = \frac{1}{A_{11}}$$

$$B_{22} = A_{22} - \frac{A_{21}A_{12}}{A_{11}}$$

$$B_{23} = A_{23} - \frac{A_{21}A_{13}}{A_{11}}$$

$$v_2 = y_2 - \frac{A_{11}y_1}{A_{11}}$$

$$E_{21} = \frac{-A_{21}}{A_{11}}$$

$$B_{32} = A_{32} - \frac{A_{31}A_{12}}{A_{11}}$$

$$B_{33} = A_{33} - \frac{A_{31}A_{13}}{A_{11}}$$

$$v_3 = y_3 - \frac{A_{31}y_1}{A_{11}}$$

$$E_{31} = \frac{-A_{31}}{A_{11}}$$

In step 2, row two of the new matrix is transformed by dividing it by the pivotal element B_{22}. Then rows one and three are transformed by deducting, from each element, the second element in the row times the newly transformed row two. This gives a new augmented matrix

$$
A_2 = \left[\begin{array}{ccc|c|ccc}
1 & 0 & C_{13} & w_1 & F_{11} & F_{12} & 0 \\
0 & 1 & C_{23} & w_2 & F_{21} & F_{22} & 0 \\
0 & 0 & C_{33} & w_3 & F_{31} & F_{32} & 1
\end{array} \right]
$$

In step 3, row three of the new matrix A_2 is transformed by dividing it by the pivotal element C_{33}. Rows one and two are then transformed by deducting, from each element, the third element in the row times the newly transformed row three. This gives a new augmented matrix

$$
A_3 = \left[\begin{array}{ccc|c|ccc}
1 & 0 & 0 & x_1 & G_{11} & G_{12} & G_{13} \\
0 & 1 & 0 & x_2 & G_{21} & G_{22} & G_{23} \\
0 & 0 & 1 & x_3 & G_{31} & G_{32} & G_{33}
\end{array} \right]
$$

This final matrix contains the complete solution to the problem. The 3×3 matrix on the left-hand side of A_3 is the identity matrix I_3. The column vector x in the middle is the solution vector. The 3×3 matrix G on the right-hand side is the inverse of the original matrix.

9.3   Regression on Two Independent Variables Using Matrices

In this section we will show how the material presented in Chapter 4 can be expressed in terms of matrices. This matrix formulation (relating to regression on two independent variables) can be generalized, with almost no change, to a regression on k independent variables.

The underlying linear model can be expressed in matrix terms as

$$Y = X\beta + u$$

Ordinary least squares regression is used to find a vector b that is an estimator of β such that $Y = Xb + e$, and the sum of the squared residuals is a minimum. Now the condition that Σe_i^2 is a minimum can be expressed by saying that $\mathbf{e'e}$ must be a minimum. (Note that $\mathbf{e'e}$ is a number, not a vector.) Because $\mathbf{e} = \mathbf{Y} - \mathbf{Xb}$, the least squares condition is that

$$\mathbf{e'e} = (\mathbf{Y} - \mathbf{Xb})'(\mathbf{Y} - \mathbf{Xb})$$

must be a minimum. Rearranging the terms using the rules of matrix algebra, including those for transposition, yields

$$\mathbf{e'e} = \mathbf{Y'Y} - 2\mathbf{b'X'Y} + \mathbf{b'(X'X)b}$$

Under certain conditions, which are met in this case, rules of differential calculus similar to those applicable to ordinary variables can also be applied to matrices. Thus to find the vector $\mathbf{b}$ that minimizes $\mathbf{e'e}$, $\mathbf{e'e}$ is differentiated with respect to $\mathbf{b}$, the derivative is set equal to zero, and the resulting equation is solved for $\mathbf{b}$. The derivative of $\mathbf{e'e}$ with respect to $\mathbf{b}$ is

$$\frac{d}{d\mathbf{b}}(\mathbf{e'e}) = -2\mathbf{X'Y} + 2(\mathbf{X'X})\mathbf{b}$$

Setting the right-hand side of this equation to zero gives $\mathbf{X'Xb} = \mathbf{X'Y}$. Because $\mathbf{X'X}$ is a square matrix, it is invertible provided that it is nonsingular. Therefore, the least squares estimator is

$$\mathbf{b} = (\mathbf{X'X})^{-1}\mathbf{X'Y}$$

In the Gamma Company example of Chapter 4

$$\mathbf{X'X} = \begin{bmatrix} \Sigma x_1^2 & \Sigma x_1 x_2 \\ \Sigma x_2 x_1 & \Sigma x_2^2 \end{bmatrix} = \begin{bmatrix} 2,120,780 & 730,408 \\ 730,408 & 560,470 \end{bmatrix}$$

Also

$$\mathbf{X'Y} = \begin{bmatrix} \Sigma x_1 y \\ \Sigma x_2 y \end{bmatrix} = \begin{bmatrix} 2,880,436 \\ 1,411,469 \end{bmatrix}$$

Thus to solve the equation $(\mathbf{X}'\mathbf{X})\mathbf{b} = \mathbf{X}'\mathbf{Y},$ the following augmented matrix is set up for the Gauss–Jordan transformation

$$\begin{bmatrix} 2{,}120{,}780 & 730{,}408 & 2{,}880{,}436 & 1 & 0 \\ 730{,}408 & 560{,}470 & 1{,}411{,}469 & 0 & 1 \end{bmatrix}$$

In the first transformation, the first row is divided by the pivotal element 2,120,780. Then the first element (730,408) times the newly transformed first row is deducted from the second row. This gives

$$\begin{bmatrix} 1 & 0.3444054 & 1.358197 & 4.715246E-07 & 0 \\ 0 & 308913.6 & 419431.5 & -0.3444054 & 1 \end{bmatrix}$$

We have used scientific notation to represent the number $4.715246E-07.$ This is the same as 4.715246×10^{-7} or 0.0000004715246. We will often use scientific notation to represent small numbers such as this.

For the second transformation, the second row is divided by the pivotal element 308,913.6. Then 0.3444054 times the newly transformed second row is deducted from the first row.

$$\begin{bmatrix} 1 & 0 & 0.8905756 & 8.554995E-07 & -1.114892E-06 \\ 0 & 1 & 1.357763 & -1.114892E-06 & 3.237152E-06 \end{bmatrix}$$

The Gauss–Jordan method has produced two matrices of interest. First

$$\mathbf{b} = \begin{bmatrix} 0.8906 \\ 1.3578 \end{bmatrix}$$

which contains the coefficients of the regression function. These are the same as the coefficients derived in Chapter 4. Second, it has produced the inverse of $\mathbf{X}'\mathbf{X}$

$$(\mathbf{X}'\mathbf{X})^{-1} = \begin{bmatrix} 8.554995E\text{-}07 & -1.114892E\text{-}06 \\ -1.114892E\text{-}06 & 3.237152E\text{-}06 \end{bmatrix}$$

That this matrix is indeed the inverse of $\mathbf{X}'\mathbf{X}$ can be verified by multiplying the two together [i.e., $(\mathbf{X}'\mathbf{X})(\mathbf{X}'\mathbf{X})^{-1} = \mathbf{I}$].

The regression constant can be calculated from $\bar{Y}$, $\mathbf{b}$, and the vector of means of the independent variables

$$a = \bar{Y} - \mathbf{b}'\bar{\mathbf{X}}$$

$$= 2502 - [0.8906 \quad 1.3578] \begin{bmatrix} 1832 \\ 911 \end{bmatrix}$$

$$= -366.4614$$

9.4 Multiple Regression Using the Correlation Matrix

In the previous section we demonstrated how multiple regression can be performed using the matrix of corrected squares and cross products as the starting point. In this section we show how it can be performed using the matrix of correlation coefficients as the starting point. In the next section we will show how this approach facilitates the computation.

The normal equations for a two-independent-variable regression, using corrected data, are

$$b_1\Sigma x_1^2 + b_2\Sigma x_1 x_2 = \Sigma x_1 y$$

$$b_1\Sigma x_1 x_2 + b_2\Sigma x_2^2 = \Sigma x_2 y$$

These normal equations can be easily changed to equations involving coefficients of correlation instead of corrected squares and cross products. Taking the first equation as an example, first the terms on both sides of the equation are divided by

$$\sqrt{\Sigma x_1^2}\sqrt{\Sigma y^2}$$

This gives

$$\frac{b_1\Sigma x_1^2}{\sqrt{\Sigma x_1^2}\sqrt{\Sigma y^2}} + \frac{b_2\Sigma x_1 x_2}{\sqrt{\Sigma x_1^2}\sqrt{\Sigma y^2}} = \frac{\Sigma x_1 y}{\sqrt{\Sigma x_1^2}\sqrt{\Sigma y^2}}$$

Next a "trick" is used in which the second expression on the left-hand side of the equation is multiplied by

$$\frac{\sqrt{\Sigma x_2^2}}{\sqrt{\Sigma x_2^2}}$$

After the terms have been rearranged and simplified, the left-hand side of the equation becomes

$$\left(\frac{b_1\sqrt{\Sigma x_1^2}}{\sqrt{\Sigma y^2}}\right) \times 1 + \left(\frac{b_2\sqrt{\Sigma x_2^2}}{\sqrt{\Sigma y^2}}\right) \times \frac{\Sigma x_1 x_2}{\sqrt{\Sigma x_1^2}\sqrt{\Sigma x_2^2}}$$

By definition of the coefficient of correlation, the right-hand side of the equation equals R_{1y} and

$$R_{12} = \frac{\Sigma x_1 x_2}{\sqrt{\Sigma x_1^2}\sqrt{\Sigma x_2^2}}$$

If the expressions in parentheses are denoted by b_1^* and b_2^*, respectively, the first normal equation can be written as

$$b_1^* \cdot 1 + b_2^* R_{12} = R_{1y}$$

where

$$b_1^* = \frac{\sqrt{\Sigma x_1^2}}{\sqrt{\Sigma y^2}}\, b_1$$

and

$$b_2^* = \frac{\sqrt{\Sigma x_2^2}}{\sqrt{\Sigma y^2}}\, b_2$$

Similarly, the second normal equation may be written as

$$b_1^* R_{21} + b_2^* \cdot 1 = R_{2y}$$

Finally, the normal equations may be written in matrix form as

$$\begin{bmatrix} 1 & R_{12} \\ R_{21} & 1 \end{bmatrix} \begin{bmatrix} b_1^* \\ b_2^* \end{bmatrix} = \begin{bmatrix} R_{1y} \\ R_{2y} \end{bmatrix}$$

If these equations are solved for **b***, it is always possible to get back to the original coefficients by decoding them as

$$b_1 = \frac{\sqrt{\Sigma y^2}}{\sqrt{\Sigma x_1^2}} b_1^*$$

$$b_2 = \frac{\sqrt{\Sigma y^2}}{\sqrt{\Sigma x_2^2}} b_2^*$$

Once b_1 and b_2 have been obtained, the regression constant can be obtained in the usual way as

$$a = \bar{Y} - b_1 \bar{X}_1 - b_2 \bar{X}_2$$

The principal advantage of using the matrix of coefficients of correlation to perform regression analysis is that some extremely useful statistics can be generated as part of the stepwise regression procedure. This will become clear in the next section.

In general terms, the normal regression equations can always be written in terms of correlation coefficients and modified regression coefficients as follows:

$$\begin{aligned}
1b_1^* + R_{12}b_2^* + \ldots + R_{1k}b_k^* &= R_{1y} \\
R_{21}b_1^* + 1b_2^* + \ldots + R_{2k}b_k^* &= R_{2y} \\
&\vdots \\
R_{k1}b_1^* + R_{k2}b_2^* + \ldots + 1b_k^* &= R_{ky}
\end{aligned}$$

The coefficient matrix is then not $\mathbf{X}'\mathbf{X}$ but

$$
\mathbf{R} = \begin{bmatrix}
1 & R_{12} & \cdots & R_{1k} \\
R_{21} & 1 & \cdots & R_{2k} \\
\cdot & \cdot & & \cdot \\
\cdot & \cdot & & \cdot \\
\cdot & \cdot & & \cdot \\
R_{k1} & R_{k2} & \cdots & 1
\end{bmatrix}
$$

and the system

$$
\mathbf{R}\mathbf{b}^* = \begin{bmatrix}
R_{1y} \\
R_{2y} \\
\cdot \\
\cdot \\
\cdot \\
R_{ky}
\end{bmatrix}
$$

is solved for $\mathbf{b}^*$, that is

$$
\mathbf{b}^* = \mathbf{R}^{-1} \begin{bmatrix}
R_{1y} \\
R_{2y} \\
\cdot \\
\cdot \\
\cdot \\
R_{ky}
\end{bmatrix}
$$

Of course, if these new normal equations are solved, the Gauss–Jordan method will yield an inverse matrix as a by-product, but this inverse matrix will be $\mathbf{R}^{-1}$ rather than $(\mathbf{X}'\mathbf{X})^{-1}$. Fortunately, to get from $\mathbf{R}^{-1}$ to $(\mathbf{X}'\mathbf{X})^{-1}$ is not difficult, as we shall now demonstrate. First, note that $\mathbf{R}$ can be derived from $\mathbf{X}'\mathbf{X}$: if a matrix $\mathbf{M}$ is defined as

$$M = \begin{bmatrix} 1/\sqrt{\Sigma x_1^2} & 0 & \cdots & 0 \\ 0 & 1/\sqrt{\Sigma x_2^2} & \cdots & 0 \\ \cdot & \cdot & & \cdot \\ \cdot & \cdot & & \cdot \\ \cdot & \cdot & & \cdot \\ 0 & 0 & \cdots & 1/\sqrt{\Sigma x_k^2} \end{bmatrix}$$

then $M(X'X)M = R$. Therefore, $X'X = M^{-1}RM^{-1}$. Using the useful property of inverse matrices that $(AB)^{-1} = B^{-1}A^{-1}$, we can write

$$(X'X)^{-1} = [(M^{-1}R)M^{-1}]^{-1}$$

$$= (M^{-1})^{-1} (M^{-1}R)^{-1}$$

and therefore

$$(X'X)^{-1} = MR^{-1}M$$

9.5 Computational Procedure for Stepwise Multiple Regression

Stepwise regression was introduced in Chapter 4 and explained a little more in Chapter 8. In this section we describe in detail the stepwise regression procedure used in the STAR Program. This procedure was developed by Efroymson [1]. A particularly lucid description of it is also given by Draper and Smith [2]. A STAR Program printout that shows all the mathematical calculations is included as Printout B.7.

To demonstrate the calculations that are involved, we shall use the Gamma Company variables:

Y REVENUE

X_1 TIME AT STANDARD

X_2 EXPENSES

X_3 COST OF SERVICES

The data are shown in Table 2.1. The process begins with the setting up of the augmented matrix of coefficients of correlation. One extra row, however, is added to the matrix, which will prove to be most useful. This row consists of the correlation of Y with itself and the X's plus a sequence of zeros. The matrix is shown as Matrix **A**, below. Notice also that, for convenience, **Y** has been shifted to the leftmost column. The addition of the new row in the augmented matrix will not affect the Gauss–Jordan transformations but will be used to generate factors for calculating partial correlation coefficients and other useful statistics.

Matrix A   Correlation Matrix

	Y	X_1	X_2	X_3	X_1	X_2	X_3
Y	1	0.8636843	0.8232684	0.8693596	0	0	0
X_1	0.8636843	1	0.6699593	0.8617923	1	0	0
X_2	0.8232684	0.6699593	1	0.8480658	0	1	0
X_3	0.8693596	0.8617923	0.8480658	1	0	0	1

For convenience, the successive augmented matrices to be used in the stepwise regression have been labeled **A, B, C, D,** and **E,** where **A** consists of correlation coefficients and **E** is the final matrix. The matrix name plus a subscript will be used to refer to specific elements of the matrix. Thus for Matrix **A,** the individual elements are referred to as follows:

$$
\mathbf{A} =
\begin{array}{|cccc|ccc|}
A_{YY} & A_{Y1} & A_{Y2} & A_{Y3} & A_{Y4} & A_{Y5} & A_{Y6} \\
A_{1Y} & A_{11} & A_{12} & A_{13} & A_{14} & A_{15} & A_{16} \\
A_{2Y} & A_{21} & A_{22} & A_{23} & A_{24} & A_{25} & A_{26} \\
A_{3Y} & A_{31} & A_{32} & A_{33} & A_{34} & A_{35} & A_{36}
\end{array}
$$

For example, $A_{23} = 0.8480658$ is in reality R_{23}, the coefficient of correlation between X_2 and X_3.

9.5.1 Step 1

1. From matrix **A**, calculate a set of so called "V statistics."

$$V_1 = A_{Y1}A_{1Y} / A_{11} = 0.7459506$$
$$V_2 = A_{Y2}A_{2Y} / A_{22} = 0.6777709$$
$$V_3 = A_{Y3}A_{3Y} / A_{33} = 0.7557861$$
$$V_4 = A_{Y4}A_{1Y} / A_{14} = 0$$
$$V_5 = A_{Y5}A_{2Y} / A_{25} = 0$$
$$V_6 = A_{Y6}A_{3Y} / A_{36} = 0$$

Note that the statistics V_1 through V_3 are simply the squares of the coefficients of correlation between the dependent variable and the independent variables. The largest V statistic (VMAX) is V_3. Therefore X_3, the variable that is most highly correlated with Y, is the first variable to be considered for admission. The F ratio used to test the significance of X_3 is

$$F = \frac{(n-k-1)\ \text{VMAX}}{A_{YY} - \text{VMAX}}$$

It can be shown that this statistic has an F distribution with 1 and $n-k-1$ degrees of freedom. It can also be written as

$$F = \frac{R_{3y}^2/1}{(1 - R_{3y}^2)/(n - k - 1)}$$

which is the same as the formula presented in Section 5.3. In this case, $n = 36$ and k is the number of variables that will be in the regression if X_3 is admitted. Therefore

$$F = \frac{34 \times 0.7557861}{1 - 0.7557861} = 105.2222$$

The critical value for an F ratio with 34 degrees of freedom at a 5% level of significance is 4.13 (Table A.4). Therefore X_3 is highly significant at the 5% level.

2.   Admit X_3 to the regression function. This is done by performing a Gauss–Jordan transformation on Matrix **A** using A_{33} as the pivotal element. The result is Matrix **B**:

Matrix B   Matrix After Transformation Using A_{33} as Pivotal Element

	Y	X_1	X_2	X_3	X_1	X_2	X_3
Y	0.24421390	0.11447690	0.08599430	0	0	0	−0.869359
X_1	0.11447690	0.25731400	−0.06089723	0	1	0	−0.861792
X_2	0.08599430	−0.06089723	0.28078450	0	0	1	−0.848065
X_3	0.86935960	0.86179230	0.84806580	1	0	0	1

At this stage, the coefficient of X_3 in the regression function could be found by decoding b_3^*

$$b_3^* = B_{3Y} = 0.86935960$$

Therefore

$$b_3 = \frac{\sqrt{\Sigma y^2}}{\sqrt{\Sigma x_3^2}} \, b_3^* = \frac{\sqrt{5,244,538}}{\sqrt{2,141,408}} \times 0.86935960 = 1.3605$$

Because $\bar{X}_3 = 815$ and $\bar{Y} = 2502$, the regression constant at this stage is

$$a = 2502 - 1.3605 \times 1815 = 32.6602$$

Therefore, if the regression were to stop at this stage, the regression function would be

$$\hat{Y} = 32.6602 + 1.3605\, X_3$$

Several other statistics of interest may be derived from Matrix **B**. The coefficient of correlation is

$$R = \sqrt{1 - B_{YY}} = \sqrt{1 - 0.2442139} = 0.8694$$

which, of course, agrees with the coefficient of correlation between Y and X_3 shown in Matrix **A** (element A_{3Y}). The standard error of the regression function is

$$s_u = \sqrt{\frac{B_{YY} \Sigma y^2}{n-k-1}}$$

$$= \sqrt{0.2442139 \times \frac{5,244,538}{34}}$$

$$= 194.0887$$

The standard error of the regression coefficient b_3 is given by

$$s_{b3} = s_u \sqrt{\frac{B_{33}}{\Sigma x_3^2}}$$

$$= 194.0887 \sqrt{\frac{1}{2,141,408}}$$

$$= 0.1326$$

The importance of B_{YY} in these calculations arises from the way in which it was derived. The Gauss–Jordan elimination method ensures that

$$B_{YY} = A_{YY} - A_{Y3} \left(\frac{A_{3Y}}{A_{33}}\right)$$

$$= R_{YY} - R_{Y3} \left(\frac{R_{3Y}}{R_{33}}\right)$$

$$= 1 - R_{Y3}^2$$

Therefore

$$R_{Y3} = \sqrt{1 - B_{YY}}$$

Also by definition of the coefficient of correlation

$$B_{YY} = 1 - R_{Y3}^2$$

$$= 1 - \frac{\Sigma \hat{y}^2}{\Sigma y^2}$$

$$= \frac{\Sigma e^2}{\Sigma y^2}$$

Therefore

$$\Sigma e^2 = B_{YY} \Sigma y^2$$

Because $s_u = \sqrt{\Sigma e^2 / (n - k - 1)}$, it can be seen that

$$s_u = \sqrt{\frac{B_{YY} \Sigma y^2}{n - k - 1}}$$

9.5.2   Step 2

1.   Using Matrix **B**, calculate the V statistics

$$V_1 = \frac{B_{Y1} B_{1Y}}{B_{11}} = 0.05092981$$

$$V_2 = \frac{B_{Y2} B_{2Y}}{B_{22}} = 0.026337$$

$$V_3 = \frac{B_{Y3} B_{3Y}}{B_{33}} = 0$$

$$V_4 = \frac{B_{Y4} B_{1Y}}{B_{14}} = 0$$

$$V_5 = \frac{B_{Y5} B_{2Y}}{B_{25}} = 0$$

$$V_6 = \frac{B_{Y6} B_{3Y}}{B_{36}} = -0.7557861$$

Notice that V_6 is negative. The statistics V_4, V_5, and V_6 will be negative when X_1, X_2, and X_3, respectively, are in the regression. This is a consequence of the Gauss–Jordan transformation. (It also provides a convenient way for a computer program to determine whether a particular variable is in the regression at any stage.)

In this case, VMAX $= V_1$. Degrees of frèedom, should X_1 be admitted, are $n-k-1 = 36-2-1 = 33$.

$$F = \frac{(n-k-1)\text{VMAX}}{B_{YY} - \text{VMAX}}$$

$$= \frac{33 \times 0.05092981}{0.2442139 - 0.05092981}$$

$$= 8.695407$$

The critical value for an F ratio with 33 degrees of freedom at a 5% level of significance is 4.14 (Table A.4). Therefore X_1 is significant at the 5% level.

An interesting feature of the V statistics is that they are directly proportional to the partial correlation coefficients that are obtained after the influence of the variables in the regression has been removed. In fact, if h_{ij} represents an element in the ith row and the jth column of the matrix, the partial correlation coefficient of X_i and Y after removing the influence of the other variables in the regression is

$$R_{iY\cdot 12\ldots(i-1)\,(i+1)\ldots k} = \sqrt{\frac{h_{iY}^2}{h_{ii}h_{YY}}}$$

From this formula and the formula for V_i (where X_i is not in the regression), it can be seen that

$$V_i = (R_{iY\cdot 12\ldots(i-1)\,(i+1)\ldots k}^2)\,h_{YY}$$

At this stage, for example, where X_3 is the only variable in the regression

$$R_{1Y\cdot 3} = \sqrt{\frac{B_{1Y}^2}{B_{11}B_{YY}}}$$

$$= \sqrt{\frac{0.11447690^2}{0.25731400 \times 0.24421390}}$$

$$= 0.4567$$

Because the V_i's bear a fixed ratio to the partial correlation coefficients, selection of the variable with the highest partial correlation coefficient is exactly the same as selection of the variable with the highest V statistic.

The F statistic, as calculated from the factors generated by the procedure, can easily be shown to be the same as the statistic discussed in Section 8.2. In this latest case

$$F = \frac{(n-k-1)V_1}{B_{YY} - V_1}$$

$$= \frac{R^2_{1Y\cdot3}B_{YY}/1}{(B_{YY} - R^2_{1Y\cdot3}B_{YY})/(n-k-1)}$$

$$= \frac{R^2_{1Y\cdot3}/1}{(1 - R^2_{1Y\cdot3})/(n-k-1)}$$

2. Because X_1 is to be admitted to the regression, the matrix is now transformed with B_{11} as the pivotal element. This gives Matrix **C**:

Matrix C   Matrix After Transformation Using B_{11} as Pivotal Element

	Y	X_1	X_2	X_3	X_1	X_2	X_3
Y	0.1932841	0	0.1130870	0	−0.4448918	0	−0.4859553
X_1	0.4448918	1	−0.2366651	0	3.8863030	0	−3.3491860
X_2	0.1130870	0	0.2663722	0	0.2366651	1	−1.0520220
X_3	0.4859553	0	1.0520220	1	−3.3491860	0	3.8863030

If the regression were terminated at this point, Matrix **C** could be used to provide information about the regression function

$$\hat{Y} = a + b_3 X_3 + b_1 X_1$$

Decoding **b*** gives

$$b_3 = \frac{\sqrt{\Sigma y^2}}{\sqrt{\Sigma x_3^2}} b_3^* = 0.7605$$

$$b_1 = \frac{\sqrt{\Sigma y^2}}{\sqrt{\Sigma x_1^2}} b_1^* = 0.6996$$

$$a = \bar{Y} - b_1 \bar{X}_1 - b_3 \bar{X}_3 = -160.0272$$

Therefore the regression function is

$$\hat{Y} = -160.0272 + 0.7605X_3 + 0.6996X_1$$

The coefficient of correlation, the standard error of regression, and the other statistics can be calculated in the same way as before.

9.5.3   Step 3

1.   From Matrix **C** calculate the V statistics

$$V_1 = \frac{C_{Y1}C_{1Y}}{C_{11}} = 0$$

$$V_2 = \frac{C_{Y2}C_{2Y}}{C_{22}} = 0.04801051$$

$$V_3 = \frac{C_{Y3}C_{3Y}}{C_{33}} = 0$$

$$V_4 = \frac{C_{Y4}C_{1Y}}{C_{14}} = -0.0592981$$

$$V_5 = \frac{C_{Y5}C_{2Y}}{C_{25}} = 0$$

$$V_6 = \frac{C_{Y6}C_{3Y}}{C_{36}} = -0.06076536$$

Because X_1 and X_3 are in the regression, V_4 and V_6 are negative.
The partial correlation coefficients for the variable not in the regression can be calculated as follows:

$$R_{2Y \cdot 13} = \sqrt{\frac{C_{2Y}^2}{C_{22}C_{YY}}} = 0.498391$$

2.   Forward selection. This time X_2 is the variable to be considered because it is the variable with the highest V statistic. VMAX $= V_2 = 0.04801051$, $n - k - 1 = 36 - 3 - 1 = 32$, and therefore

$$F = \frac{(n-k-1)\ \text{VMAX}}{C_{YY} - \text{VMAX}} = 10.57546$$

The critical value for an F ratio with 32 degrees of freedom at a 5% level of significance is 4.15 (Table A.4). Therefore X_2 is significant at the 5% level.

3.   Admit X_2 and perform the necessary Gauss–Jordan transformation using C_{33} as the pivotal element. Matrix **D** is

Matrix D . Matrix After Transformation Using C_{22} as Pivotal Element

	Y	X_1 X_2 X_3			X_1	X_2	X_3
Y	0.14527360	0	0	0	−0.5453667	−0.4245450	−0.03932479
X_1	0.54536670	1	0	0	4.0965740	0.8884751	−4.28388100
X_2	0.42454490	0	1	0	0.8884751	3.7541450	−3.94944300
X_3	0.03932479	0	0	1	−4.2838810	−3.9494430	8.04120300

If the regression were to stop at this point, the regression coefficients and constant could be calculated to give the function

$$\hat{Y} = -363.9794 + 0.2990X_3 + 0.2145X_1 + 0.3994X_2$$

9.5.4   Step 4

1.   From Matrix **D**, calculate the V statistics

$$V_1 = \frac{D_{Y1}D_{1Y}}{D_{11}} = 0$$

$$V_2 = \frac{D_{Y2}D_{2Y}}{D_{22}} = 0$$

$$V_3 = \frac{D_{Y3}D_{3Y}}{D_{33}} = 0$$

$$V_4 = \frac{D_{Y4}D_{1Y}}{D_{14}} = -0.07260331$$

$$V_5 = \frac{D_{Y5}D_{2Y}}{D_{25}} = -0.04801051$$

$$V_6 = \frac{D_{Y6}D_{3Y}}{D_{36}} = -0.0001923142$$

2.   Backward elimination. VMIN $= V_6 = -0.0001923142$, and therefore the related F value is

$$F = \frac{(n-k-1)|\text{VMIN}|}{D_{YY}}$$

$$= \frac{32 \times 0.0001923142}{0.14527360}$$

$$= 0.04236183$$

The critical value for an F ratio with 32 degrees of freedom at a 5% level of significance is 4.15 (Table A.4). Because the calculated F ratio is less than this, X_3 is no longer significant at the 5% level and therefore must be eliminated.

The removal of a variable from the regression function takes exactly the same form as the admission of a variable, except that the pivotal element is taken from the right-hand side of the matrix. In this case, the Gauss-Jordan transformation is applied to **D** using D_{36} as the pivotal element. The result is Matrix **E**.

Matrix E   Matrix After Transformation Using D_{36} as Pivotal Element

	Y	X_1	X_2	X_3	X_1	X_2	X_3
Y	0.145465900	0	0	0.004890412	-0.5663167	-0.4438594	0
X_1	0.566316700	1	0	0.532741400	1.8143730	-1.2155570	0
X_2	0.443859400	0	1	0.491150800	-1.2155570	1.8143730	0
X_3	0.004890412	0	0	0.124359500	-0.5327414	-0.4911508	1

3.   From Matrix **E**, calculate the V statistics

$$V_1 = \frac{E_{Y1}E_{1Y}}{E_{11}} = 0$$

$$V_2 = \frac{E_{Y2}E_{2Y}}{E_{22}} = 0$$

$$V_3 = \frac{E_{Y3}E_{3Y}}{E_{33}} = 0.0001923142$$

$$V_4 = \frac{E_{Y4}E_{1Y}}{E_{14}} = -0.1767633$$

$$V_5 = \frac{E_{Y5}E_{2Y}}{E_{25}} = -0.1085836$$

$$V_6 = \frac{E_{Y6}E_{3Y}}{E_{36}} = 0$$

4. Backward elimination. VMIN $= V_5 = -0.1085835$, and therefore the related F value is

$$F = \frac{(n-k-1)\ |\text{VMIN}|}{E_{YY}}$$

$$= \frac{33 \times 0.1085835}{0.1454695}$$

$$= 24.63297$$

The $n-k-1$ is now 33. The critical value for an F ratio with 33 degrees of freedom at a 5% level of significance is 4.14 (Table A.4). Because the calculated F ratio exceeds this, X_2 is still significant at the 5% level and therefore must be retained.

5. Forward selection. Because there are no further variables to test, the procedure ends at this point with two statistically significant independent variables. The final function is

$$\hat{Y} = a + b_1X_1 + b_2X_2$$

As before

$$b_1 = \frac{\sqrt{\Sigma y^2}}{\sqrt{\Sigma x_1^2}}\ b_1^*$$

$$= \frac{\sqrt{5,244,538}}{\sqrt{2,120,780}} \times 0.5663167$$

$$= 0.8906$$

$$b_2 = \frac{\sqrt{\Sigma y^2}}{\Sigma x_2^2} b_2^*$$

$$= \frac{\sqrt{5,244,538}}{\sqrt{560,470}} \times 0.44385940$$

$$= 1.3578$$

$$a = \bar{Y} - b_1 \bar{X}_1 - b_2 \bar{X}_2$$
$$= -366.4614$$

Therefore

$$\hat{Y} = -366.4614 + 0.8906\, X_1 + 1.3578\, X_2$$

is the final regression function. Furthermore

$$R = \sqrt{1 - E_{YY}}$$
$$= \sqrt{1 - 0.1452736}$$
$$= 0.9244$$

$$s_u = \sqrt{\frac{E_{YY}\, \Sigma y^2}{n - k - 1}}$$

$$= \sqrt{\frac{0.1454659 \times 5,244,538}{33}}$$

$$= 152.0471$$

$$s_{b1} = s_u \sqrt{\frac{E_{11}}{\Sigma x_1^2}}$$

$$= 152.0471 \sqrt{\frac{1.8143730}{2,120,780}}$$

$$= 0.1406$$

$$s_{b2} = s_u \sqrt{\frac{E_{22}}{\Sigma x_2^2}}$$

$$= 152.0471 \sqrt{\frac{1.1814373}{560,470}}$$

$$= 0.2736$$

9.5.5   A more efficient computer procedure

As the augmented matrix is transformed in each step, some of the columns contain only zeros and ones, depending on whether a variable is included in or excluded from the regression. In computer terms, the zeros and the ones take up just as much storage as the other numbers. Because the Program can determine at any stage whether a particular variable is in or out of the regression by testing the sign of the V statistic, it is really unnecessary to store the trivial zeros and ones.

The STAR Program, therefore, uses a somewhat more efficient procedure than the one that we have presented. It merges, into one submatrix, the two submatrices that are shown in the example as the middle and the right-hand submatrices. Thus the final Matrix **E** is

Matrix E   In Compact Form

	Y	X_1	X_2	X_3
Y	0.145465900	-0.5663167	-0.4438594	0.004890412
X_1	0.566316700	1.8143730	-1.2155570	0.532741400
X_2	0.443859400	-1.2155570	1.8143730	0.491150800
X_3	0.004890412	-0.5327414	-0.4911508	0.124359500

Whether a variable is in or out of the regression is determined by the sign of the V statistic.

9.5.6   Refinement of the F test

A refined form of the F test has proved to be quite useful in stepwise regression and is the one actually used by the STAR Program. It results in admission requirements for new independent variables becoming tighter as more variables are admitted. The test is based on *target confidence levels* (probabilities) rather than critical F values.

Instead of calculating critical F values that correspond to predetermined levels of significance, the STAR Program calculates probabilities that correspond to the calculated F ratios. If there is only one variable to be tested, the F probability that corresponds to the F ratio is computed. If it equals or exceeds 95% the variable is admitted. In the case of only one independent variable, this test is exactly equivalent to the standard F test.

If a second variable is to be tested, however, the target confidence level for its admission is raised from 95% to $T_2 = 95/P_1$ percent, where P_1 is the confidence level that corresponds to the F ratio for the admission of the first variable. If the second variable is admitted (at a confidence level of P_2), the target confidence for the third variable is $T_3 = T_2 / P_2$. The process continues along these lines. At each step the target admission requirement for the next variable becomes the previous target divided by the confidence level at which the previous variable was admitted.

The confidence level for eliminating a variable is kept constant at 95% by the STAR Program. If a variable is to be eliminated, the target for the next admission becomes the present target for admission multiplied by the confidence level at which that variable was admitted. This has the effect of reducing the target to what it would have been had the eliminated variable not been admitted in the first place.

9.6   Audit Interface Calculations in Matrix Terms

As regards the audit interface, the only significant difference between regression with one independent variable and multivariable regression is the calculation of the estimated standard error. The number of degrees of freedom will also be less given the same number of observations. Therefore, where the regression function

$$Y_t = a + b_1X_{1t} + b_2X_{2t} + \dots + b_kX_{kt} + e_t$$

is used to predict a value Y_t, the standardized residual

$$\frac{Y_t - \hat{Y}_t}{s(e_t)}$$

has a t distribution with $n - k - 1$ degrees of freedom (see Chapter 3).

It can be shown that the standard error of the residual e_t is given by

$$s(e_t) = s_u \sqrt{1 + \frac{1}{n} + \mathbf{c}_t'(\mathbf{X}'\mathbf{X})^{-1}\mathbf{c}_t}$$

where $(\mathbf{X}'\mathbf{X})^{-1}$ is the inverse of the matrix of corrected squares and cross products, and

$$
\mathbf{c}_t = \begin{bmatrix} X_{1t} - \bar{X}_1 \\ X_{2t} - \bar{X}_2 \\ \cdot \\ \cdot \\ \cdot \\ X_{kt} - \bar{X}_k \end{bmatrix}
$$

In Chapter 3 we discussed the case of one independent variable. There we showed that

$$
(\mathbf{X}'\mathbf{X})^{-1} = \frac{1}{\Sigma x^2}
$$

and

$$
\mathbf{c}_t = X_t - \bar{X}
$$

The Gauss–Jordan procedure automatically produces the inverse matrix expressed in terms of the coefficients of correlation. In the present example, this is the 2×2 matrix in the middle of $\mathbf{E}$ and corresponds to the variables in the final regression function.

$$
\mathbf{R}^{-1} = \begin{bmatrix} 1.814373 & -1.215557 \\ -1.215557 & 1.814373 \end{bmatrix}
$$

The Program converts this inverse matrix to one that is expressed in terms of corrected squares and cross products. It uses the relationship $(\mathbf{X}'\mathbf{X})^{-1} = \mathbf{M}\mathbf{R}^{-1}\mathbf{M}$ derived in Section 9.4. Therefore

$$
(\mathbf{X}'\mathbf{X})^{-1} = \begin{bmatrix} \dfrac{1.814373}{2,120,780} & \dfrac{-1.215557}{\sqrt{2,120,780}\ \sqrt{560,470}} \\[2ex] \dfrac{-1.215557}{\sqrt{2,120,780}\ \sqrt{560,470}} & \dfrac{1.814373}{560,470} \end{bmatrix}
$$

$$= \begin{bmatrix} 0.0000008555389 & -0.000001114956 \\ -0.0000011149560 & 0.000003237270 \end{bmatrix}$$

This matrix is used in the calculation of the estimated standard error. For example, in period 48 for Gamma Company

$$X_{1,48} - \bar{X}_1 = 2389 - 1842 = 557$$
$$X_{2,48} - \bar{X}_2 = 1159 - 911 = 248$$

and therefore

$$\mathbf{c}_t = \begin{bmatrix} 557 \\ 248 \end{bmatrix}$$

The matrix calculation factor $\mathbf{c}'_t(\mathbf{X}'\mathbf{X})^{-1}\mathbf{c}_t$ is

$$\begin{bmatrix} 557 & 248 \end{bmatrix} \begin{bmatrix} 0.0000008555389 & -0.000001114956 \\ -0.0000011149560 & 0.000003237270 \end{bmatrix} \begin{bmatrix} 557 \\ 248 \end{bmatrix}$$

$$= 0.156504$$

The standard error is therefore

$$s(e_{48}) = 152.0471 \sqrt{1 + \frac{1}{36} + 0.156504} = 165.4648$$

Hence $(Y_{48} - \hat{Y}_{48})/165.4648$ has a t distribution with 33 degrees of freedom $(36-2-1=33)$.

All the remaining calculations for identifying excesses and computing optional sample sizes are essentially the same as set forth in Chapter 5, where they were dealt with in the context of a function with one independent variable.

References

1. M. A. Efroymson, *Multiple Regression Analysis.* Article 17 in A. Ralston and H. S. Wilf, Eds., *Mathematical Methods for Digital Computers.* New York: Wiley, 1962.
2. N. R. Draper and H. Smith, *Applied Regression Analysis.* New York: Wiley, 1981.

General References

S. Chatterjee, *Regression Analysis by Example.* New York: Wiley, 1977.

M. Ezekiel and K. A. Fox, *Methods of Correlation and Regression Analysis,* 3rd ed. New York: Wiley, 1959.

A. Koutsoyiannis, *Theory of Econometrics,* 2nd ed. London: Macmillan, 1977.

M. S. Lewis-Beck, *Applied Regression: An Introduction.* Beverly Hills, CA: Sage Publications, 1980.

J. Neper, *Applied Linear Regression Models.* Homewood, IL: R. D. Irwin, 1983.

K. W. Smillie, *An Introduction to Regression and Correlation.* New York: Academic Press, 1966.

STATISTICAL TABLES

Table A.1   Reliability factors (R) and related reliability level percentages (Rel %)

R	Rel %	R	Rel %	R	Rel %	R	Rel %
0.1	9.5	1.1	66.7	2.1	87.8	3.1	95.5
0.2	18.1	1.2	69.9	2.2	88.9	3.2	95.9
0.3	25.9	1.3	72.7	2.3	90.0	3.3	96.3
0.4	33.0	1.4	75.3	2.4	90.9	3.4	96.7
0.5	39.3	1.5	77.7	2.5	91.8	3.5	97.0
0.6	45.1	1.6	79.8	2.6	92.6	3.6	97.3
0.7	50.3	1.7	81.7	2.7	93.3	3.7	97.5
0.8	55.1	1.8	83.5	2.8	93.9	3.8	97.8
0.9	59.3	1.9	85.0	2.9	94.5	3.9	98.0
1.0	63.2	2.0	86.5	3.0	95.0	4.0	98.2

Reliability factors can be derived from the reliability level percent by the formula
$R = -\log(1 - (\text{Rel } \% / 100))$, where log is the natural logarithm.

Table A.2 shows the probability that a t-distributed random variable (with degrees of freedom shown in the column heading) will be less than the t value in the leftmost column. For example, the probability that a t variable with 30 degrees of freedom will be less than 0.6 is 72.2%. This represents the area under the curve of the t distribution to the left of 0.6. Because the curve is symmetrical, 72.2% is also the probability that the t variable will be greater than -0.6. The rightmost column represents the cumulative probabilities for the normal distribution because the t distribution is identical to the normal distribution for infinite degrees of freedom.

237

Table A.2   Cumulative probabilities of the t distribution

t	df = 5	df = 10	df = 30	df = 60	df = 120	df = ∞
0.00	50.0	50.0	50.0	50.0	50.0	50.0
0.05	51.9	51.9	52.0	52.0	52.0	52.0
0.10	53.8	53.9	53.9	53.9	54.0	54.0
0.15	55.7	55.8	55.9	55.9	55.9	56.0
0.20	57.5	57.7	57.8	57.9	57.9	57.9
0.25	59.4	59.6	59.7	59.8	59.8	59.9
0.30	61.2	61.5	61.6	61.7	61.8	61.8
0.35	63.0	63.3	63.5	63.6	63.7	63.7
0.40	64.7	65.1	65.3	65.4	65.5	65.5
0.45	66.4	66.9	67.1	67.2	67.3	67.4
0.50	68.1	68.6	68.9	69.0	69.1	69.1
0.55	69.7	70.3	70.6	70.7	70.8	70.9
0.60	71.3	71.9	72.2	72.3	72.5	72.6
0.65	72.8	73.5	73.8	74.0	74.2	74.2
0.70	74.2	75.0	75.4	75.5	75.7	75.8
0.75	75.6	76.5	76.9	77.0	77.3	77.3
0.80	77.0	77.9	78.3	78.5	78.7	78.8
0.85	78.3	79.2	79.7	79.9	80.1	80.2
0.90	79.5	80.5	81.1	81.2	81.5	81.6
0.95	80.7	81.8	82.3	82.5	82.8	82.9
1.00	81.8	83.0	83.5	83.7	84.0	84.1
1.05	82.9	84.1	84.7	84.9	85.2	85.3
1.10	83.9	85.1	85.8	86.0	86.3	86.4
1.15	84.9	86.2	86.8	87.0	87.4	87.5
1.20	85.8	87.1	87.8	88.0	88.4	88.5
1.25	86.7	88.0	88.7	89.0	89.3	89.4
1.30	87.5	88.9	89.6	89.8	90.2	90.3
1.35	88.3	89.7	90.4	90.6	91.0	91.2
1.40	89.0	90.4	91.2	91.4	91.8	91.9
1.45	89.7	91.1	91.9	92.1	92.5	92.6
1.50	90.3	91.8	92.5	92.8	93.2	93.3
1.55	90.9	92.4	93.2	93.4	93.8	93.9
1.60	91.5	93.0	93.7	94.0	94.4	94.5
1.65	92.0	93.5	94.3	94.5	94.9	95.1
1.70	92.5	94.0	94.8	95.0	95.4	95.5
1.75	93.0	94.5	95.2	95.5	95.9	96.0
1.80	93.4	94.9	95.7	95.9	96.3	96.4
1.85	93.8	95.3	96.0	96.3	96.7	96.8
1.90	94.2	95.7	96.4	96.6	97.0	97.1
1.95	94.6	96.0	96.7	97.0	97.3	97.4
2.00	94.9	96.3	97.0	97.3	97.6	97.7

Table A.3 F distribution, upper 1% points

Degrees of freedom for numerator

	1	2	3	4	5	6	7	8	9	10	12	15	20	24	30	40	60	120	∞
1	4,052	5,000	5,403	5,625	5,764	5,859	5,928	5,982	6,023	6,056	6,106	6,157	6,209	6,235	6,261	6,287	6,313	6,339	6,366
2	98.5	99.0	99.2	99.2	99.3	99.3	99.4	99.4	99.4	99.4	99.4	99.4	99.4	99.5	99.5	99.5	99.5	99.5	99.5
3	34.1	30.8	29.5	28.7	28.2	27.9	27.7	27.5	27.3	27.2	27.1	26.9	26.7	26.6	26.5	26.4	26.3	26.2	26.1
4	21.2	18.0	16.7	16.0	15.5	15.2	15.0	14.8	14.7	14.5	14.4	14.2	14.0	13.9	13.8	13.7	13.7	13.6	13.5
5	16.3	13.3	12.1	11.4	11.0	10.7	10.5	10.3	10.2	10.1	9.89	9.72	9.55	9.47	9.38	9.29	9.20	9.11	9.02
6	13.7	10.9	9.78	9.15	8.75	8.47	8.26	8.10	7.98	7.87	7.72	7.56	7.40	7.31	7.23	7.14	7.06	6.97	6.88
7	12.2	9.55	8.45	7.85	7.46	7.19	6.99	6.84	6.72	6.62	6.47	6.31	6.16	6.07	5.99	5.91	5.82	5.74	5.65
8	11.3	8.65	7.59	7.01	6.63	6.37	6.18	6.03	5.91	5.81	5.67	5.52	5.36	5.28	5.20	5.12	5.03	4.95	4.86
9	10.6	8.02	6.99	6.42	6.06	5.80	5.61	5.47	5.35	5.26	5.11	4.96	4.81	4.73	4.65	4.57	4.48	4.40	4.31
10	10.0	7.56	6.55	5.99	5.64	5.39	5.20	5.06	4.94	4.85	4.71	4.56	4.41	4.33	4.25	4.17	4.08	4.00	3.91
11	9.65	7.21	6.22	5.67	5.32	5.07	4.89	4.74	4.63	4.54	4.40	4.25	4.10	4.02	3.94	3.86	3.78	3.69	3.60
12	9.33	6.93	5.95	5.41	5.06	4.82	4.64	4.50	4.39	4.30	4.16	4.01	3.86	3.78	3.70	3.62	3.54	3.45	3.36
13	9.07	6.70	5.74	5.21	4.86	4.62	4.44	4.30	4.19	4.10	3.96	3.82	3.66	3.59	3.51	3.43	3.34	3.25	3.17
14	8.86	6.51	5.56	5.04	4.70	4.46	4.28	4.14	4.03	3.94	3.80	3.66	3.51	3.43	3.35	3.27	3.18	3.09	3.00
15	8.68	6.36	5.42	4.89	4.56	4.32	4.14	4.00	3.89	3.80	3.67	3.52	3.37	3.29	3.21	3.13	3.05	2.96	2.87
16	8.53	6.23	5.29	4.77	4.44	4.20	4.03	3.89	3.78	3.69	3.55	3.41	3.26	3.18	3.10	3.02	2.93	2.84	2.75
17	8.40	6.11	5.19	4.67	4.34	4.10	3.93	3.79	3.68	3.59	3.46	3.31	3.16	3.08	3.00	2.92	2.83	2.75	2.65
18	8.29	6.01	5.09	4.58	4.25	4.01	3.84	3.71	3.60	3.51	3.37	3.23	3.08	3.00	2.92	2.84	2.75	2.66	2.57
19	8.19	5.93	5.01	4.50	4.17	3.94	3.77	3.63	3.52	3.43	3.30	3.15	3.00	2.92	2.84	2.76	2.67	2.58	2.49
20	8.10	5.85	4.94	4.43	4.10	3.87	3.70	3.56	3.46	3.37	3.23	3.09	2.94	2.86	2.78	2.69	2.61	2.52	2.42
21	8.02	5.78	4.87	4.37	4.04	3.81	3.64	3.51	3.40	3.31	3.17	3.03	2.88	2.80	2.72	2.64	2.55	2.46	2.36
22	7.95	5.72	4.82	4.31	3.99	3.76	3.59	3.45	3.35	3.26	3.12	2.98	2.83	2.75	2.67	2.58	2.50	2.40	2.31
23	7.88	5.66	4.76	4.26	3.94	3.71	3.54	3.41	3.30	3.21	3.07	2.93	2.78	2.70	2.62	2.54	2.45	2.35	2.26
24	7.82	5.61	4.72	4.22	3.90	3.67	3.50	3.36	3.26	3.17	3.03	2.89	2.74	2.66	2.58	2.49	2.40	2.31	2.21
25	7.77	5.57	4.68	4.18	3.86	3.63	3.46	3.32	3.22	3.13	2.99	2.85	2.70	2.62	2.53	2.45	2.36	2.27	2.17
30	7.56	5.39	4.51	4.02	3.70	3.47	3.30	3.17	3.07	2.98	2.84	2.70	2.55	2.47	2.39	2.30	2.21	2.11	2.01
40	7.31	5.18	4.31	3.83	3.51	3.29	3.12	2.99	2.89	2.80	2.66	2.52	2.37	2.29	2.20	2.11	2.02	1.92	1.80
60	7.08	4.98	4.13	3.65	3.34	3.12	2.95	2.82	2.72	2.63	2.50	2.35	2.20	2.12	2.03	1.94	1.84	1.73	1.60
120	6.85	4.79	3.95	3.48	3.17	2.96	2.79	2.66	2.56	2.47	2.34	2.19	2.03	1.95	1.86	1.76	1.66	1.53	1.38
∞	6.63	4.61	3.78	3.32	3.02	2.80	2.64	2.51	2.41	2.32	2.18	2.04	1.88	1.79	1.70	1.59	1.47	1.32	1.00

Degrees of freedom for denominator

Interpolation should be performed using reciprocals of the degrees of freedom.

This table is reproduced with the permission of the Biometrika Trustees from M. Merrington, C.M. Thompson, "Tables of percentage points of the inverted beta (F) distribution," Biometrika, vol. 33, p. 73, 1943.

Table A.4 *F* distribution, upper 5% points

Degrees of freedom for numerator

Denom	1	2	3	4	5	6	7	8	9	10	12	15	20	24	30	40	60	120	∞
1	161	200	216	225	230	234	237	239	241	242	244	246	248	249	250	251	252	253	254
2	18.5	19.0	19.2	19.2	19.3	19.3	19.4	19.4	19.4	19.4	19.4	19.4	19.4	19.5	19.5	19.5	19.5	19.5	19.5
3	10.1	9.55	9.28	9.12	9.01	8.94	8.89	8.85	8.81	8.79	8.74	8.70	8.66	8.64	8.62	8.59	8.57	8.55	8.53
4	7.71	6.94	6.59	6.39	6.26	6.16	6.09	6.04	6.00	5.96	5.91	5.86	5.80	5.77	5.75	5.72	5.69	5.66	5.63
5	6.61	5.79	5.41	5.19	5.05	4.95	4.88	4.82	4.77	4.74	4.68	4.62	4.56	4.53	4.50	4.46	4.43	4.40	4.37
6	5.99	5.14	4.76	4.53	4.39	4.28	4.21	4.15	4.10	4.06	4.00	3.94	3.87	3.84	3.81	3.77	3.74	3.70	3.67
7	5.59	4.74	4.35	4.12	3.97	3.87	3.79	3.73	3.68	3.64	3.57	3.51	3.44	3.41	3.38	3.34	3.30	3.27	3.23
8	5.32	4.46	4.07	3.84	3.69	3.58	3.50	3.44	3.39	3.35	3.28	3.22	3.15	3.12	3.08	3.04	3.01	2.97	2.93
9	5.12	4.26	3.86	3.63	3.48	3.37	3.29	3.23	3.18	3.14	3.07	3.01	2.94	2.90	2.86	2.83	2.79	2.75	2.71
10	4.96	4.10	3.71	3.48	3.33	3.22	3.14	3.07	3.02	2.98	2.91	2.85	2.77	2.74	2.70	2.66	2.62	2.58	2.54
11	4.84	3.98	3.59	3.36	3.20	3.09	3.01	2.95	2.90	2.85	2.79	2.72	2.65	2.61	2.57	2.53	2.49	2.45	2.40
12	4.75	3.89	3.49	3.26	3.11	3.00	2.91	2.85	2.80	2.75	2.69	2.62	2.54	2.51	2.47	2.43	2.38	2.34	2.30
13	4.67	3.81	3.41	3.18	3.03	2.92	2.83	2.77	2.71	2.67	2.60	2.53	2.46	2.42	2.38	2.34	2.30	2.25	2.21
14	4.60	3.74	3.34	3.11	2.96	2.85	2.76	2.70	2.65	2.60	2.53	2.46	2.39	2.35	2.31	2.27	2.22	2.18	2.13
15	4.54	3.68	3.29	3.06	2.90	2.79	2.71	2.64	2.59	2.54	2.48	2.40	2.33	2.29	2.25	2.20	2.16	2.11	2.07
16	4.49	3.63	3.24	3.01	2.85	2.74	2.66	2.59	2.54	2.49	2.42	2.35	2.28	2.24	2.19	2.15	2.11	2.06	2.01
17	4.45	3.59	3.20	2.96	2.81	2.70	2.61	2.55	2.49	2.45	2.38	2.31	2.23	2.19	2.15	2.10	2.06	2.01	1.96
18	4.41	3.55	3.16	2.93	2.77	2.66	2.58	2.51	2.46	2.41	2.34	2.27	2.19	2.15	2.11	2.06	2.02	1.97	1.92
19	4.38	3.52	3.13	2.90	2.74	2.63	2.54	2.48	2.42	2.38	2.31	2.23	2.16	2.11	2.07	2.03	1.98	1.93	1.88
20	4.35	3.49	3.10	2.87	2.71	2.60	2.51	2.45	2.39	2.35	2.28	2.20	2.12	2.08	2.04	1.99	1.95	1.90	1.84
21	4.32	3.47	3.07	2.84	2.68	2.57	2.49	2.42	2.37	2.32	2.25	2.18	2.10	2.05	2.01	1.96	1.92	1.87	1.81
22	4.30	3.44	3.05	2.82	2.66	2.55	2.46	2.40	2.34	2.30	2.23	2.15	2.07	2.03	1.98	1.94	1.89	1.84	1.78
23	4.28	3.42	3.03	2.80	2.64	2.53	2.44	2.37	2.32	2.27	2.20	2.13	2.05	2.01	1.96	1.91	1.86	1.81	1.76
24	4.26	3.40	3.01	2.78	2.62	2.51	2.42	2.36	2.30	2.25	2.18	2.11	2.03	1.98	1.94	1.89	1.84	1.79	1.73
25	4.24	3.39	2.99	2.76	2.60	2.49	2.40	2.34	2.28	2.24	2.16	2.09	2.01	1.96	1.92	1.87	1.82	1.77	1.71
30	4.17	3.32	2.92	2.69	2.53	2.42	2.33	2.27	2.21	2.16	2.09	2.01	1.93	1.89	1.84	1.79	1.74	1.68	1.62
40	4.08	3.23	2.84	2.61	2.45	2.34	2.25	2.18	2.12	2.08	2.00	1.92	1.84	1.79	1.74	1.69	1.64	1.58	1.51
60	4.00	3.15	2.76	2.53	2.37	2.25	2.17	2.10	2.04	1.99	1.92	1.84	1.75	1.70	1.65	1.59	1.53	1.47	1.39
120	3.92	3.07	2.68	2.45	2.29	2.18	2.09	2.02	1.96	1.91	1.83	1.75	1.66	1.61	1.55	1.50	1.43	1.35	1.25
∞	3.84	3.00	2.60	2.37	2.21	2.10	2.01	1.94	1.88	1.83	1.75	1.67	1.57	1.52	1.46	1.39	1.32	1.22	1.00

Degrees of freedom for denominator

Interpolation should be performed using reciprocals of the degrees of freedom.

This table is reproduced with the permission of the Biometrika Trustees from M. Merrington, C.M. Thompson, "Tables of percentage points of the inverted beta (F) distribution," *Biometrika*, vol. 33, p. 73, 1943.

Table A.5 Durbin–Watson statistic (d)—significance points: 1%

n	$k' = 1$		$k' = 2$		$k' = 3$		$k' = 4$		$k' = 5$	
	d_L	d_U	d_L	d_U	d_L	d_U	d_L	d_U	d_L	d_U
15	0.81	1.07	0.70	1.25	0.59	1.46	0.49	1.70	0.39	1.96
16	0.84	1.09	0.74	1.25	0.63	1.44	0.53	1.66	0.44	1.90
17	0.87	1.10	0.77	1.25	0.67	1.43	0.57	1.63	0.48	1.85
18	0.90	1.12	0.80	1.26	0.71	1.42	0.61	1.60	0.52	1.80
19	0.93	1.13	0.83	1.26	0.74	1.41	0.65	1.58	0.56	1.77
20	0.95	1.15	0.86	1.27	0.77	1.41	0.68	1.57	0.60	1.74
21	0.97	1.16	0.89	1.27	0.80	1.41	0.72	1.55	0.63	1.71
22	1.00	1.17	0.91	1.28	0.83	1.40	0.75	1.54	0.66	1.69
23	1.02	1.19	0.94	1.29	0.86	1.40	0.77	1.53	0.70	1.67
24	1.04	1.20	0.96	1.30	0.88	1.41	0.80	1.53	0.72	1.66
25	1.05	1.21	0.98	1.30	0.90	1.41	0.83	1.52	0.75	1.65
26	1.07	1.22	1.00	1.31	0.93	1.41	0.85	1.52	0.78	1.64
27	1.09	1.23	1.02	1.32	0.95	1.41	0.88	1.51	0.81	1.63
28	1.10	1.24	1.04	1.32	0.97	1.41	0.90	1.51	0.83	1.62
29	1.12	1.25	1.05	1.33	0.99	1.42	0.92	1.51	0.85	1.61
30	1.13	1.26	1.07	1.34	1.01	1.42	0.94	1.51	0.88	1.61
31	1.15	1.27	1.08	1.34	1.02	1.42	0.96	1.51	0.90	1.60
32	1.16	1.28	1.10	1.35	1.04	1.43	0.98	1.51	0.92	1.60
33	1.17	1.29	1.11	1.36	1.05	1.43	1.00	1.51	0.94	1.59
34	1.18	1.30	1.13	1.36	1.07	1.43	1.01	1.51	0.95	1.59
35	1.19	1.31	1.14	1.37	1.08	1.44	1.03	1.51	0.97	1.59
36	1.21	1.32	1.15	1.38	1.10	1.44	1.04	1.51	0.99	1.59
37	1.22	1.32	1.16	1.38	1.11	1.45	1.06	1.51	1.00	1.59
38	1.23	1.33	1.18	1.39	1.12	1.45	1.07	1.52	1.02	1.58
39	1.24	1.34	1.19	1.39	1.14	1.45	1.09	1.52	1.03	1.58
40	1.25	1.34	1.20	1.40	1.15	1.46	1.10	1.52	1.05	1.58
45	1.29	1.38	1.24	1.42	1.20	1.48	1.16	1.53	1.11	1.58
50	1.32	1.40	1.28	1.45	1.24	1.49	1.20	1.54	1.16	1.59
55	1.36	1.43	1.32	1.47	1.28	1.51	1.25	1.55	1.21	1.59
60	1.38	1.45	1.35	1.48	1.32	1.52	1.28	1.56	1.25	1.60
65	1.41	1.47	1.38	1.50	1.35	1.53	1.31	1.57	1.28	1.61
70	1.43	1.49	1.40	1.52	1.37	1.55	1.34	1.58	1.31	1.61
75	1.45	1.50	1.42	1.53	1.39	1.56	1.37	1.59	1.34	1.62
80	1.47	1.52	1.44	1.54	1.42	1.57	1.39	1.60	1.36	1.62
85	1.48	1.53	1.46	1.55	1.43	1.58	1.41	1.60	1.39	1.63
90	1.50	1.54	1.47	1.56	1.45	1.59	1.43	1.61	1.41	1.64
95	1.51	1.55	1.49	1.57	1.47	1.60	1.45	1.62	1.42	1.64
100	1.52	1.56	1.50	1.58	1.48	1.60	1.46	1.63	1.44	1.65

n = number of observations.
k' = number of explanatory variables.
This Table is reproduced from *Biometrika*, vol. 41, p. 175, 1951, with the permission of the Trustees.

Table A.6 Durbin-Watson statistic (d)—significance points: 5%

n	$k' = 1$		$k' = 2$		$k' = 3$		$k' = 4$		$k' = 5$	
	d_L	d_U	d_L	d_U	d_L	d_U	d_L	d_U	d_L	d_U
15	1.08	1.36	0.95	1.54	0.82	1.75	0.69	1.97	0.56	2.21
16	1.10	1.37	0.98	1.54	0.86	1.73	0.74	1.93	0.62	2.15
17	1.13	1.38	1.02	1.54	0.90	1.71	0.78	1.90	0.67	2.10
18	1.16	1.39	1.05	1.53	0.93	1.69	0.82	1.87	0.71	2.06
19	1.18	1.40	1.08	1.53	0.97	1.68	0.86	1.85	0.75	2.02
20	1.20	1.41	1.10	1.54	1.00	1.68	0.90	1.83	0.79	1.99
21	1.22	1.42	1.13	1.54	1.03	1.67	0.93	1.81	0.83	1.96
22	1.24	1.43	1.15	1.54	1.05	1.66	0.96	1.80	0.86	1.94
23	1.26	1.44	1.17	1.54	1.08	1.66	0.99	1.79	0.90	1.92
24	1.27	1.45	1.19	1.55	1.10	1.66	1.01	1.78	0.93	1.90
25	1.29	1.45	1.21	1.55	1.12	1.66	1.04	1.77	0.95	1.89
26	1.30	1.46	1.22	1.55	1.14	1.65	1.06	1.76	0.98	1.88
27	1.32	1.47	1.24	1.56	1.16	1.65	1.08	1.76	1.01	1.86
28	1.33	1.48	1.26	1.56	1.18	1.65	1.10	1.75	1.03	1.85
29	1.34	1.48	1.27	1.56	1.20	1.65	1.12	1.74	1.05	1.84
30	1.35	1.49	1.28	1.57	1.21	1.65	1.14	1.74	1.07	1.83
31	1.36	1.50	1.30	1.57	1.23	1.65	1.16	1.74	1.09	1.83
32	1.37	1.50	1.31	1.57	1.24	1.65	1.18	1.73	1.11	1.82

n										
33	1.38	1.51	1.32	1.58	1.26	1.65	1.19	1.73	1.13	1.81
34	1.39	1.51	1.33	1.58	1.27	1.65	1.21	1.73	1.15	1.81
35	1.40	1.52	1.34	1.58	1.28	1.65	1.22	1.73	1.16	1.80
36	1.41	1.52	1.35	1.59	1.29	1.65	1.24	1.73	1.18	1.80
37	1.42	1.53	1.36	1.59	1.31	1.66	1.25	1.72	1.19	1.80
38	1.43	1.54	1.37	1.59	1.32	1.66	1.26	1.72	1.21	1.79
39	1.43	1.54	1.38	1.60	1.33	1.66	1.27	1.72	1.22	1.79
40	1.44	1.54	1.39	1.60	1.34	1.66	1.29	1.72	1.23	1.79
45	1.48	1.57	1.43	1.62	1.38	1.67	1.34	1.72	1.29	1.78
50	1.50	1.59	1.46	1.63	1.42	1.67	1.38	1.72	1.34	1.77
55	1.53	1.60	1.49	1.64	1.45	1.68	1.41	1.72	1.38	1.77
60	1.55	1.62	1.51	1.65	1.48	1.69	1.44	1.73	1.41	1.77
65	1.57	1.63	1.54	1.66	1.50	1.70	1.47	1.73	1.44	1.77
70	1.58	1.64	1.55	1.67	1.52	1.70	1.49	1.74	1.46	1.77
75	1.60	1.65	1.57	1.68	1.54	1.71	1.51	1.74	1.49	1.77
80	1.61	1.66	1.59	1.69	1.56	1.72	1.53	1.74	1.51	1.77
85	1.62	1.67	1.60	1.70	1.57	1.72	1.55	1.75	1.52	1.77
90	1.63	1.68	1.61	1.70	1.59	1.73	1.57	1.75	1.54	1.78
95	1.64	1.69	1.62	1.71	1.60	1.73	1.58	1.75	1.56	1.78
100	1.65	1.69	1.63	1.72	1.61	1.74	1.59	1.76	1.57	1.78

Source: This table is reproduced from *Biometrika*, vol. 41, p. 173, 1951, with the permission of the Trustees.

n = number of observations.

k' = number of explanatory variables.

Table A.7 Reliability factors and related precision adjustment factors

Reliability Factors (R)	0.7	0.8	0.9	1.0	1.1	1.2	1.3	1.4	1.6	2.0	2.3	3.0	4.6
Reliability Levels	50%	55%	59%	63%	66%	69%	72%	75%	80%	86%	90%	95%	99%
Rank of Errors[a]	Precision Adjustment Factors (p) For Reliability Levels Shown Above												
	For Errors of Overstatement[b]												
1	1.01	1.05	1.11	1.15	1.20	1.24	1.28	1.32	1.39	1.51	1.59	1.75	2.04
2	1.01	1.04	1.08	1.12	1.15	1.18	1.21	1.24	1.28	1.38	1.44	1.56	1.77
3	1.00	1.04	1.07	1.10	1.13	1.15	1.17	1.20	1.24	1.31	1.36	1.46	1.64
4	1.00	1.03	1.06	1.09	1.11	1.13	1.15	1.17	1.21	1.27	1.32	1.40	1.56
5	1.00	1.03	1.05	1.08	1.10	1.12	1.14	1.16	1.19	1.25	1.29	1.36	1.50
6	1.00	1.03	1.05	1.07	1.09	1.11	1.13	1.14	1.17	1.23	1.26	1.33	1.46
7	1.00	1.02	1.04	1.07	1.09	1.10	1.12	1.13	1.16	1.21	1.24	1.31	1.43
8	1.00	1.02	1.04	1.06	1.08	1.10	1.11	1.12	1.15	1.20	1.23	1.29	1.40
9	1.00	1.02	1.04	1.06	1.08	1.09	1.10	1.12	1.14	1.19	1.22	1.28	1.38
10	1.00	1.02	1.04	1.06	1.07	1.09	1.10	1.11	1.14	1.18	1.21	1.26	1.36
11	1.00	1.02	1.04	1.05	1.07	1.08	1.10	1.11	1.13	1.17	1.20	1.25	1.35
12	1.00	1.02	1.03	1.05	1.07	1.08	1.09	1.10	1.13	1.16	1.19	1.24	1.34
13	1.00	1.02	1.03	1.05	1.06	1.08	1.09	1.10	1.12	1.16	1.18	1.23	1.33
14	1.00	1.02	1.03	1.05	1.06	1.07	1.08	1.10	1.12	1.15	1.18	1.22	1.32
15–19	1.00	1.02	1.03	1.05	1.06	1.07	1.08	1.09	1.11	1.15	1.17	1.22	1.31
20–24	1.00	1.01	1.03	1.04	1.05	1.06	1.07	1.08	1.10	1.13	1.15	1.19	1.26
25–29	1.00	1.01	1.03	1.04	1.05	1.06	1.06	1.07	1.09	1.11	1.13	1.17	1.24
30–39	1.00	1.01	1.02	1.03	1.04	1.05	1.06	1.06	1.08	1.10	1.12	1.15	1.22
40–49	1.00	1.00	1.02	1.03	1.04	1.05	1.05	1.06	1.07	1.09	1.10	1.13	1.19

244

For Errors of Understatement[b] (Note 2)

[a]	.00	.05	.10	.14	.22	.28	.31	.35	.40	.45	.49	.58	.67
1	.00	.05	.10	.14	.22	.28	.31	.35	.40	.45	.49	.58	.67
2	.14	.30	.42	.49	.60	.66	.70	.74	.78	.82	.87	.92	.96
3	.29	.46	.57	.62	.71	.76	.78	.81	.84	.88	.91	.95	.99
4	.39	.54	.64	.69	.76	.80	.82	.85	.87	.90	.92	.95	.99
5	.45	.60	.68	.73	.79	.83	.85	.87	.89	.91	.93	.96	.99
6	.51	.64	.71	.75	.81	.84	.86	.88	.90	.92	.94	.96	.99
7	.54	.67	.74	.77	.83	.86	.87	.89	.91	.93	.95	.97	.99
8	.57	.69	.76	.79	.84	.87	.88	.90	.91	.93	.95	.97	.99
9	.60	.71	.77	.80	.85	.88	.89	.90	.92	.94	.95	.97	.99
10	.62	.73	.78	.81	.86	.88	.90	.91	.92	.94	.96	.97	.99
11	.64	.74	.79	.82	.86	.89	.90	.91	.93	.94	.96	.98	1.00
12	.65	.75	.80	.83	.87	.89	.90	.92	.93	.94	.96	.98	1.00
13	.66	.76	.81	.84	.87	.90	.91	.92	.93	.95	.96	.98	1.00
14	.67	.77	.82	.84	.88	.90	.91	.92	.94	.95	.96	.98	1.00
15–19	.68	.78	.83	.85	.88	.90	.91	.93	.94	.95	.96	.98	1.00
20–24	.73	.81	.85	.87	.90	.92	.93	.94	.95	.96	.96	.98	1.00
25–29	.76	.83	.87	.89	.91	.93	.93	.94	.95	.96	.97	.98	1.00
30–39	.78	.85	.88	.90	.92	.93	.94	.95	.96	.96	.97	.98	1.00
40–49	.80	.87	.90	.91	.93	.94	.95	.95	.96	.97	.98	.99	1.00

[a]This column refers to the rank of the estimated population errors (E_l). Errors of overstatement and of understatement should be ranked separately, and within each group the ranking should be from the largest to the smallest amount of error.
[b]The distinction between errors of overstatement and of understatement should be based on their effect on the recorded amount of the dependent variable.

B

STAR PROGRAM PRINTOUTS

B.1   Gamma Company Printout

This application is introduced in Chapter 2. The regression base statistics are discussed in Chapter 3. The audit interface calculations are explained in Chapter 5.

```
      Deloitte                              STAR              CAL 2502
   Haskins+Sells          Computer Applications Library     Release 2.1
-------------------------------------------------------------------------
```

STAR — Statistical Techniques for Analytical Review

REPORT PRINTED ON APRIL 24, 1985 AT 21:24

JOB   :GAMMA
CLIENT :GAMMA COMPANY
YEAR END :DECEMBER 31 1984

APPLICATION NUMBER # 1 (REVENUE) REPORT TYPE 4

REPORT REVIEWED BY :   DATE :


```
=========================================================================
```


SPECIFICATIONS FOR MODEL

NAME OF VARIABLE	SOURCE/DESCRIPTION OF VARIABLE	UNITS	BYPASS
Y REVENUE	C09	1000	NONE
X1 TIME AT STANDARD	M07 = (C01*C04+C02*C05+C03*C06)/1000	1000	NONE

NUMBER OF OBSERVATIONS :
USED TO GENERATE MODEL   36
USED FOR PROJECTIONS   12

   TOTAL   48
                                   ====
NO OBSERVATIONS HAVE BEEN BYPASSED

THE DATA PROFILE IS TIME SERIES

THERE ARE 12 PERIODS PER YEAR

STEPWISE MULTIPLE REGRESSION MODEL

| | INPUT DATA | | REGRESSION FUNCTION ETC. | |
DESCRIPTION	MEAN	STANDARD ERROR	CONSTANT OR COEFFICIENT	STANDARD ERROR
CONSTANT			13.7629	
INDEPENDENT VARIABLES				
X1 TIME AT STANDARD	1832.0000	246.1553	1.3582	0.1359
DEPENDENT VARIABLE				
Y REVENUE	2502.0000	387.0976		
Y' REGRESSION ESTIMATE			2502.0000	197.9585
COEFFICIENT OF :				
CORRELATION			0.8637	
REGRESSION IMPROVEMENT			0.4886	
RESIDUAL VARIATION			0.0791	

===

REGRESSION ESTIMATE [Y'(t)] OF REVENUE FOR OBSERVATION t :
Y'(t) = 13.7629 + 1.3582*X1(t)

VARIABLES USED

OBS#	Y	X1
1	2107	1574
2	1915	1503
3	1873	1645
4	1978	1380
5	2010	1580
6	1969	1576
7	2228	1752
8	2152	1549
9	2439	1652
10	2318	1650
11	2244	1496
12	2357	1671
13	2103	1679
14	2457	1782
15	2606	1652
16	2493	1756
17	2264	1555
18	2058	1621
19	2516	1982
20	2533	2050
21	2958	1959
22	2564	1836
23	2318	2006
24	2928	2164
25	2754	1780
26	2678	2054
27	3189	2265
28	3067	2117
29	2735	1955
30	3029	2059
31	2531	2059
32	2765	2096
33	3074	2201
34	2651	2016
35	3056	2197
36	3155	2083
	90072	65952

RESULTS BASED ON THE REGRESSION FUNCTION

```
          RECORDED   REGRESSION              RESIDUALS GRAPHED IN UNITS
OBS#       AMOUNT     ESTIMATE    RESIDUAL   OF 1 STD. ERROR ( 197.958)   OBS#

                                            -4 -3 -2 -1  0  1  2  3  4
                                            -I—I—I—I—I—I—I—I—I-
    1       2107        2152        -45 -I      I     *I       I     I-      1
    2       1915        2055       -140 -I      I   * I        I     I-      2
    3       1873        2248       -375 -I      *     I        I     I-      3
    4       1978        1888         90 -I      I        I*    I     I-      4
    5       2010        2160       -150 -I      I   *  I       I     I-      5
    6       1969        2154       -185 -I      I   *  I       I     I-      6
    7       2228        2393       -165 -I      I   *  I       I     I-      7
    8       2152        2118         34 -I      I        I*    I     I-      8
    9       2439        2258        181 -I      I        I  *  I     I-      9
   10       2318        2255         63 -I      I        I*    I     I-     10
   11       2244        2046        198 -I      I        I  *  I     I-     11
   12       2357        2283         74 -I      I        I*    I     I-     12
                                            -I—I—I—I—I—I—I—I—I-
   13       2103        2294       -191 -I      I   *  I       I     I-     13
   14       2457        2434         23 -I      I        *     I     I-     14
   15       2606        2258        348 -I      I        I     *I    I-     15
   16       2493        2399         94 -I      I        I*    I     I-     16
   17       2264        2126        138 -I      I        I *   I     I-     17
   18       2058        2215       -157 -I      I   *  I       I     I-     18
   19       2516        2706       -190 -I      I   *  I       I     I-     19
   20       2533        2798       -265 -I      I  *   I       I     I-     20
   21       2958        2674        284 -I      I        I  *  I     I-     21
   22       2564        2507         57 -I      I        I*    I     I-     22
   23       2318        2738       -420 -I      *     I        I     I-     23
   24       2928        2953        -25 -I      I        *     I     I-     24
                                            -I—I—I—I—I—I—I—I—I-
   25       2754        2431        323 -I      I        I     *I    I-     25
   26       2678        2804       -126 -I      I   *  I       I     I-     26
   27       3189        3090         99 -I      I        I*    I     I-     27
   28       3067        2889        178 -I      I        I  *  I     I-     28
   29       2735        2669         66 -I      I        I*    I     I-     29
   30       3029        2810        219 -I      I        I  *  I     I-     30
   31       2531        2810       -279 -I      I *      I     I     I-     31
   32       2765        2861        -96 -I      I     *I       I     I-     32
   33       3074        3003         71 -I      I        I*    I     I-     33
   34       2651        2752       -101 -I      I   *  I       I     I-     34
   35       3056        2998         58 -I      I        I*    I     I-     35
   36       3155        2843        312 -I      I        I     *I    I-     36
                                            -I—I—I—I—I—I—I—I—I-
   37       2757        2832        -75 -I      I     *I       I     I-     37
   38       2869        2708        161 -I      I        I  *  I     I-     38
   39       3168        3200        -32 -I      I        *     I     I-     39
   40       3210        3075        135 -I      I        I  *  I     I-     40
   41       2958        2956          2 -I      I        *     I     I-     41
   42       2698        2748        -50 -I      I     *I       I     I-     42
   43       3412        3396         16 -I      I        *     I     I-     43
   44       2872        2973       -101 -I      I   *  I       I     I-     44
   45       3263        3063        200 -I      I        I  *  I     I-     45
   46       3506        3430         76 -I      I        I*    I     I-     46
   47       3452        3259        193 -I      I        I  *  I     I-     47
   48       2993        3259       -266 -I      I  *   I       I     I-     48
                                            -I—I—I—I—I—I—I—I—I-
```

251

AUDIT OF PROJECTION DATA

MONETARY PRECISION = 600 (SAME UNITS AS DEPENDENT VARIABLE)
RELIABILITY FACTOR = 3
DIRECTION OF TEST IS UNDERSTATEMENT

---------------------------- REGRESSION PROJECTIONS ----------------------------

| | | | | | OPTIONAL SAMPLE DATA | | |
OBS NO	RECORDED AMOUNT	REGRESSION ESTIMATE	RESIDUAL	EXCESS TO BE INVESTIGATED	SELECTION INTERVAL	RANDOM START	MAXIMUM ITEMS
37	2757	2832	−75				
38	2869	2708	161				
39	3168	3200	−32				
40	3210	3075	135				
41	2958	2956	2				
42	2698	2748	−50				
43	3412	3396	16				
44	2872	2973	−101				
45	3263	3063	200				
46	3506	3430	76				
47	3452	3259	193				
48	2993	3259	−266	138	384	331	8
	37158	36899	259	138			8

===

VARIABLES USED

OBS#	Y	X1
37	2757	2075
38	2869	1984
39	3168	2346
40	3210	2254
41	2958	2166
42	2698	2013
43	3412	2490
44	2872	2179
45	3263	2245
46	3506	2515
47	3452	2389
48	2993	2389
	37158	27045

===

END OF REPORT ON APPLICATION 1

252

B.2   Universal Chemicals Printout

This application is used in Chapter 4 and again in Chapter 8 to explain the tests that the STAR Program applies to test for discontinuity in the base period.

```
       Deloitte                           STAR              CAL 2502
   Haskins+Sells          Computer Applications Library     Release 2.1
--------------------------------------------------------------------------


STAR — Statistical Techniques for Analytical Review

REPORT PRINTED ON APRIL 25, 1985 AT 18:18


JOB      :CHEM
CLIENT   :UNIVERSAL CHEMICALS
YEAR END :DECEMBER 31 1974


APPLICATION NUMBER # 1 (PRODUCTION COSTS) REPORT TYPE 4


REPORT REVIEWED BY :                        DATE :



=========================================================================


SPECIFICATIONS FOR MODEL

    NAME OF VARIABLE      SOURCE/DESCRIPTION OF VARIABLE      UNITS    BYPASS
    ----------------      -----------------------------      -----    ------
    Y    PRODUCTION COSTS CO4                                1000 NONE
    X1   QUANTITY PROD    CO1                                   1 NONE

NUMBER OF OBSERVATIONS :
USED TO GENERATE MODEL          36
USED FOR PROJECTIONS            12
                              ----
    TOTAL                       48
                              ====

NO OBSERVATIONS HAVE BEEN BYPASSED

THE DATA PROFILE IS TIME SERIES

THERE ARE 12  PERIODS PER YEAR
```

STEPWISE MULTIPLE REGRESSION MODEL

	INPUT DATA		REGRESSION FUNCTION ETC.	
DESCRIPTION	MEAN	STANDARD ERROR	CONSTANT OR COEFFICIENT	STANDARD ERROR
CONSTANT			−67.9933	
INDEPENDENT VARIABLES X1 QUANTITY PROD	645.3055	168.9909	0.9266	0.0657
DEPENDENT VARIABLE Y PRODUCTION COSTS	529.9167	169.4258		
Y′ REGRESSION ESTIMATE			529.9167	65.6605
COEFFICIENT OF : CORRELATION			0.9242	
REGRESSION IMPROVEMENT			0.6125	
RESIDUAL VARIATION			0.1239	

===

REGRESSION ESTIMATE [Y′(t)] OF PRODUCTION COSTS FOR OBSERVATION t :
Y′(t) = −67.9933 + .9266*X1(t)

VARIABLES USED

OBS#	Y	X1
1	312	388
2	320	392
3	320	422
4	363	494
5	512	721
6	334	470
7	390	567
8	185	263
9	528	683
10	395	483
11	380	499
12	375	496
13	568	739
14	448	604
15	613	787
16	452	644
17	540	734
18	531	653
19	621	815
20	363	467
21	515	698
22	605	825
23	546	717
24	629	805
25	414	581
26	528	614
27	1010	1152
28	699	733
29	831	916
30	638	673
31	675	707
32	710	750
33	711	692
34	723	742
35	660	679
36	633	626
	19077	23231

RESULTS BASED ON THE REGRESSION FUNCTION

OBS#	RECORDED AMOUNT	REGRESSION ESTIMATE	RESIDUAL	RESIDUALS GRAPHED IN UNITS OF 1 STD. ERROR (65.6605)	OBS#

```
                 RECORDED   REGRESSION            RESIDUALS GRAPHED IN UNITS
      OBS#       AMOUNT     ESTIMATE   RESIDUAL   OF 1 STD. ERROR ( 65.6605)   OBS#

                                                 -4 -3 -2 -1  0  1  2  3  4
                                                 -I—I—I—I—I—I—I—I—I-
       1          312        292          20 -I      I      I*    I      I-      1
       2          320        295          25 -I      I      I*    I      I-      2
       3          320        323          -3 -I      I      *     I      I-      3
       4          363        390         -27 -I      I    *I      I      I-      4
       5          512        600         -88 -I    I *     I      I      I-      5
       6          334        367         -33 -I      I   * I      I      I-      6
       7          390        457         -67 -I      I *   I      I      I-      7
       8          185        176           9 -I      I      *     I      I-      8
       9          528        565         -37 -I      I   * I      I      I-      9
      10          395        380          15 -I      I      I*    I      I-     10
      11          380        394         -14 -I      I    *I      I      I-     11
      12          375        392         -17 -I      I    *I      I      I-     12
                                                 -I—I—I—I—I—I—I—I—I-
      13          568        617         -49 -I      I  * I      I      I-     13
      14          448        492         -44 -I      I  * I      I      I-     14
      15          613        661         -48 -I      I  * I      I      I-     15
      16          452        529         -77 -I    I *     I      I      I-     16
      17          540        612         -72 -I      I *   I      I      I-     17
      18          531        537          -6 -I      I      *     I      I-     18
      19          621        687         -66 -I      I *   I      I      I-     19
      20          363        365          -2 -I      I      *     I      I-     20
      21          515        579         -64 -I      I *   I      I      I-     21
      22          605        696         -91 -I    I *     I      I      I-     22
      23          546        596         -50 -I      I  * I      I      I-     23
      24          629        678         -49 -I      I  * I      I      I-     24
                                                 -I—I—I—I—I—I—I—I—I-
      25          414        470         -56 -I      I  * I      I      I-     25
      26          528        501          27 -I      I      I*    I      I-     26
      27         1010        999          11 -I      I      *     I      I-     27
      28          699        611          88 -I      I      I  *  I      I-     28
      29          831        781          50 -I      I      I *   I      I-     29
      30          638        556          82 -I      I      I  *  I      I-     30
      31          675        587          88 -I      I      I  *  I      I-     31
      32          710        627          83 -I      I      I  *  I      I-     32
      33          711        573         138 -I      I      I      *       I-   33
      34          723        620         103 -I      I      I    *I      I-     34
      35          660        561          99 -I      I      I    *I      I-     35
      36          633        512         121 -I      I      I      *       I-   36
                                                 -I—I—I—I—I—I—I—I—I-
      37          820        672         148 -I      I      I      I*    I-     37
      38          591        481         110 -I      I      I    *I      I-     38
      39          601        484         117 -I      I      I    *I      I-     39
      40          371        291          80 -I      I      I    * I      I-    40
      41          688        527         161 -I      I      I      I*    I-     41
      42          551        413         138 -I      I      I      *       I-   42
      43          793        584         209 -I      I      I      I    * I-    43
      44          513        388         125 -I      I      I      *       I-   44
      45          587        421         166 -I      I      I      I *    I-    45
      46          387        266         121 -I      I      I      *       I-   46
      47          579        396         183 -I      I      I      I *    I-    47
      48          486        325         161 -I      I      I      I*    I-     48
                                                 -I—I—I—I—I—I—I—I—I-
```

THERE IS AN INDICATION OF DISCONTINUITY IN THE BASE PROFILE.
THIS MODEL SHOULD NOT BE USED FOR AUDIT PURPOSES.

END OF REPORT ON APPLICATION 1

B.3   Autocorp, Inc. Printout

This application is used in Chapter 4 and again in Chapter 8 to explain the tests that the STAR Program applies to test for autocorrelation of the residuals.

```
        Deloitte                                STAR              CAL 2502
    Haskins+Sells          Computer Applications Library       Release 2.1
-----------------------------------------------------------------------------
```

STAR — Statistical Techniques for Analytical Review

REPORT PRINTED ON APRIL 25, 1985 AT 18:21

JOB   :AUTOCORP
CLIENT   :AUTOCORP INC.
YEAR END :12/31/82

APPLICATION NUMBER # 1 (WAGES) REPORT TYPE 4

REPORT REVIEWED BY :   DATE :


```
=============================================================================
```

SPECIFICATIONS FOR MODEL

NAME OF VARIABLE	SOURCE/DESCRIPTION OF VARIABLE	UNITS	BYPASS
Y WAGES	C02	1	NONE
X1 HOURS	C01	1	NONE

NUMBER OF OBSERVATIONS :
USED TO GENERATE MODEL   36
USED FOR PROJECTIONS   3

    TOTAL   39
                               ====

NO OBSERVATIONS HAVE BEEN BYPASSED

THE DATA PROFILE IS TIME SERIES

THERE ARE 12 PERIODS PER YEAR

STEPWISE MULTIPLE REGRESSION MODEL

	INPUT DATA		REGRESSION FUNCTION ETC.	
DESCRIPTION	MEAN	STANDARD ERROR	CONSTANT OR COEFFICIENT	STANDARD ERROR
CONSTANT			−68.0822	
INDEPENDENT VARIABLES				
X1 HOURS	367.6667	35.0846	2.5554	0.2553
DEPENDENT VARIABLE				
Y WAGES	871.4445	103.7626		
Y' REGRESSION ESTIMATE			871.4445	53.0004
COEFFICIENT OF :				
CORRELATION			0.8640	
REGRESSION IMPROVEMENT			0.4892	
RESIDUAL VARIATION			0.0608	

==

REGRESSION ESTIMATE [Y'(t)] OF WAGES FOR OBSERVATION t :
Y'(t) = −68.0822 + 2.5554*X1(t)

VARIABLES USED

OBS#	Y	X1
1	649	287
2	660	303
3	766	355
4	747	347
5	804	356
6	686	299
7	709	312
8	745	319
9	904	370
10	968	384
11	824	342
12	806	328
13	928	373
14	884	346
15	881	362
16	901	396
17	986	411
18	863	346
19	987	393
20	989	377
21	945	389
22	980	401
23	885	363
24	942	390
25	986	406
26	887	370
27	989	401
28	1042	425
29	943	394
30	905	383
31	963	382
32	945	419
33	820	352
34	862	378
35	786	360
36	805	417
	31372	13236

RESULTS BASED ON THE REGRESSION FUNCTION

OBS#	RECORDED AMOUNT	REGRESSION ESTIMATE	RESIDUAL	RESIDUALS GRAPHED IN UNITS OF 1 STD. ERROR (53.0004)	OBS#

```
                                          -4 -3 -2 -1  0  1  2  3  4
                                          -I--I--I--I--I--I--I--I--I-
  1      649        665       -16  -I        I     *I        I       I-    1
  2      660        706       -46  -I        I  *   I        I       I-    2
  3      766        839       -73  -I        I *    I        I       I-    3
  4      747        819       -72  -I        I *    I        I       I-    4
  5      804        842       -38  -I        I   *  I        I       I-    5
  6      686        696       -10  -I        I     *I        I       I-    6
  7      709        729       -20  -I        I     *I        I       I-    7
  8      745        747        -2  -I        I      *        I       I-    8
  9      904        877        27  -I        I      I *      I       I-    9
 10      968        913        55  -I        I      I  *     I       I-   10
 11      824        806        18  -I        I      I*       I       I-   11
 12      806        770        36  -I        I      I *      I       I-   12
                                          -I--I--I--I--I--I--I--I--I-
 13      928        885        43  -I        I      I *      I       I-   13
 14      884        816        68  -I        I      I   *    I       I-   14
 15      881        857        24  -I        I      I*       I       I-   15
 16      901        944       -43  -I        I   *  I        I       I-   16
 17      986        982         4  -I        I      *        I       I-   17
 18      863        816        47  -I        I      I  *     I       I-   18
 19      987        936        51  -I        I      I  *     I       I-   19
 20      989        895        94  -I        I      I    *I          I-   20
 21      945        926        19  -I        I      I*       I       I-   21
 22      980        957        23  -I        I      I*       I       I-   22
 23      885        860        25  -I        I      I*       I       I-   23
 24      942        929        13  -I        I      I*       I       I-   24
                                          -I--I--I--I--I--I--I--I--I-
 25      986        969        17  -I        I      I*       I       I-   25
 26      887        877        10  -I        I      I*       I       I-   26
 27      989        957        32  -I        I      I *      I       I-   27
 28     1042       1018        24  -I        I      I*       I       I-   28
 29      943        939         4  -I        I      *        I       I-   29
 30      905        911        -6  -I        I      *        I       I-   30
 31      963        908        55  -I        I      I  *     I       I-   31
 32      945       1003       -58  -I        I  *   I        I       I-   32
 33      820        831       -11  -I        I     *I        I       I-   33
 34      862        898       -36  -I        I   *  I        I       I-   34
 35      786        852       -66  -I        I *    I        I       I-   35
 36      805        998      -193  -I*       I      I        I       I-   36
                                          -I--I--I--I--I--I--I--I--I-
 37      867       1061      -194  -I*       I      I        I       I-   37
 38      925       1164      -239  -*        I      I        I       I-   38
 39     1200       1304      -104  -I        *      I        I       I-   39
                                          -I--I--I--I--I--I--I--I--I-
```

THERE IS AN INDICATION OF DISCONTINUITY BETWEEN BASE AND PROJECTION PROFILES.

ABNORMALITY IN THE BASE IS INDICATED BY:
    LEFT SKEWNESS — THIS MAY BE CAUSED BY LARGE NEGATIVE RESIDUALS
    KURTOSIS
CORRECTION OF THE ABNORMALITY COULD IMPROVE THE RESULTS.
THERE IS AN INDICATION OF AUTOCORRELATION IN THE BASE PROFILE.
    GENERALIZED LEAST SQUARES REGRESSION WILL NOW BE USED.
    COEFFICIENT OF AUTOCORRELATION = .4756
THERE IS AN INDICATION OF AUTOCORRELATION IN THE BASE PROFILE.
    GENERALIZED LEAST SQUARES REGRESSION WILL NOW BE USED.
    COEFFICIENT OF AUTOCORRELATION = .6209

REGRESSION ESTIMATE [Y'(t)] OF WAGES FOR OBSERVATION t :
Y'(1) = 118.8505 + 2.0386*X1(1) + SQR(1-.6209^2)*e(1)
Y'(t) = 118.8505 + 2.0386*X1(t) + .6209*e(t-1), for t > 1
where
e(t) = Y(t) - (118.8505 + 2.0386*X1(t))
STANDARD ERROR   = 50.4997
COEFFICIENT OF RESIDUAL VARIATION = .0579

RESULTS BASED ON THE REGRESSION FUNCTION

OBS#	RECORDED AMOUNT	REGRESSION ESTIMATE	RESIDUAL	RESIDUALS GRAPHED IN UNITS OF 1 STD. ERROR (50.4997)	OBS#
				-4 -3 -2 -1 0 1 2 3 4	
				-I—I—I—I—I—I—I—I—I-	
1	649	661	-12	-I I *I I I-	1
2	660	702	-42	-I I * I I I-	2
3	766	795	-29	-I I * I I I-	3
4	747	779	-32	-I I * I I I-	4
5	804	795	9	-I I I* I I-	5
6	686	703	-17	-I I *I I I-	6
7	709	729	-20	-I I *I I I-	7
8	745	741	4	-I I * I I-	8
9	904	858	46	-I I I * I I-	9
10	968	921	47	-I I I * I I-	10
11	824	857	-33	-I I * I I I-	11
12	806	792	14	-I I I* I I-	12
				-I—I—I—I—I—I—I—I—I-	
13	928	891	37	-I I I * I I-	13
14	884	854	30	-I I I * I I-	14
15	881	894	-13	-I I *I I I-	15
16	901	941	-40	-I I * I I I-	16
17	986	941	45	-I I I * I I-	17
18	863	842	21	-I I I* I I-	18
19	987	944	43	-I I I * I I-	19
20	989	929	60	-I I I * I I-	20
21	945	975	-30	-I I * I I I-	21
22	980	957	23	-I I I* I I-	22
23	885	886	-1	-I I * I I-	23
24	942	930	12	-I I I* I I-	24
				-I—I—I—I—I—I—I—I—I-	
25	986	964	22	-I I I* I I-	25
26	887	898	-11	-I I *I I I-	26
27	989	945	44	-I I I * I I-	27
28	1042	1018	24	-I I I* I I-	28
29	943	957	-14	-I I *I I I-	29
30	905	913	-8	-I I * I I-	30
31	963	901	62	-I I I * I I-	31
32	945	1014	-69	-I I * I I I-	32
33	820	819	1	-I I * I I-	33
34	862	879	-17	-I I *I I I-	34
35	786	836	-50	-I I * I I I-	35
36	805	928	-123	-I *I I I I-	36
				-I—I—I—I—I—I—I—I—I-	
37	867	918	-51	-I I * I I I-	37
38	925	1007	-82	-I I* I I I-	38
39	1200	1104	96	-I I I * I-	39
				-I—I—I—I—I—I—I—I—I-	

AUDIT OF PROJECTION DATA

MONETARY PRECISION = 200 (SAME UNITS AS DEPENDENT VARIABLE)
RELIABILITY FACTOR = 1
DIRECTION OF TEST IS OVERSTATEMENT

————————————————— REGRESSION PROJECTIONS —————————————————

| | | | | | OPTIONAL SAMPLE DATA | | |
OBS NO	RECORDED AMOUNT	REGRESSION ESTIMATE	RESIDUAL	EXCESS TO BE INVESTIGATED	SELECTION INTERVAL	RANDOM START	MAXIMUM ITEMS
37	867	918	−51				
38	925	1007	−82				
39	1200	1104	96	16	416	166	3
	2992	3029	−37	16			3

VARIABLES USED

OBS#	Y	X1
37	867	442
38	925	482
39	1200	537
	2992	1461

END OF REPORT ON APPLICATION 1

B.4   Heteroco, Inc. Printout

This application is used in Chapter 4 and again in Chapter 8 to explain the tests that the STAR Program applies to test for heteroscedasticity of the residuals.

Deloitte Haskins+Sells	STAR Computer Applications Library	CAL 2502 Release 2.1

STAR — Statistical Techniques for Analytical Review

REPORT PRINTED ON APRIL 25, 1985 AT 18:27

```
JOB       :HETEROCO
CLIENT    :HETEROCO INC.
YEAR END :09/21/82
```

APPLICATION NUMBER # 1 (SALES) REPORT TYPE 4

REPORT REVIEWED BY :   DATE :

===

SPECIFICATIONS FOR MODEL

NAME OF VARIABLE		SOURCE/DESCRIPTION OF VARIABLE	UNITS	BYPASS
Y	SALES	C03	1	NONE
X1	RENT COST	C01	1000	NONE
X2	FLOOR AREA	C02	1	NONE

```
NUMBER OF OBSERVATIONS :
USED TO GENERATE MODEL          30
USED FOR PROJECTIONS             1
                               ___
    TOTAL                       31
                               ===
```

NO OBSERVATIONS HAVE BEEN BYPASSED

THE DATA PROFILE IS CROSS-SECTIONAL

STEPWISE MULTIPLE REGRESSION MODEL

	INPUT DATA		REGRESSION FUNCTION ETC.	
DESCRIPTION	MEAN	STANDARD ERROR	CONSTANT OR COEFFICIENT	STANDARD ERROR
CONSTANT			29.6635	
INDEPENDENT VARIABLES				
X1 RENT COST	370.0000	268.9019	2.9450	0.0306
X2 FLOOR AREA	1997.6670	84.0230	0.8393	0.0979
DEPENDENT VARIABLE				
Y SALES	2795.9331	794.4219		
Y' REGRESSION ESTIMATE			2795.9331	44.2681
COEFFICIENT OF :				
CORRELATION			0.9986	
REGRESSION IMPROVEMENT			0.9443	
RESIDUAL VARIATION			0.0158	

==

REGRESSION ESTIMATE [Y'(t)] OF SALES FOR OBSERVATION t :
Y'(t) = 29.6635 + 2.945*X1(t) + .8393*X2(t)

OBS#	VARIABLES USED Y	X1	X2
1	2787	347	2050
2	3095	437	2052
3	3184	517	1944
4	2084	139	1978
5	2287	189	2022
6	3228	551	1901
7	4842	1076	2058
8	2210	194	1912
9	2565	276	2081
10	2494	297	1912
11	2422	241	2030
12	3090	444	2077
13	2287	229	1899
14	2669	297	2151
15	3204	467	2123
16	2105	171	1886
17	2440	229	2096
18	3126	479	1970
19	4776	1002	1951
20	2030	100	2035
21	2070	138	1963
22	4949	1144	1945
23	2862	371	2087
24	2347	185	2082
25	2912	388	2030
26	2259	234	1875
27	2730	393	1822
28	2106	153	1944
29	2274	200	1967
30	2444	212	2087
	83878	11100	59930

RESULTS BASED ON THE REGRESSION FUNCTION

OBS#	RECORDED AMOUNT	REGRESSION ESTIMATE	RESIDUAL	RESIDUALS GRAPHED IN UNITS OF 1 STD. ERROR (44.2681)	OBS#
				-4 -3 -2 -1 0 1 2 3 4	
				-I—I—I—I—I—I—I—I—I-	
1	2787	2772	15	-I I I* I I-	1
2	3095	3039	56	-I I I * I I-	2
3	3184	3184	0	-I I * I I-	3
4	2084	2099	-15	-I I *I I I-	4
5	2287	2283	4	-I I * I I-	5
6	3228	3248	-20	-I I *I I I-	6
7	4842	4926	-84	-I * I I I-	7
8	2210	2206	4	-I I * I I-	8
9	2565	2589	-24	-I I * I I I-	9
10	2494	2509	-15	-I I *I I I-	10
11	2422	2443	-21	-I I *I I I-	11
12	3090	3080	10	-I I I* I I-	12
13	2287	2298	-11	-I I *I I I-	13
14	2669	2710	-41	-I I * I I I-	14
15	3204	3187	17	-I I I* I I-	15
16	2105	2116	-11	-I I *I I I-	16
17	2440	2463	-23	-I I * I I I-	17
18	3126	3094	32	-I I I * I I-	18
19	4776	4618	158	-I I I I *I-	19
20	2030	2032	-2	-I I * I I-	20
21	2070	2084	-14	-I I *I I I-	21
22	4949	5031	-82	-I * I I I-	22
23	2862	2874	-12	-I I *I I I-	23
24	2347	2322	25	-I I I * I I-	24
25	2912	2876	36	-I I I * I I-	25
26	2259	2292	-33	-I I * I I I-	26
27	2730	2716	14	-I I I* I I-	27
28	2106	2112	-6	-I I * I I-	28
29	2274	2270	4	-I I * I I-	29
30	2444	2406	38	-I I I * I I-	30
				-I—I—I—I—I—I—I—I—I-	
31	2200	2592	-392	-* I I I I-	31
				-I—I—I—I—I—I—I—I—I-	

===

THERE IS AN INDICATION OF DISCONTINUITY BETWEEN BASE AND PROJECTION PROFILES.

ABNORMALITY IN THE BASE IS INDICATED BY:
   RIGHT SKEWNESS — THIS MAY BE CAUSED BY LARGE POSITIVE RESIDUALS
   KURTOSIS
CORRECTION OF THE ABNORMALITY COULD IMPROVE THE RESULTS.
THERE IS AN INDICATION OF HETEROSCEDASTICITY IN THE BASE PROFILE.
   THE RESIDUALS ARE SIGNIFICANTLY CORRELATED WITH X1, RENT COST
   WEIGHTED LEAST SQUARES REGRESSION WILL NOW BE USED.

REGRESSION ESTIMATE [Y'(t)] OF SALES FOR OBSERVATION t :
Y'(t) = -97.3944 + 2.9701*X1(t) + .8987*X2(t)
STANDARD ERROR (t)   = .0863*X1(t)
COEFFICIENT OF RESIDUAL VARIATION = .0114

RESULTS BASED ON THE REGRESSION FUNCTION

OBS#	RECORDED AMOUNT	REGRESSION ESTIMATE	RESIDUAL	RESIDUALS GRAPHED IN UNITS OF 1 STD. ERROR (VARIABLE)	OBS#
				-4 -3 -2 -1 0 1 2 3 4	
				-I—I—I—I—I—I—I—I—I-	
1	2787	2775	12	-I I I* I I-	1
2	3095	3045	50	-I I I * I I-	2
3	3184	3185	-1	-I I * I I-	3
4	2084	2093	-9	-I I * I I I-	4
5	2287	2281	6	-I I I* I I-	5
6	3228	3247	-19	-I I *I I I-	6
7	4842	4948	-106	-I I * I I I-	7
8	2210	2197	13	-I I I * I I-	8
9	2565	2592	-27	-I I * I I I-	9
10	2494	2503	-9	-I I *I I I-	10
11	2422	2443	-21	-I I * I I I-	11
12	3090	3088	2	-I I * I I-	12
13	2287	2289	-2	-I I * I I-	13
14	2669	2718	-49	-I * I I I-	14
15	3204	3198	6	-I I * I I-	15
16	2105	2105	-0	-I I * I I-	16
17	2440	2466	-26	-I I * I I I-	17
18	3126	3096	30	-I I I * I I-	18
19	4776	4632	144	-I I I *I I-	19
20	2030	2028	2	-I I I* I I-	20
21	2070	2077	-7	-I I * I I I-	21
22	4949	5048	-99	-I I * I I I-	22
23	2862	2880	-18	-I I * I I I-	23
24	2347	2323	24	-I I I * I I-	24
25	2912	2879	33	-I I I * I I-	25
26	2259	2283	-24	-I I * I I I-	26
27	2730	2707	23	-I I I * I I-	27
28	2106	2104	2	-I I * I I-	28
29	2274	2264	10	-I I I * I I-	29
30	2444	2408	36	-I I I * I-	30
				-I—I—I—I—I—I—I—I—I-	
31	2200	2591	-391	-* I I I I-	31
				-I—I—I—I—I—I—I—I—I-	

AUDIT OF PROJECTION DATA

MONETARY PRECISION = 1000 (SAME UNITS AS DEPENDENT VARIABLE)
RELIABILITY FACTOR = 1
DIRECTION OF TEST IS UNDERSTATEMENT

---------------------- REGRESSION PROJECTIONS ----------------------

				OPTIONAL SAMPLE DATA		
OBS	RECORDED	REGRESSION		EXCESS TO BE	SELECTION	RANDOM	MAXIMUM
NO	AMOUNT	ESTIMATE	RESIDUAL	INVESTIGATED	INTERVAL	START	ITEMS
31	2200	2591	−391	316	999	251	3
	2200	2591	−391	316			3

VARIABLES USED

OBS#	Y	X1	X2
31	2200	300	2000
	2200	300	2000

END OF REPORT ON APPLICATION 1

B.5   Paranormal Productions Printout

This application is used in Chapter 4 and again in Chapter 8 to explain the tests that the STAR Program applies to test for abnormality of the residuals.

Deloitte	STAR	CAL 2502
Haskins+Sells	Computer Applications Library	Release 2.1

STAR — Statistical Techniques for Analytical Review

REPORT PRINTED ON APRIL 25, 1985 AT 18:29

JOB   : PARA
CLIENT   : PARANORMAL PRODUCTIONS
YEAR END : DECEMBER 31 1984

APPLICATION NUMBER # 1 (PRODUCTION) REPORT TYPE 4

REPORT REVIEWED BY :   DATE :

==

SPECIFICATIONS FOR MODEL

NAME OF VARIABLE		SOURCE/DESCRIPTION OF VARIABLE	UNITS	BYPASS
Y	PRODUCTION	CO_2	1	NONE
X1	HOURS	CO_1	1	NONE

NUMBER OF OBSERVATIONS :
USED TO GENERATE MODEL   40
                                ———
   TOTAL   40
                                ====

NO OBSERVATIONS HAVE BEEN BYPASSED

THE DATA PROFILE IS CROSS-SECTIONAL

STEPWISE MULTIPLE REGRESSION MODEL

DESCRIPTION	INPUT DATA		REGRESSION FUNCTION ETC.	
	MEAN	STANDARD ERROR	CONSTANT OR COEFFICIENT	STANDARD ERROR
CONSTANT			−0.0131	
INDEPENDENT VARIABLES X1 HOURS	69.0250	20.9058	0.7662	0.0354
DEPENDENT VARIABLE Y PRODUCTION Y′ REGRESSION ESTIMATE	52.8750	16.6552	52.8750	4.6212
COEFFICIENT OF : CORRELATION REGRESSION IMPROVEMENT RESIDUAL VARIATION			0.9618 0.7225 0.0874	

REGRESSION ESTIMATE [Y′(t)] OF PRODUCTION FOR OBSERVATION t :
Y′(t) = −.0131 + .7662*X1(t)

VARIABLES USED

OBS#	Y	X1
1	31	39
2	32	39
3	32	42
4	36	49
5	41	72
6	33	47
7	39	57
8	19	26
9	53	68
10	40	48
11	38	50
12	38	50
13	56	74
14	45	60
15	62	79
16	45	64
17	55	73
18	53	65
19	61	82
20	37	47
21	52	70
22	51	83
23	55	72
24	62	81
25	41	58
26	53	61
27	100	134
28	70	85
29	82	106
30	65	79
31	67	86
32	61	92
33	71	84
34	72	91
35	66	83
36	62	76
37	82	97
38	60	72
39	60	73
40	37	47
	2115	2761

RESULTS BASED ON THE REGRESSION FUNCTION

```
            RECORDED    REGRESSION                 RESIDUALS GRAPHED IN UNITS
   OBS#      AMOUNT      ESTIMATE    RESIDUAL      OF 1 STD. ERROR ( 4.62120)    OBS#
   ----     --------    ----------   --------      ---------------------------   ----
                                                  -4 -3 -2 -1  0  1  2  3  4
                                                  -I—I—I—I—I—I—I—I—I-
    1          31          30           1       -I     I      I*    I      I-      1
    2          32          30           2       -I     I      I*    I      I-      2
    3          32          32          -0       -I     I      *     I      I-      3
    4          36          38          -2       -I     I     *I     I      I-      4
    5          41          55         -14       -I  *  I      I     I      I-      5
    6          33          36          -3       -I     I   *  I     I      I-      6
    7          39          44          -5       -I     I   *  I     I      I-      7
    8          19          20          -1       -I     I     *I     I      I-      8
    9          53          52           1       -I     I      I*    I      I-      9
   10          40          37           3       -I     I      I *   I      I-     10
   11          38          38          -0       -I     I      *     I      I-     11
   12          38          38          -0       -I     I      *     I      I-     12
   13          56          57          -1       -I     I      *     I      I-     13
   14          45          46          -1       -I     I     *I     I      I-     14
   15          62          61           1       -I     I      I*    I      I-     15
   16          45          49          -4       -I     I   *  I     I      I-     16
   17          55          56          -1       -I     I     *I     I      I-     17
   18          53          50           3       -I     I      I *   I      I-     18
   19          61          63          -2       -I     I     *I     I      I-     19
   20          37          36           1       -I     I      I*    I      I-     20
   21          52          54          -2       -I     I     *I     I      I-     21
   22          51          64         -13       -I  *  I      I     I      I-     22
   23          55          55          -0       -I     I      *     I      I-     23
   24          62          62          -0       -I     I      *     I      I-     24
   25          41          44          -3       -I     I   *  I     I      I-     25
   26          53          47           6       -I     I      I  *  I      I-     26
   27         100         103          -3       -I     I   *  I     I      I-     27
   28          70          65           5       -I     I      I  *  I      I-     28
   29          82          81           1       -I     I      I*    I .    I-     29
   30          65          61           4       -I     I      I  *  I      I-     30
   31          67          66           1       -I     I      I*    I.     I-     31
   32          61          70          -9       -I     *      I     I      I-     32
   33          71          64           7       -I     I      I  *  I      I-     33
   34          72          70           2       -I     I      I*    I      I-     34
   35          66          64           2       -I     I      I *   I      I-     35
   36          62          58           4       -I     I      I *   I      I-     36
   37          82          74           8       -I     I      I    *I      I-     37
   38          60          55           5       -I     I      I  *  I      I-     38
   39          60          56           4       -I     I      I  *  I      I-     39
   40          37          36           1       -I     I      I*    I      I-     40
                                                  -I—I—I—I—I—I—I—I—I-
```

==

ABNORMALITY IN THE BASE IS INDICATED BY:
    LEFT SKEWNESS — THIS MAY BE CAUSED BY LARGE NEGATIVE RESIDUALS
    KURTOSIS
CORRECTION OF THE ABNORMALITY COULD IMPROVE THE RESULTS.

END OF REPORT ON APPLICATION 1

B.6 ABC Trading Company Printout

This application illustrates how the STAR Program can be applied in an Ending Balance Projection. The application is not specifically dealt with in the text, although a general reference to ending balance projection is contained in Section 6.3.1.

In this application COLLECTIONS was regressed against SALES, and SALES lagged by various periods in order to develop a model that could be used to estimate collections in the period between the date at which receivables were confirmed and the balance sheet date. The estimated collections were then used to project the ending balance of accounts receivable. Notice that the audit interface calculations are related to the ending balance.

```
        Deloitte                              STAR                CAL 2502
    Haskins+Sells            Computer Applications Library        Release 2.1
--------------------------------------------------------------------------------
```

STAR -- Statistical Techniques for Analytical Review

REPORT PRINTED ON APRIL 25, 1985 AT 18:38

JOB   :ABC
CLIENT   :ABC COMPANY
YEAR END :DECEMBER 31 1983

APPLICATION NUMBER # 1 (COLLECTIONS) REPORT TYPE 4

REPORT REVIEWED BY :   DATE :


```
================================================================================
```


SPECIFICATIONS FOR MODEL

NAME OF VARIABLE	SOURCE/DESCRIPTION OF VARIABLE	UNITS	BYPASS	
Y COLLECTIONS	C01	1000	NONE	
X1 SALES	C02	1000	NONE	
X2 SALES −1	L03 = C02(SALES) LAGGED 1	1000	THRU	1
X3 SALES −2	L04 = C02(SALES) LAGGED 2	1000	THRU	2
X4 SALES −3	L05 = C02(SALES) LAGGED 3	1000	THRU	3
X5 SALES −4	L06 = C02(SALES) LAGGED 4	1000	THRU	4

NUMBER OF OBSERVATIONS :
BYPASSED AT BEGINNING (ALL VARIABLES)   4
USED TO GENERATE MODEL   42
USED FOR PROJECTIONS   2

   TOTAL   48
                                        ====
THE MAXIMUM BYPASS HAS BEEN APPLIED TO ALL VARIABLES

THE DATA PROFILE IS TIME SERIES

THERE ARE 12 PERIODS PER YEAR

STEPWISE MULTIPLE REGRESSION MODEL

	INPUT DATA		REGRESSION FUNCTION ETC.	
DESCRIPTION	MEAN	STANDARD ERROR	CONSTANT OR COEFFICIENT	STANDARD ERROR
CONSTANT			7.9310	
INDEPENDENT VARIABLES				
X2 SALES −1	196.6905	37.2431	0.3010	0.0625
X3 SALES −2	194.1190	37.2009	0.2244	0.0603
X4 SALES −3	191.4048	36.8829	0.2447	0.0605
X5 SALES −4	188.7381	36.4411	0.1908	0.0632
DEPENDENT VARIABLE				
Y COLLECTIONS	193.5238	31.7585		
Y′ REGRESSION ESTIMATE			193.5238	9.9656
COEFFICIENT OF :				
CORRELATION			0.9545	
REGRESSION IMPROVEMENT			0.6862	
RESIDUAL VARIATION			0.0515	

REGRESSION ESTIMATE [Y′(t)] OF COLLECTIONS FOR OBSERVATION t :
Y′(t) = 7.931 + .301*X2(t) + .2244*X3(t) + .2447*X4(t) + .1908*X5(t)

VARIABLES USED

OBS#	Y	X2	X3	X4	X5
5	141	136	142	140	140
6	152	172	136	142	140
7	164	161	172	136	142
8	157	172	161	172	136
9	166	147	172	161	172
10	153	144	147	172	161
11	133	116	144	147	172
12	147	178	116	144	147
13	165	184	178	116	144
14	168	150	184	178	116
15	174	211	150	184	178
16	168	185	211	150	184
17	171	149	185	211	150
18	173	179	149	185	211
19	177	171	179	149	185
20	195	193	171	179	149
21	202	202	193	171	179
22	188	201	202	193	171
23	186	169	201	202	193
24	209	196	169	201	202
25	187	161	196	169	201
26	177	161	161	196	169
27	192	257	161	161	196
28	193	187	257	161	161
29	184	193	187	257	161
30	203	182	193	187	257
31	182	202	182	193	187
32	204	248	202	182	193
33	200	197	248	202	182
34	225	214	197	248	202
35	223	215	214	197	248
36	213	234	215	214	197
37	230	213	234	215	214
38	219	234	213	234	215
39	227	221	234	213	234
40	240	258	221	234	213
41	220	221	258	221	234
42	262	239	221	258	221
43	235	252	239	221	258
44	230	252	252	239	221
45	247	254	252	252	239
46	246	250	254	252	252
	8128	8261	8153	8039	7927

RESULTS BASED ON THE REGRESSION FUNCTION

OBS#	RECORDED AMOUNT	REGRESSION ESTIMATE	RESIDUAL	RESIDUALS GRAPHED IN UNITS OF 1 STD. ERROR (9.96560)	OBS#
				-4 -3 -2 -1 0 1 2 3 4	
				-I—I—I—I—I—I—I—I—I-	
5	141	142	-1	-I I * I I-	5
6	152	152	0	-I I * I I-	6
7	164	155	9	-I I I * I I-	7
8	157	164	-7	-I I * I I I-	8
9	166	163	3	-I I I* I I-	9
10	153	157	-4	-I I *I I I-	10
11	133	144	-11	-I I * I I I-	11
12	147	151	-4	-I I *I I I-	12
				-I—I—I—I—I—I—I—I—I-	
13	165	159	6	-I I I * I I-	13
14	168	160	8	-I I I * I I-	14
15	174	184	-10	-I I * I I I-	15
16	168	183	-15	-I I * I I I-	16
17	171	175	-4	-I I *I I I-	17
18	173	181	-8	-I I * I I I-	18
19	177	171	6	-I I I * I I-	19
20	195	177	18	-I I I * I-	20
21	202	188	14	-I I I * I I-	21
22	188	194	-6	-I I * I I I-	22
23	186	190	-4	-I I *I I I-	23
24	209	193	16	-I I I *I I-	24
				-I—I—I—I—I—I—I—I—I-	
25	187	180	7	-I I I * I I-	25
26	177	173	4	-I I I* I I-	26
27	192	198	-6	-I I * I I I-	27
28	193	192	1	-I I * I I-	28
29	184	202	-18	-I I* I I I-	29
30	203	201	2	-I I I* I I-	30
31	182	192	-10	-I I * I I I-	31
32	204	209	-5	-I I * I I I-	32
33	200	207	-7	-I I * I I I-	33
34	225	216	9	-I I I * I I-	34
35	223	216	7	-I I I * I I-	35
36	213	217	-4	-I I *I I I-	36
				-I—I—I—I—I—I—I—I—I-	
37	230	218	12	-I I I * I I-	37
38	219	224	-5	-I I * I I I-	38
39	227	224	3	-I I I* I I-	39
40	240	233	7	-I I I * I I-	40
41	220	231	-11	-I I * I I I-	41
42	262	235	27	-I I I I * I-	42
43	235	241	-6	-I I * I I I-	43
44	230	241	-11	-I I * I I I-	44
45	247	248	-1	-I I * I I-	45
46	246	250	-4	-I I *I I I-	46
				-I—I—I—I—I—I—I—I—I-	
47	249	254	-5	-I I * I I I-	47
48	240	256	-16	-I I* I I I-	48
				-I—I—I—I—I—I—I—I—I-	

ENDING BALANCE PROJECTION

MONETARY PRECISION = 25 (SAME UNITS AS DEPENDENT VARIABLE)
RELIABILITY FACTOR = 1
DEPENDENT VARIABLE IS TESTED FOR UNDERSTATEMENT
 DEPENDENT VARIABLE IS CREDIT COMPONENT
 RECORDED RECEIVABLES   300 (ASSET)
 ESTIMATED RECEIVABLES   279
                                                       ─────────
 RESIDUAL   21
                                                       ═════════

 EXCESS TO BE INVESTIGATED   4

OPTIONAL SAMPLE DATA :
 SELECTION INTERVAL   77
 RANDOM START   55
 MAXIMUM SAMPLE SIZE   4

==

VARIABLES USED
OBS#   Y   X2   X3   X4   X5
─────   ───────   ───────   ───────   ───────   ───────
  47   249   265   250   254   252
  48   240   263   265   250   254
        ───────   ───────   ───────   ───────   ───────
          489   528   515   504   506
        ═══════   ═══════   ═══════   ═══════   ═══════

==

END OF REPORT ON APPLICATION 1

B.7 Gamma Company Mathematical Printout

One of the reports that the STAR Program can produce is one that details all the mathematical calculations performed by the Program. The printout shown here is a detailed mathematical printout for the Gamma Company application that is used in Chapter 9 to explain stepwise multiple regression.

```
       Deloitte                              STAR              CAL 2502
    Haskins+Sells        Computer Applications Library       Release 2.1
----------------------------------------------------------------------------


STAR — Statistical Techniques for Analytical Review

REPORT PRINTED ON APRIL 25, 1985 AT 18:34


JOB      :GAMMA
CLIENT   :GAMMA COMPANY
YEAR END :DECEMBER 31 1984

APPLICATION NUMBER # 2 (REVENUE) REPORT TYPE 8


REPORT REVIEWED BY :                        DATE :



================================================================================


SPECIFICATIONS FOR MODEL

    NAME OF VARIABLE        SOURCE/DESCRIPTION OF VARIABLE      UNITS   BYPASS
    --------------------    -----------------------------      -----  -------
    Y    REVENUE           C09                                 1000   NONE
    X1   TIME AT STANDARD  M07 = (C01*C04+C02*C05+C03*C06)/1000 1000   NONE
    X2   EXPENSES          C08                                 1000   NONE
    X3   COST OF SERVICES  C10                                 1000   NONE

NUMBER OF OBSERVATIONS :
USED TO GENERATE MODEL            36
USED FOR PROJECTIONS              12
                                 ----
    TOTAL                         48
                                 ====
NO OBSERVATIONS HAVE BEEN BYPASSED

THE DATA PROFILE IS TIME SERIES

THERE ARE 12  PERIODS PER YEAR
```

**** COMPUTING OLS FUNCTION ****

MATRIX OF CORRECTED SQUARES AND CROSS-PRODUCTS OBSERVATIONS 1 THRU 36

	Y	X1	X2	X3
Y	5.244560E+06	2.880400E+06	1.411464E+06	2.913424E+06
X1	2.880400E+06	2.120736E+06	7.304080E+05	1.836520E+06
X2	1.411464E+06	7.304080E+05	5.604640E+05	9.290800E+05
X3	2.913424E+06	1.836520E+06	9.290800E+05	2.141408E+06

MATRIX OF COEFFICIENTS OF CORRELATION OBSERVATIONS 1 THRU 36

	Y	X1	X2	X3
Y	1.000000E+00	8.636843E-01	8.232684E-01	8.693596E-01
X1	8.636843E-01	1.000000E+00	6.699593E-01	8.617923E-01
X2	8.232684E-01	6.699593E-01	1.000000E+00	8.480657E-01
X3	8.693596E-01	8.617923E-01	8.480657E-01	1.000000E+00

STEP NUMBER 1   OBSERVATIONS 1 THRU 36

MOST SIGNIFICANT NEW VARIABLE / LEAST SIGNIFICANT OLD VARIABLE

MOST SIGNIFICANT NEW VARIABLE = X3 COST OF SERVICES :VMAX = .7557861

TEST FOR ADMISSION OF X3
F-VALUE (1 , 34) = 105.2222
SIGNIFICANCE LEVEL = .999999   ;   CRITICAL LEVEL = .95
X3 COST OF SERVICES ADMITTED. TARGET SIGNIFICANCE BECOMES .9500009

MATRIX AFTER TRANSFORMATION USING (X3,X3) AS PIVOTAL ELEMENT

	Y	X1	X2	X3
Y	2.442139E-01	1.144769E-01	8.599424E-02	-8.693596E-01
X1	1.144769E-01	2.573140E-01	-6.089729E-02	-8.617923E-01
X2	8.599424E-02	-6.089729E-02	2.807845E-01	-8.480657E-01
X3	8.693596E-01	8.617923E-01	8.480657E-01	1.000000E+00

STEP NUMBER 2   OBSERVATIONS 1 THRU 36

VARIABLES IN FOLLOWING STEP 2

VARIABLE	COEFFICIENT	STANDARD ERROR
X3 COST OF SERVICES	1.360518E+00	1.326327E-01
CONSTANT	3.266016E+01	
ERROR SUM OF SQUARES	1.280794E+06	
STANDARD ERROR	1.940887E+02	

DEGREES OF FREEDOM = 34

MOST SIGNIFICANT NEW VARIABLE / LEAST SIGNIFICANT OLD VARIABLE

MOST SIGNIFICANT NEW VARIABLE = X1 TIME AT STANDARD :VMAX = 5.092981E-02

LEAST SIGNIFICANT OLD VARIABLE = X3 COST OF SERVICES :VMIN =-.7557861

TEST FOR ADMISSION OF X1
F-VALUE (1 , 33) = 8.695407
SIGNIFICANCE LEVEL = .9942205   ;   CRITICAL LEVEL = .9500009
X1 TIME AT STANDARD ADMITTED. TARGET SIGNIFICANCE BECOMES .9555234

MATRIX AFTER TRANSFORMATION USING (X1,X1) AS PIVOTAL ELEMENT

```
            Y            X1            X2            X3
Y     1.932841E-01 -4.448918E-01  1.130869E-01 -4.859553E-01
X1    4.448918E-01  3.886303E+00 -2.366653E-01 -3.349186E+00
X2    1.130869E-01  2.366653E-01  2.663722E-01 -1.052022E+00
X3    4.859553E-01 -3.349186E+00  1.052022E+00  3.886303E+00
```


STEP NUMBER 3   OBSERVATIONS 1 THRU 36

VARIABLES IN FOLLOWING STEP 3
VARIABLE   COEFFICIENT   STANDARD ERROR
X1 TIME AT STANDARD   6.996254E-01 2.372579E-01
X3 COST OF SERVICES   7.605034E-01 2.361099E-01
    CONSTANT   -1.600272E+02
    ERROR SUM OF SQUARES   1.013690E+06
    STANDARD ERROR   1.752652E+02
DEGREES OF FREEDOM = 33

MOST SIGNIFICANT NEW VARIABLE / LEAST SIGNIFICANT OLD VARIABLE

MOST SIGNIFICANT NEW VARIABLE = X2 EXPENSES :VMAX = 4.801048E-02

LEAST SIGNIFICANT OLD VARIABLE = X1 TIME AT STANDARD :VMIN =-5.092981E-02

TEST FOR RETENTION OF X1
F-VALUE (1 , 33) = 8.695408
SIGNIFICANCE LEVEL = .9942205   ;   CRITICAL LEVEL = .95
X1 TIME AT STANDARD RETAINED.

TEST FOR ADMISSION OF X2
F-VALUE (1 , 32) = 10.57546
SIGNIFICANCE LEVEL = .9972123   ;   CRITICAL LEVEL = .9555234
X2 EXPENSES ADMITTED. TARGET SIGNIFICANCE BECOMES .9581946

MATRIX AFTER TRANSFORMATION USING (X2,X2) AS PIVOTAL ELEMENT

	Y	X1	X2	X3
Y	1.452736E-01	-5.453668E-01	-4.245448E-01	-3.932479E-02
X1	5.453668E-01	4.096574E+00	8.884760E-01	-4.283882E+00
X2	4.245448E-01	8.884760E-01	3.754145E+00	-3.949444E+00
X3	3.932476E-02	-4.283882E+00	-3.949444E+00	8.041205E+00

STEP NUMBER 4 OBSERVATIONS 1 THRU 36

VARIABLES IN FOLLOWING STEP 4

VARIABLE		COEFFICIENT	STANDARD ERROR
X1	TIME AT STANDARD	8.576298E-01	2.144569E-01
X2	EXPENSES	1.298686E+00	3.993508E-01
X3	COST OF SERVICES	6.154190E-02	2.990086E-01
	CONSTANT	-3.639794E+02	
	ERROR SUM OF SQUARES	7.618960E+05	
	STANDARD ERROR	1.543025E+02	

DEGREES OF FREEDOM = 32

MOST SIGNIFICANT NEW VARIABLE / LEAST SIGNIFICANT OLD VARIABLE

LEAST SIGNIFICANT OLD VARIABLE = X3 COST OF SERVICES :VMIN =-1.923142E-04

TEST FOR RETENTION OF X3
F-VALUE (1 , 32) = 4.236183E-02
SIGNIFICANCE LEVEL = .1804 ; CRITICAL LEVEL = .95
X3 COST OF SERVICES ELIMINATED.
SIGNIFICANCE ON ADMISSION .999999 ; TARGET SIGNIFICANCE BECOMES .9581936

MATRIX AFTER TRANSFORMATION USING (X3,X3) AS PIVOTAL ELEMENT

	Y	X1	X2	X3
Y	1.454659E-01	-5.663167E-01	-4.438593E-01	4.890411E-03
X1	5.663167E-01	1.814373E+00	-1.215556E+00	5.327414E-01
X2	4.438592E-01	-1.215556E+00	1.814373E+00	4.911508E-01
X3	4.890407E-03	-5.327414E-01	-4.911508E-01	1.243595E-01

STEP NUMBER 5 OBSERVATIONS 1 THRU 36

VARIABLES IN FOLLOWING STEP 5

VARIABLE		COEFFICIENT	STANDARD ERROR
X1	TIME AT STANDARD	8.905752E-01	1.406365E-01
X2	EXPENSES	1.357769E+00	2.735694E-01
	CONSTANT	-3.664614E+02	
	ERROR SUM OF SQUARES	7.629046E+05	
	STANDARD ERROR	1.520471E+02	

DEGREES OF FREEDOM = 33

MOST SIGNIFICANT NEW VARIABLE / LEAST SIGNIFICANT OLD VARIABLE

LEAST SIGNIFICANT OLD VARIABLE = X2 EXPENSES :VMIN =-.1085835

TEST FOR RETENTION OF X2
F-VALUE (1 , 33) = 24.63297
SIGNIFICANCE LEVEL = .9999676   ;   CRITICAL LEVEL = .95
X2 EXPENSES RETAINED.

STEPWISE MULTIPLE REGRESSION MODEL

	INPUT DATA		REGRESSION FUNCTION ETC.	
DESCRIPTION	MEAN	STANDARD ERROR	CONSTANT OR COEFFICIENT	STANDARD ERROR
CONSTANT			−366.4614	
INDEPENDENT VARIABLES				
X1 TIME AT STANDARD	1832.0000	246.1553	0.8906	0.1406
X2 EXPENSES	911.0000	126.5435	1.3578	0.2736
DEPENDENT VARIABLE				
Y REVENUE	2502.0000	387.0976		
Y' REGRESSION ESTIMATE			2502.0000	152.0471
COEFFICIENT OF :				
CORRELATION			0.9244	
REGRESSION IMPROVEMENT			0.6072	
RESIDUAL VARIATION			0.0608	

===

REGRESSION ESTIMATE [Y'(t)] OF REVENUE FOR OBSERVATION t :
Y'(t) = −366.4614 + .8906*X1(t) + 1.3578*X2(t)

VARIABLES USED

OBS#	Y	X1	X2
1	2107	1574	802
2	1915	1503	785
3	1873	1645	711
4	1978	1380	844
5	2010	1580	761
6	1969	1576	716
7	2228	1752	724
8	2152	1549	753
9	2439	1652	1020
10	2318	1650	878
11	2244	1496	841
12	2357	1671	900
13	2103	1679	794
14	2457	1782	873
15	2606	1652	929
16	2493	1756	875
17	2264	1555	794
18	2058	1621	813
19	2516	1982	886
20	2533	2050	913
21	2958	1959	990
22	2564	1836	963
23	2318	2006	855
24	2928	2164	1058
25	2754	1780	1059
26	2678	2054	966
27	3189	2265	983
28	3067	2117	956
29	2735	1955	1077
30	3029	2059	1108
31	2531	2059	813
32	2765	2096	1101
33	3074	2201	1186
34	2651	2016	1092
35	3056	2197	915
36	3155	2083	1062
	90072	65952	32796

RESULTS BASED ON THE REGRESSION FUNCTION

OBS#	RECORDED AMOUNT	REGRESSION ESTIMATE	RESIDUAL	RESIDUALS GRAPHED IN UNITS OF 1 STD. ERROR (152.047)	OBS#
				-4 -3 -2 -1 0 1 2 3 4	
				-I—I—I—I—I—I—I—I—I-	
1	2107	2124	-17	-I I * I I-	1
2	1915	2038	-123	-I I * I I I-	2
3	1873	2064	-191	-I I * I I I-	3
4	1978	2008	-30	-I I *I I I-	4
5	2010	2074	-64	-I I *I I I-	5
6	1969	2009	-40	-I I *I I I-	6
7	2228	2177	51	-I I I* I I-	7
8	2152	2035	117	-I I I * I I-	8
9	2439	2490	-51	-I I *I I I-	9
10	2318	2295	23	-I I * I I-	10
11	2244	2108	136	-I I I * I I-	11
12	2357	2344	13	-I I * I I-	12
				-I—I—I—I—I—I—I—I—I-	
13	2103	2207	-104	-I I * I I I-	13
14	2457	2406	51	-I I I* I I-	14
15	2606	2366	240	-I I I *I I-	15
16	2493	2385	108	-I I I * I I-	16
17	2264	2096	168	-I I I * I I-	17
18	2058	2181	-123	-I I * I I I-	18
19	2516	2602	-86	-I I * I I I-	19
20	2533	2699	-166	-I I * I I I-	20
21	2958	2722	236	-I I I *I I-	21
22	2564	2576	-12	-I I * I I-	22
23	2318	2581	-263	-I I* I I I-	23
24	2928	2997	-69	-I I *I I I-	24
				-I—I—I—I—I—I—I—I—I-	
25	2754	2657	97	-I I I * I I-	25
26	2678	2774	-96	-I I * I I I-	26
27	3189	2985	204	-I I I * I I-	27
28	3067	2817	250	-I I I *I I-	28
29	2735	2837	-102	-I I * I I I-	29
30	3029	2972	57	-I I I* I I-	30
31	2531	2571	-40	-I I *I I I-	31
32	2765	2995	-230	-I I* I I I-	32
33	3074	3204	-130	-I I * I I I-	33
34	2651	2912	-261	-I I* I I I-	34
35	3056	2832	224	-I I I * I I-	35
36	3155	2931	224	-I I I * I I-	36
				-I—I—I—I—I—I—I—I—I-	
37	2757	2716	41	-I I I* I I-	37
38	2869	2757	112	-I I I * I I-	38
39	3168	3128	40	-I I I* I I-	39
40	3210	2939	271	-I I I *I I-	40
41	2958	3393	-435	-I * I I I I-	41
42	2698	2997	-299	-I * I I I-	42
43	3412	3167	245	-I I I *I I-	43
44	2872	3171	-299	-I * I I I-	44
45	3263	3440	-177	-I I * I I I-	45
46	3506	3421	85	-I I I * I I-	46
47	3452	3590	-138	-I I * I I I-	47
48	2993	3335	-342	-I *I I I I-	48
				-I—I—I—I—I—I—I—I—I-	

MATRIX OF CORRECTED SQUARES AND CROSS-PRODUCTS OBSERVATIONS 1 THRU 24

	Y	X1	X2	X3
Y	1.969328E+06	1.004376E+06	5.457720E+05	1.107512E+06
X1	1.004376E+06	8.960160E+05	2.473440E+05	7.554560E+05
X2	5.457720E+05	2.473440E+05	2.050160E+05	3.878800E+05
X3	1.107512E+06	7.554560E+05	3.878800E+05	1.033152E+06

MATRIX OF COEFFICIENTS OF CORRELATION OBSERVATIONS 1 THRU 24

	Y	X1	X2	X3
Y	1.000000E+00	7.561003E-01	8.589311E-01	7.764390E-01
X1	7.561003E-01	1.000000E+00	5.770981E-01	7.851799E-01
X2	8.589311E-01	5.770981E-01	1.000000E+00	8.427939E-01
X3	7.764390E-01	7.851799E-01	8.427939E-01	1.000000E+00

MATRIX AFTER TRANSFORMATION USING (X1,X1) AS PIVOTAL ELEMENT

	Y	X1	X2	X3
Y	4.283124E-01	-7.561003E-01	4.225870E-01	1.827642E-01
X1	7.561003E-01	1.000000E+00	5.770981E-01	7.851799E-01
X2	4.225870E-01	-5.770981E-01	6.669579E-01	3.896682E-01
X3	1.827642E-01	-7.851799E-01	3.896682E-01	3.834926E-01

MATRIX AFTER TRANSFORMATION USING (X2,X2) AS PIVOTAL ELEMENT

	Y	X1	X2	X3
Y	1.605596E-01	-3.904488E-01	-6.336038E-01	-6.413099E-02
X1	3.904488E-01	1.499345E+00	-8.652691E-01	4.480120E-01
X2	6.336038E-01	-8.652691E-01	1.499345E+00	5.842471E-01
X3	-6.413101E-02	-4.480120E-01	-5.842471E-01	1.558301E-01

MATRIX OF CORRECTED SQUARES AND CROSS-PRODUCTS OBSERVATIONS 25 THRU 36

	Y	X1	X2	X3
Y	5.607840E+05	1.879760E+05	5.834800E+04	1.225120E+05
X1	1.879760E+05	1.749560E+05	-1.901200E+04	3.414000E+04
X2	5.834800E+04	-1.901200E+04	1.153230E+05	4.050800E+04
X3	1.225120E+05	3.414000E+04	4.050800E+04	6.427200E+04

MATRIX OF COEFFICIENTS OF CORRELATION OBSERVATIONS 25 THRU 36

	Y	X1	X2	X3
Y	1.000000E+00	6.001229E-01	2.294406E-01	6.453123E-01
X1	6.001229E-01	1.000000E+00	-1.338460E-01	3.219498E-01
X2	2.294406E-01	-1.338460E-01	1.000000E+00	4.705133E-01
X3	6.453123E-01	3.219498E-01	4.705133E-01	1.000000E+00

MATRIX AFTER TRANSFORMATION USING (X1,X1) AS PIVOTAL ELEMENT

	Y	X1	X2	X3
Y	6.398525E-01	-6.001229E-01	3.097646E-01	4.521028E-01
X1	6.001229E-01	1.000000E+00	-1.338460E-01	3.219498E-01
X2	3.097646E-01	1.338460E-01	9.820852E-01	5.136051E-01
X3	4.521028E-01	-3.219498E-01	5.136051E-01	8.963483E-01

MATRIX AFTER TRANSFORMATION USING (X2,X2) AS PIVOTAL ELEMENT

	Y	X1	X2	X3
Y	5.421480E-01	-6.423400E-01	-3.154152E-01	2.901039E-01
X1	6.423400E-01	1.018242E+00	1.362876E-01	3.919478E-01
X2	3.154152E-01	1.362876E-01	1.018242E+00	5.229740E-01
X3	2.901039E-01	-3.919478E-01	-5.229740E-01	6.277462E-01

CHOW TEST FOR DISCONTINUITY
FIRST SET OF BASE OBSERVATIONS DF = 21 ; SSE = 316194.5
SECOND SET OF BASE OBSERVATIONS DF = 9 ; SSE = 304027.9
TOTAL BASE   DF = 33 ; SSE = 762904.6
F-RATIO (3 , 30) = 2.300502
CRITICAL F-VALUE 4.414 ; SIGNIFICANCE LEVEL .01
NO DISCONTINUITY INDICATED

MATRIX OF CORRECTED SQUARES AND CROSS-PRODUCTS OBSERVATIONS 1 THRU 48

	Y	X1	X2	X3
Y	9.270848E+06	5.604704E+06	2.655952E+06	5.307904E+06
X1	5.604704E+06	4.066832E+06	1.583968E+06	3.538544E+06
X2	2.655952E+06	1.583968E+06	1.250940E+06	1.994720E+06
X3	5.307904E+06	3.538544E+06	1.994720E+06	4.037856E+06

MATRIX OF COEFFICIENTS OF CORRELATION OBSERVATIONS 1 THRU 48

	Y	X1	X2	X3
Y	1.000000E+00	9.127774E-01	7.799060E-01	8.675368E-01
X1	9.127774E-01	1.000000E+00	7.022634E-01	8.732147E-01
X2	7.799060E-01	7.022634E-01	1.000000E+00	8.875406E-01
X3	8.675368E-01	8.732147E-01	8.875406E-01	1.000000E+00

MATRIX AFTER TRANSFORMATION USING (X1,X1) AS PIVOTAL ELEMENT

	Y	X1	X2	X3
Y	1.668375E-01	-9.127774E-01	1.388959E-01	7.048619E-02
X1	9.127774E-01	1.000000E+00	7.022634E-01	8.732147E-01
X2	1.388959E-01	-7.022634E-01	5.068262E-01	2.743139E-01
X3	7.048619E-02	-8.732147E-01	2.743139E-01	2.374961E-01

MATRIX AFTER TRANSFORMATION USING (X2,X2) AS PIVOTAL ELEMENT

	Y	X1	X2	X3
Y	1.287730E-01	-7.203219E-01	-2.740503E-01	-4.689612E-03
X1	7.203219E-01	1.973063E+00	-1.385610E+00	4.931227E-01
X2	2.740503E-01	-1.385610E+00	1.973063E+00	5.412386E-01
X3	-4.689619E-03	-4.931227E-01	-5.412386E-01	8.902684E-02

CHOW TEST FOR DISCONTINUITY BETWEEN BASE & PROJECTION
SET OF BASE OBSERVATIONS   SSE = 762904.6
AUGMENTED SET OF OBSERVATIONS SSE = 1193835
F-RATIO (12 , 33) = 1.55335
CRITICAL F-VALUE 2.777534 ; SIGNIFICANCE LEVEL .01
NO DISCONTINUITY INDICATED

REGRESSION FUNCTION
	CONSTANT	-3.664614E+02
X1	TIME AT STANDARD	8.905752E-01
X2	EXPENSES	1.357769E+00
	STANDARD ERROR	1.520471E+02

```
STATISTICS RELATING TO RESIDUALS
S1 = SUM[T=2,N]((E(T)-E(T-1))^2) = 1240746
S2 = SUM[T=2,N](E(T)*E(T-1))     = 117142.8
S3 = SUM[T=2,N](E(T)^2)          = 762554.5

M0 = SUM[T=1,N](ABS(E(T)))       = 4396.613
M2 = SUM[T=1,N](E(T)^2)          = 762851.6
M3 = SUM[T=1,N](E(T)^3)          = 1.480595E+07
M4 = SUM[T=1,N](E(T)^4)          = 3.406346E+10


CROSS-PRODUCTS OF ABSOLUTE RESIDUALS WITH X VARIABLES
X1 VS E = 8346093
X2 VS E = 4096318
X3 VS E = 8197876


TESTS FOR ABNORMALITY
SAMPLE MOMENTS AND K-STATISTICS
M2 =  762851.6 ; K2 =  21852.52
M3 =  411276.3 ; K3 =  451491.9
M4 =  9.462073E+08 ; K4 = -4.001709E+08
TEST FOR SKEWNESS
TEST STATISTIC .312839  ;  CRITICAL VALUE 2.355929
TEST FOR KURTOSIS
TEST STATISTIC-.8809617  ;  CRITICAL VALUE 2.158879
NO ABNORMALITIES


TEST FOR HETEROSCEDASTICITY
ABSOLUTE RESIDUALS MOST HIGHLY CORRELATED WITH TIME AT STANDARD
COEFFICIENT OF CORRELATION =  .4211447
F-TEST :
DF1 = 1 ; DF2 = 34 ; F = 7.330493 ; CRITICAL F( .01 ) = 7.446706


DURBIN-WATSON TEST FOR AUTOCORRELATION
DURBIN-WATSON STATISTIC D-W = 1240746 / 762904.6 = 1.626345
CRITICAL VALUES :
  F-VALUE = F( 35 , 39 , .01 ) = 2.167555
  D-VALUE = D( 35 , 39 , .01 ) = 1.375174
NO AUTOCORRELATION INDICATED
RHO =  117142.8 / 762554.5   = .1536189


INVERSE MATRIX FOR STD ERROR CALCS
X1.X1 = 8.555389E-07 ; X1.X2 =-1.114956E-06 ;
X2.X1 =-1.114956E-06 ; X2.X2 = 3.23727E-06 ;
```

AUDIT OF PROJECTION DATA

MONETARY PRECISION = 600 (SAME UNITS AS DEPENDENT VARIABLE)
RELIABILITY FACTOR = 3
DIRECTION OF TEST IS UNDERSTATEMENT

———————————————— REGRESSION PROJECTIONS ————————————————

OPTIONAL SAMPLE DATA

| OBS | RECORDED | REGRESSION | | EXCESS TO BE | SELECTION | RANDOM | MAXIMUM |
| NO | AMOUNT | ESTIMATE | RESIDUAL | INVESTIGATED | INTERVAL | START | ITEMS |

PERIOD 37
CALCULATION OF EXCESS TO BE INVESTIGATED
STANDARD ERROR OF THE RESIDUAL   157.9676
CALCULATION FACTOR (CXI)   5.161541E-02
t-VALUE OF MP (MP / STANDARD ERROR)   3.798248
MOST ADVERSE NUMBER OF PERIODS TO SPREAD ERROR   4
MOST ADVERSE RISK   .4723575
t-VALUE OF RISK LINE   -6.969731E-02
t-VALUE OF CUTOFF POINT   .8798646
CUTOFF VALUE (t-VALUE * STANDARD ERROR)   138.9901
RESIDUAL   41.30591
EXCESS TO BE INVESTIGATED   0
   37   2757   2716   41

PERIOD 38
CALCULATION OF EXCESS TO BE INVESTIGATED
STANDARD ERROR OF THE RESIDUAL   155.2658
CALCULATION FACTOR (CXI)   1.500848E-02
t-VALUE OF MP (MP / STANDARD ERROR)   3.864341
MOST ADVERSE NUMBER OF PERIODS TO SPREAD ERROR   4
MOST ADVERSE RISK   .4723575
t-VALUE OF RISK LINE   -6.969731E-02
t-VALUE OF CUTOFF POINT   .896388
CUTOFF VALUE (t-VALUE * STANDARD ERROR)   139.1784
RESIDUAL   112.1489
EXCESS TO BE INVESTIGATED   0
   38   2869   2757   112

PERIOD 39
CALCULATION OF EXCESS TO BE INVESTIGATED
STANDARD ERROR OF THE RESIDUAL   163.8627
CALCULATION FACTOR (CXI)   .1336806
t-VALUE OF MP (MP / STANDARD ERROR)   3.661603
MOST ADVERSE NUMBER OF PERIODS TO SPREAD ERROR   4
MOST ADVERSE RISK   .4723575
t-VALUE OF RISK LINE   -6.969731E-02
t-VALUE OF CUTOFF POINT   .8457034
CUTOFF VALUE (t-VALUE * STANDARD ERROR)   138.5792
RESIDUAL   39.88135
EXCESS TO BE INVESTIGATED   0
   39   3168   3128   40

```
PERIOD 40
CALCULATION OF EXCESS TO BE INVESTIGATED
STANDARD ERROR OF THE RESIDUAL                       162.651
CALCULATION FACTOR (CXI)                             .1165672
t-VALUE OF MP (MP / STANDARD ERROR)                  3.68888
MOST ADVERSE NUMBER OF PERIODS TO SPREAD ERROR   4
MOST ADVERSE RISK                                    .4723575
t-VALUE OF RISK LINE                                 -6.969731E-02
t-VALUE OF CUTOFF POINT                              .8525228
CUTOFF VALUE (t-VALUE * STANDARD ERROR)              138.6637
RESIDUAL                                             271.0776
EXCESS TO BE INVESTIGATED                            0
   40     3210      2939      271


PERIOD 41
CALCULATION OF EXCESS TO BE INVESTIGATED
STANDARD ERROR OF THE RESIDUAL                       180.9273
CALCULATION FACTOR (CXI)                             .3881851
t-VALUE OF MP (MP / STANDARD ERROR)                  3.316249
MOST ADVERSE NUMBER OF PERIODS TO SPREAD ERROR   4
MOST ADVERSE RISK                                    .4723575
t-VALUE OF RISK LINE                                 -6.969731E-02
t-VALUE OF CUTOFF POINT                              .759365
CUTOFF VALUE (t-VALUE * STANDARD ERROR)              137.3899
RESIDUAL                                             -434.7969
EXCESS TO BE INVESTIGATED                            297.407

OPTIONAL SAMPLE CALULATIONS
t-VALUE OF RESIDUAL                                  1.574096
RISK ASSOCIATED WITH t-VALUE                         .9374976
MOST ADVERSE RISK                                    .4723575
RISK FOR CMA SAMPLE                                  .5038493
RELIABILITY FACTOR FOR CMA SAMPLE                    .6854782
SELECTION INTERVAL FOR CMA SAMPLE                    218
RANDOM START                                         149
RECORDED Y-VALUE                                     2958
SAMPLE SIZE                                          15
   41     2958      3393     -435      297        218       149      15
```

```
PERIOD 42
CALCULATION OF EXCESS TO BE INVESTIGATED
STANDARD ERROR OF THE RESIDUAL                       163.2241
CALCULATION FACTOR (CXI)                             .1246458
t-VALUE OF MP (MP / STANDARD ERROR)                  3.675928
MOST ADVERSE NUMBER OF PERIODS TO SPREAD ERROR       4
MOST ADVERSE RISK                                    .4723575
t-VALUE OF RISK LINE                                 -6.969731E-02
t-VALUE OF CUTOFF POINT                              .8492848
CUTOFF VALUE (t-VALUE * STANDARD ERROR)              138.6237
RESIDUAL                                             -299.2051
EXCESS TO BE INVESTIGATED                            160.5814

OPTIONAL SAMPLE CALULATIONS
t-VALUE OF RESIDUAL                                  .9141119
RISK ASSOCIATED WITH t-VALUE                         .8163555
MOST ADVERSE RISK                                    .4723575
RISK FOR CMA SAMPLE                                  .5786173
RELIABILITY FACTOR FOR CMA SAMPLE                    .5471139
SELECTION INTERVAL FOR CMA SAMPLE                    274
RANDOM START                                         236
RECORDED Y-VALUE                                     2698
SAMPLE SIZE                                          11
    42    2698    2997    -299    161    274    236    11


PERIOD 43
CALCULATION OF EXCESS TO BE INVESTIGATED
STANDARD ERROR OF THE RESIDUAL                       174.9522
CALCULATION FACTOR (CXI)                             .2962054
t-VALUE OF MP (MP / STANDARD ERROR)                  3.429508
MOST ADVERSE NUMBER OF PERIODS TO SPREAD ERROR       4
MOST ADVERSE RISK                                    .4723575
t-VALUE OF RISK LINE                                 -6.969731E-02
t-VALUE OF CUTOFF POINT                              .7876797
CUTOFF VALUE (t-VALUE * STANDARD ERROR)              137.8063
RESIDUAL                                             245.251
EXCESS TO BE INVESTIGATED                            0
    43    3412    3167    245
```

```
PERIOD 44
CALCULATION OF EXCESS TO BE INVESTIGATED
STANDARD ERROR OF THE RESIDUAL                    163.2704
CALCULATION FACTOR (CXI)                          .1253003
t-VALUE OF MP (MP / STANDARD ERROR)               3.674885
MOST ADVERSE NUMBER OF PERIODS TO SPREAD ERROR    4
MOST ADVERSE RISK                                 .4723575
t-VALUE OF RISK LINE                              -6.969731E-02
t-VALUE OF CUTOFF POINT                           .8490239
CUTOFF VALUE (t-VALUE * STANDARD ERROR)           138.6205
RESIDUAL                                          -298.8384
EXCESS TO BE INVESTIGATED                         160.2179

OPTIONAL SAMPLE CALULATIONS
t-VALUE OF RESIDUAL                               .9116065
RISK ASSOCIATED WITH t-VALUE                      .8157063
MOST ADVERSE RISK                                 .4723575
RISK FOR CMA SAMPLE                               .5790779
RELIABILITY FACTOR FOR CMA SAMPLE                 .5463182
SELECTION INTERVAL FOR CMA SAMPLE                 274
RANDOM START                                      204
RECORDED Y-VALUE                                  2872
SAMPLE SIZE                                       11
   44     2872     3171     -299      160      274      204      11


PERIOD 45
CALCULATION OF EXCESS TO BE INVESTIGATED
STANDARD ERROR OF THE RESIDUAL                    177.1828
CALCULATION FACTOR (CXI)                          .3301822
t-VALUE OF MP (MP / STANDARD ERROR)               3.386333
MOST ADVERSE NUMBER OF PERIODS TO SPREAD ERROR    4
MOST ADVERSE RISK                                 .4723575
t-VALUE OF RISK LINE                              -6.969731E-02
t-VALUE OF CUTOFF POINT                           .7768858
CUTOFF VALUE (t-VALUE * STANDARD ERROR)           137.6508
RESIDUAL                                          -177.0703
EXCESS TO BE INVESTIGATED                         39.41948

OPTIONAL SAMPLE CALULATIONS
t-VALUE OF RESIDUAL                               .1527818
RISK ASSOCIATED WITH t-VALUE                      .5602497
MOST ADVERSE RISK                                 .4723575
RISK FOR CMA SAMPLE                               .8431196
RELIABILITY FACTOR FOR CMA SAMPLE                 .1706464
SELECTION INTERVAL FOR CMA SAMPLE                 879
RANDOM START                                      228
RECORDED Y-VALUE                                  3263
SAMPLE SIZE                                       4
   45     3263     3440     -177       39      879      228       4
```

PERIOD 46
CALCULATION OF EXCESS TO BE INVESTIGATED
STANDARD ERROR OF THE RESIDUAL   169.8489
CALCULATION FACTOR (CXI)   .2200913
t-VALUE OF MP (MP / STANDARD ERROR)   3.532553
MOST ADVERSE NUMBER OF PERIODS TO SPREAD ERROR   4
MOST ADVERSE RISK   .4723575
t-VALUE OF RISK LINE   -6.969731E-02
t-VALUE OF CUTOFF POINT   .8134408
CUTOFF VALUE (t-VALUE * STANDARD ERROR)   138.162
RESIDUAL   84.80811
EXCESS TO BE INVESTIGATED   0
     46   3506   3421   85

PERIOD 47
CALCULATION OF EXCESS TO BE INVESTIGATED
STANDARD ERROR OF THE RESIDUAL   177.7756
CALCULATION FACTOR (CXI)   .3392835
t-VALUE OF MP (MP / STANDARD ERROR)   3.375042
MOST ADVERSE NUMBER OF PERIODS TO SPREAD ERROR   4
MOST ADVERSE RISK   .4723575
t-VALUE OF RISK LINE   -6.969731E-02
t-VALUE OF CUTOFF POINT   .7740631
CUTOFF VALUE (t-VALUE * STANDARD ERROR)   137.6095
RESIDUAL   -138.0376
EXCESS TO BE INVESTIGATED   0
     47   3452   3590   -138

PERIOD 48
CALCULATION OF EXCESS TO BE INVESTIGATED
STANDARD ERROR OF THE RESIDUAL   165.4648
CALCULATION FACTOR (CXI)   .156504
t-VALUE OF MP (MP / STANDARD ERROR)   3.626148
MOST ADVERSE NUMBER OF PERIODS TO SPREAD ERROR   4
MOST ADVERSE RISK   .4723575
t-VALUE OF RISK LINE   -6.969731E-02
t-VALUE OF CUTOFF POINT   .8368397
CUTOFF VALUE (t-VALUE * STANDARD ERROR)   138.4675
RESIDUAL   -341.7769
EXCESS TO BE INVESTIGATED   203.3093

OPTIONAL SAMPLE CALULATIONS
t-VALUE OF RESIDUAL   1.159019
RISK ASSOCIATED WITH t-VALUE   .8726167
MOST ADVERSE RISK   .4723575
RISK FOR CMA SAMPLE   .5413115
RELIABILITY FACTOR FOR CMA SAMPLE   .6137603
SELECTION INTERVAL FOR CMA SAMPLE   244
RANDOM START   223
RECORDED Y-VALUE   2993
SAMPLE SIZE   13
     48   2993   3335   -342   203   244   223   13
          -------- -------- -------- --------   --------
             37158   38054   -896   860   54
          ======== ======== ======== ========   ========

VARIABLES USED

OBS#	Y	X1	X2
37	2757	2075	909
38	2869	1984	999
39	3168	2346	1035
40	3210	2254	956
41	2958	2166	1348
42	2698	2013	1157
43	3412	2490	969
44	2872	2179	1176
45	3263	2245	1331
46	3506	2515	1140
47	3452	2389	1347
48	2993	2389	1159
	37158	27045	13526

==

END OF REPORT ON APPLICATION 2

INDEX

297